REDNECK IN RED CHINA
An American Southerner's Life in Modern China

REDNECK IN RED CHINA
An American Southerner's Life in Modern China

Dan Trotter

North American Business Press
Atlanta – Seattle – South Florida - Toronto

North American Business Press, Inc

Atlanta, Georgia
Seattle, Washington
South Florida
Toronto, Canada

Redneck in Red China: An American Southerner's Life in Modern China

ISBN: 9780982843475

Along with trade books for various business disciplines, the North American Business Press also publishes a variety of academic-peer reviewed journals.

Library of Congress Control Number: 2012951020

Library of Congress
Cataloging in Publication Division
101 Independence Ave., SE
Washington, DC 20540-4320
Printed in theUnited States of America

First Edition

TABLE OF CONTENTS

ACKNOWLEDGEMENTS

Grateful appreciation is extended to the Shantou University Publishing Foundation, without whose financial assistance this book would not have been published. I would also like to thank Xu Zongling, Dean of Shantou University Business School, for the wonderful support and assistance I have received at Shantou University, which has afforded me the time and facilities to enable me to write the book. Likewise, I am indebted to Malcolm Doubles, the former movie star and former Provost of Coker College, Hartsville, South Carolina, who sent me from Coker College to China when I didn't even know where the Yellow River or Beijing was. I know this book would never have happened if it had not been for Mac Doubles, because I never would have gone to China. I say he is a former movie star because he appeared in *A Time to Remember* (1998), starring Charlie Leung. You will recognize him as the most distinguished foreigner in the movie, and the movie is available at Amazon.com and on Netflix, and you ought to watch it. Special thanks also go to my friend, neighbor, colleague and editor, Dr. Robert Tian, whose ideas and encouragement launched me on this project, and whose unfailing enthusiasm kept me going once I started. I would also like to thank Marius Lazau and Dr. David Smith of the North American Business Press for all the assistance they provided along the way. Helen Throckmorton provided much-appreciated editorial assistance. Two Chinese women living in southern America also deserve special thanks: Lu Shan and Zhou Saijing, who helped me with Chinese language problems, whose life experiences provided me with some of the material herein, and who have now attended more NASCAR races than I have. There are too many individual Chinese to name, many of whom were my students, whom I would like to thank for all the time you spent with me, regaling me with stories of your native land, and of your life in China. I want to also especially thank my neighbor Edmund Ball, who has been encouraging me for years to write a book, even when I didn't feel like it. And special thanks to my childhood friend Bill Harritt, who urged me to write this book about China, and who, although he won't be able to read the book, already knows that heaven is a lot like Dixie. Les and Cheryl Buford, and Steve and Sandra Atkerson, left Dixie long enough to come visit Linda and me in China several times, and I should here acknowledge their friendship and encouragement. My friend and former neighbor Dan Bausum is worthy of special mention, because he regaled me with hours of stories about his missionary ancestors in China, and because his great-aunt Ruth Bausum was Hudson Taylor's *meipo*, and Ruth Bausum was the spitting image of Dan's daughter Sarah, who was the childhood friend of my daughter Brittany. Last, but certainly not least, I want to thank my wife Linda, and my three children Tara, Tyler, and Brittany. They cheerfully went to China in 1995 when I didn't want to go. Tyler designed the jacket cover. My son-in-law Chris Neiger, a professional writer, encouraged me when I reached the stage where a writer's manuscript repulses him. Linda shared almost all of the experiences contained in the book, and also kept me in food and laundry so that I had the time to write, and she helped me remember a lot of stories I had forgotten. She also contributed many anecdotes derived from her years of teaching English to Chinese university students. Not many women would have missed five Christmases and Thanksgivings in a row so I could live in China. She also proofread the manuscript. She is another person whose contributions were critically necessary for the existence of this book. I fear I have failed to acknowledge someone's contribution. If so, please let me know, and I'll flatter you in the acknowledgments of the second edition, I promise!

This book is written for Westerners who are curious enough to penetrate the exotic mystery of modern China, even though I know it is impossible for Westerners ever fully to do so. At a time when overly broad stereotypes about the Chinese abound in the West, Redneck in Red China is designed to help the Western reader to ameliorate the untoward effects of these over-generalizations. The reader will discover that not all Chinese eat cats and dogs, and most Chinese love Americans; some students even wear American flag T-shirts. At a time when geopolitical tensions between the superpowers dominate the headlines, I think it would be useful for Americans to be able to better understand those with whom we are competing.

I have come to love China and the Chinese people. Even after years of living in China, I still light up when I see a Chinese cashier in a Chinese restaurant in the United States, or a Chinese actor or actress in a Western movie. In my considered opinion, the Chinese people are the most interesting and most charming people on earth. When I find a willing Chinese person, I sit and talk with him, or with her, for hours. I am convinced that Chinese people do not themselves realize how fascinating they are. After my first trip to China, I became obsessed with the desire to go back. When I finally did get back to China, I asked a foreigner who had lived in China for years why I had such strong feelings about this land. The foreigner responded that I was afflicted with "Sino-citis." This was a disease to which many foreigners were highly susceptible. He said there was no cure, and that once the Chinese germ entered your bloodstream, it was like herpes – it would never, ever go away.

That I would become addicted to China was somewhat of a shock to me. I knew nothing about China except for the impressions garnered from reading the news. Lack of knowledge about something inevitably gives rise to overly broad stereotypes, both good and bad. One positive stereotype I had of the Chinese for years was that "all" Chinese were highly intelligent and mathematical. It took me a long time to realize that all those Chinese students in the science departments of Western universities were a biased sample. To come to the United States to study requires extremely high academic competence and intelligence. These are needed in order to obtain admission to the university and a visa, and therefore, what I was observing was not typical of what I might see in a college in China. The stereotype of the brilliant Chinese is pervasive in America. I remember sitting on an academic search committee, and hearing arguments made for the Chinese applicant. One committee member argued that since everybody thinks the Chinese are so smart, it would make the college look good to hire a Chinese.

I held other, negative stereotypes, some of which are shared by many Americans. I thought of China as "Communist." My consciousness was filled with goose-stepping PLA soldiers marching in lockstep beneath Chairman Mao's unsmiling painting overlooking Tiananmen Square, in Beijing. When I first arrived in Shanghai in 1995, I was expecting to see blue Mao hats and blue Mao jackets everywhere, filling a dull gray cityscape, populated by unsmiling, cowed citizens who shuffled slave-like through their dreary world. Instead, I was bombarded with color, bustle, and excitement. The booming economy didn't have people standing in line for bread like all those old pictures of communist Russia. There were colorful white banners containing red characters strung across the streets. There were women in fashionable black and grey skirts, with modern hairdos, wearing stiletto heels. Cell phones were everywhere. I will never forget that first bus ride in China, as the bus took my family to our first residence. My concept of what I would encounter when I arrived would be seriously challenged, in a way I have never experienced before. I had been up for 48 hours because the rookie travel agent we hired flew us the wrong way around the world. Jet-lagged as I was, I nevertheless knew I was facing a phenomenon I couldn't figure out. I was thinking I was in communist China, but in point of fact, I was in modern China, and modern China is not communist China.

However, old stereotypes die hard. I remember being embarrassed by a friend when I introduced him to a Chinese student who had come to visit our family in the United States. I had told him some good things about China, and his response to me, in the presence of the Chinese student, was, "it is amazing how a communist country could do that." He then proceeded to express a laundry list of stereotypes: the inhumane orphanages, the thought control and lack of freedom, the dangerous products, the bellicose nature of the government. I suspect these stereotypes are ubiquitous in America. While I am not attempting to whitewash the more unpleasant aspects of life in the People's Republic, and, in fact, I document some things that might be quite offputting to a squeamish Westerner, I also try to give a well-rounded presentation of many aspects of Chinese life, so that the interested Westerner may form a realistic picture of the Chinese people and their country. If I succeed, perhaps the reader will come to understand the Chinese as a distinct people, regardless of the Chinese government's international and domestic policies. A people is not its government.

What the reader will find in this book is life experience, not politics or ideology. It is written from my viewpoint, and thus subject to my limitations of experience, as well as my preconceived notions. As I contemplate that, I am comforted with the sure knowledge that any other foreign writer who set out to expound on things Chinese is in exactly the same boat as I am. I am also blessed with the knowledge that I have a repository of stored memories of Chinese people from all over the Middle Kingdom who have enriched my life immeasurably, and who will never, ever be thought of by me as goose-stepping, America-hating soldiers, or hidebound leftist ideologues. I could have written endlessly concerning these pleasant memories in China, but my purpose is rather to focus on those aspects of Chinese life that a Westerner could never understand without having lived there, themselves.

There are many travel books and cross-cultural books designed to help the foreigner understand China. These are written by authors who have as much understanding of China as I do of Swahili. The authors are like a dragonfly, soaring down on a great pool of water, only to bounce back off, rather than swimming in the water. I have become immersed in China, off and on for sixteen years, and although I have more understanding that the travel author who backpacks around the country for a week or two, I do not claim omniscience on this topic. It is very, very hard to understand China. And that's why I love this country so much. There is never a day that goes by in which foreigners fail to discuss animatedly among themselves why so-and-so is doing this or that. I truly believe that the Chinese are the most fascinating people on earth. I still remember discussing China in Shanghai with a lady from Texas. She ended her conversation with this question: "How can you help but love the Chinese?"

Well, you can't. And because I love the Chinese, I do not want to cause offense. When operating cross-culturally, it is a sure bet that somewhere along the way, someone is going to get offended. I think about the time when a student took my checkbook without permission, and started examining its entries. I was ticked off at first, but I took a deep breath, and reminded myself that this is China, and things are different over here. The difference in culture creates many humorous situations. So much of humor is cross-cultural: the Star Wars bar scene, Gulliver in the land of the Lilliputians, the African Eddie Murphy in New York City in the movie Trading Places, the libertine holed up on an Amish farm hiding from mobsters. Humor arises when the unexpected collides with the normal. This happens all the time to foreigners in China, and so it is very easy to write about humorous stuff. However, it is also possible that when one laughs at the predicament of a libertine on an Amish farm, an Amish person, upon hearing the laughter, might perhaps think that one is laughing at him, and not at the predicament. I would hope that no Chinese would ever think I am poking fun at him or her, personally or culturally. I love the Chinese culture, as I love my own Southern American culture. As a (white) southerner, I never take offense at all the redneck jokes that circulate through the country, and I enjoy the cultural dissonance between my region and the rest of the country, a difference that produces so much humor. I would hope that any Chinese who might read this book would take the humor in the same good-natured way.

This book grew from a set of emails I sent home during my employment as a university professor in China. My aim was to give my friends and family a good laugh in the process of telling them what I was up to. Several of those friends and family suggested putting the emails in a book. I carried the idea around for a while, when my friend Dr. Robert Tian, the editor of North American Business Press' Modern China Series, not knowing that I was kicking around an idea for a book, asked me to write the first volume of the series. I told him I was already going to do a book, and my book wouldn't work for him, because it was going to be a humorous, travel-memoir sort of book. Dr. Tian suggested that I supplement my experiences with research, and write the book for him.

At first, I thought writing a book this way would produce a monstrous tertium quid, a book composed of mutually antagonistic sections of humor and academic writing. I wanted the book to be readable, and as someone who has read plenty of dry-as-dust academic writing, I was afraid such writing would pollute the book. I'll give you an example of what I was worried about. The following was written by an academic who is an expert on things Chinese, commenting on a book by another China expert:

> Farquharad opts Bourdieu's concept of habitus to define
> the "bodies and appetites" she intends to interrogate.
> "Habitus is made up of the mundane conditions of daily
> life and the practices of (broadly construed) bodies," and
> "is always generated in collective social practice"(p. 9).
> *Appetites* focuses on the gustatory, medical, and sexual
> aspects of contemporary Chinese habitus. (Sisson, 2003)

I apologize for having made you read that. I think these scholars were writing about food and sex in China. But even if they were, normal people aren't ever going to read nonsense like that. I have written plenty about food and sex in this book, and much, much more, I hope in a way that you might find more enjoyable. I use a combination of personal experiences and scholarly research. When I used scholarly research, I tried to strip it of academic stuffiness. I think the attempt to mix a light touch with scholarly information is pleasing, just like those beautiful babies born to mixed Chinese and Westerner couples whose culture seems incompatible, but who nevertheless produce beautiful offspring.

The book is topically organized, and so you can read it in any order you please. One chapter does not depend on the next. The topics I have included should be helpful to academics, students, and businessmen who plan to travel to the People's Republic. However, for those who have no intention to travel to China, but who are possessed of wit, imagination, and curiosity, this book should serve you well. I have included many topics that might be considered anthropological, because I have tried to understand China in the contrasting light of Western culture. The topics are somewhat biased towards the academic world and business, because I have been a business professor at four Chinese universities.

And speaking of Chinese universities, before I begin I would like to especially thank Shantou University for their financial assistance towards the publishing of this book, through the Shantou University Publishing Foundation. Without Shantou University's help, this book would never have been published.

I hope you enjoy reading this book as much as I did living it.

CHAPTER REFERENCES

Sisson, Kathy. (2003) From Mao to Viagra: What a Long, Strange Trip It's Been. Review of Appetites: Food and Sex in Post- Socialist China by Judith Farquhar. The Journal of Sex Research 40(2):225-227.

I didn't want to go China, at first. However, when, in the spring of 1995, Mac Doubles, the Dean of the Faculty of Coker College in Hartsville, S.C. came running across the campus, knocked on my office door, and breathlessly asked me, "Would you like to teach in China?" I really had no choice but to say yes. I had just started my career as a professor, and in order to get tenure I had vowed to myself never to turn down a request from above. It seemed that Mac had met some high-level officials at Shanghai International Studies University (SISU, Chinese name Shanghai Waiguo Yuyan Daxue, alternate English name Shanghai Foreign Languages University). SISU had decided to convert one of its English colleges to a law college, and since I was an ex-lawyer, I was the logical choice. I figured if POWs can survive prison camp, I could survive China. Needless to say, my attitude was very bad.

I arrived in Shanghai in late August 1995 with my wife Linda, my fifteen-year old daughter Tara, my thirteen-year old son Tyler, and my ten-year old daughter Brittany. I didn't know how to say "Hello" or "Goodbye" in Chinese. I didn't know how to hold chopsticks. I didn't know how to use a squatty potty. I knew exactly four things about Chinese geography – I knew there were two big cities, Beijing and Shanghai, and two big rivers, the Yellow River and the Yangtze. I had no idea which city or which river was north or south.

My lousy attitude was not enhanced by our travel arrangements. Our newbie travel agent, a sister of a friend, had flown us the wrong way around the world. From the time we left our front door till we arrived in Shanghai, forty-eight sleepless hours had elapsed. When we arrived, our host, a delightful SISU professor named Yu Jianhua, insisted on taking us to a restaurant to eat. There is something in the Chinese soul that impels Chinese hosts to take foreigners to restaurants, regardless of their mental or physical condition. In 2010, my Chinese boss took an arriving teacher, put him in the hospital the first night because the teacher was quite sick, checked him out of the hospital the same night, and took him out to eat before he took him back home!

We checked into our room the first night, tortured for lack of sleep. The air conditioner, an antique window unit that was also home to one of the several mice who shared our apartment, was equipped with a clattering fan that put cold air into one of the rooms for just so long as the condenser remained unfrozen, which unfortunately, was not too long. The next day, we dragged all the mattresses from the two bedrooms, and placed all four of them on the floor of the living room, under the air conditioner. One could only operate the toilet by removing the water tank top, after which one could manipulate the ball valve and flapper. I remember how, one day, later in the trip, I opened the bathroom door and observed a plumber who had been called to fix the toilet. He was sitting on the edge of the tub, holding his head in his hand. A horizontal stream of water reached from somewhere within the toilet's plumbing, and ended at the wall across the bathroom extending up from the side of the tub. I still remember the tub and its showerhead. The showerhead began leaking inside the wall. I informed the desk downstairs, and several weeks later, when the repairmen had gotten around to coming up to fix it, the leak had spread through all the interior walls of our apartment. The mold on all the interior walls was thick enough to write in, and and it smelled somewhat similar to water drains in the street, which, like all Chinese sewers I have examined by sniffing, conveniently mixed rainwater and sewage.

Upon awakening the morning after the first night, my first thought was, I'm thirsty, and my family has no water. I grew up in middle-class America; I've never been confronted with a desperate feeling that I've got to have water. I took the big wad of Chinese currency that Yu Jianhua had given us, and along with my family, I ventured into the street. We wandered down that street, named Guang Ling Yi Lu, crowded with vendors' stalls, bicycles, pedicabs, taxis, pedestrians, mopeds, electric bicycles, motor scooters, and motorcycles. There wasn't enough room for an ant to walk across. Later, we would see old men balancing their qi, walking backwards through all that chaos, without turning their heads, without getting hit.   Brittany almost stepped into an open unmarked manhole, one of millions in China. One of the children found a McDonald's wrapper on the street, and pounced on it. Never has litter looked so sweet. We meandered our way into the "Japanese Super Market" at the end of the street, which was owned by Japanese, but looked just like any other Chinese supermarket. We recognized hardly any food on the shelves, nor the English translations on the wrappers. I remembered hearing Ricky Nelson's Traveling Man over the store speakers, and squeezing my face really hard to keep from crying. That song was one of my five or so favorites as a teenager. It became number one that afternoon. That emotional high was not topped until sixteen years later, when a Chinese student asked me if I had heard a particular song before. She then started singing a song in Chinese to the tune of Jambalaya, and I realized that the Chinese had discovered Hank Williams. I have yet to discover how the song's translator translated pirogue and bayou. In the Japanese supermarket, we found bottled water. I took it to the checkout counter, held the wad of bills in my hand out to the sales clerk, and she dutifully and honestly picked out the correct change for me.

That was the first day. I had already calculated there were about 120 days in the semester I was assigned to be there. I decided to approach this like prisoners do in the movies. I would count each day, and mark it down, cross-hatching at every fifth day. I would pay no attention to weekends. Each day would be equal, and I would survive that day, then go on to the next day, until I went home to South Carolina.

At about the eightieth day, I was on my rusty bicycle at a traffic light in downtown Shanghai, surrounded by the typical ocean of people that surrounds one in Shanghai. Even the Chinese people think Shanghai is extraordinarily crowded. One time, my family was immersed in a crowd, on a wide Shanghai sidewalk. I saw road construction up ahead, which narrowed the sidewalk into a sort of bottleneck. True to Bernoulli's principle, the crowd started moving faster as we approached the bottleneck. By the time we reached it, my youngest daughter had been squeezed tight against the wall of pedestrians beside her, her feet were lifted off the ground, and we, along with her, shot through the bottleneck at a running speed. As I sat on my bicycle on day eighty-something, surrounded by that sea of people, waiting for the traffic light to change, and as a motorcycle ran over my foot, I thought how beautiful Shanghai was. I looked at the flashing neon, the outsized five- or six-story TV screens, and then it suddenly occurred to me that I had lost track of my days in Chinese prison. I knew I was somewhere around eighty. I tried to calculate the correct number, and then I stopped. I realized at that point that I just didn't care anymore what day it was, because I loved this place.

It's real hard to explain why I love China. A foreigner once told me he couldn't explain it either, except that once it got into your blood stream, it was like herpes – it wasn't ever going to go away. This book will attempt to describe China for you, with a view to understanding the people and its culture. But the attempt will fail. I read once of a Western reporter asking an "old China hand" back in the 1930s, that since the old foreigner understood China, would he please help the reporter explain it to his readers back home. The old China hand responded, "Young man, let me tell you something. No foreigner will ever understand China." And so it is. However, the same thing is said concerning the sexes, that they will never understand each other, but what fun it is to try.

I have adapted a somewhat unusual approach to this. I will intersperse informal emails I have written home over the years with scholarly research. The emails are lighthearted, humorous, and ironic. They form a counterweight to the scholarly material. Business and anthropology scholars, many of them Chinese, have written most of the scholarly material. I am convinced that if anyone really desired to understand modern China, business and anthropology research would be the proper vehicle. I am also convinced that very few people will ever read that research. Hopefully this book will be one of many channels that will funnel some knowledge to the West of an incredibly complex, ancient, ever-changing, critically important nation.

CHINESE TRANSPORTATION AND CHINESE TRAFFIC

There are several ways to move around China: airplane, boat, train, bus, car, subways, three-wheeled vehicles, motorcycle, motor scooter, mo-ped, electric bicycle, bicycle, and on foot. I have tried them all, except for the motorized two-wheel vehicles. It is very unlikely that you will feel both safe and comfortable, regardless of the particular transportation you are using. The domestic airlines tend to fly at low altitudes where the air is rough, and they are almost always late. Nonetheless, they seem safe enough, unless you are flying an airliner made in Russia, and there seem to be quite a few of those. One passenger boat, on which I traveled from Tianjin to Shanghai, managed to ram the dock in Shanghai, throwing my wife and me to the deck, and gouging a large hole in the concrete wharf, exposing the reinforcing rods within. Another tour boat that took us through what was left of the famous Three Gorges was so hot that the passengers walked into the restaurant wearing only their underwear. I remember how strange it was for me to be sleeping in a room that held four passengers - my wife, me, our college-age travel guide, and a Beijing man who conversed with us in his Garfield undies. I rode a bus in Shanghai in 1995 which had sparks falling out of the front panel. The panel had been opened for the driver to peridically rewire after connections had burnt up. At about the same time, I rode a "slow train," as they are called, which looked like a train arriving in Moscow from Siberia at about the time of the 1917 Revolution. There were chickens and peasants and bai jiu (white liquor) bottles, and suitcases jammed into an antique train car that seemed to travel at about 20 mph. A gnarled old man would periodically tap the fan above the green-and-yellow compartment, and the fan would spark and buzz and try to turn, in order to swirl the sweltering heat around a little bit in the blue cigarette smoke which engulfed the train car. Sadly, those colorful days are over, and most dilapidated equipment has been replaced with modern trains that will take you to where you want to go in style and comfort, and with speed; this, of course, assuming they don't run off the rails and cause death and mayhem. I rode with a friend from Beijing to Harbin in a train in which we slept on nice sheets, watched color TV, and arrived after an all-night trip fresh as daisies. Likewise, many of the buses in many of the cities have been replaced with air conditioned, color TV-equipped units.

One train ride from Shanghai to Beijing was particularly memorable because of the restroom facilities on the train. I tried to use the restroom while we were stopped at the station in Shanghai preparing to leave, but the attendant would not let me. I found out later that the reason was that the squatty potties in the train had no storage containers, and that the products of elimination were dumped straight through the hole of the squatty potty onto the tracks. Only when the train was moving through the countryside could passengers use the facilities. So I had to wait till the train was in motion. I really didn't want to wrestle with a moving squatty potty, so I tried to put off the inevitable. I didn't realize that, by waiting, this gave all the other passengers an opportunity to use the restroom. I also didn't realize that no one would clean the restroom during the trip. When I finally entered the restroom, I was grief-stricken to see that the squatty potty was lurching all over the place because of the movement of the train, that there were two shoe-sized platforms on each side of the squatty potty on which one had to place his feet, and a handle across the wall in front, which one could hold in order to balance oneself on the shoe pads. But the most disconcerting thing was the one-inch deep pool of feces and water that covered the whole restroom floor, and which surrounded the shoepads. Somehow I had to step over the feces, stand on the shoepads, lower my trousers, and avoid getting thrown into the feces every time the train lurched or braked. I have rarely known such despair.

I rode one overnight train from Shandong province to Beijing, and didn't have to worry about the state of the restrooms, because I couldn't physically make my way to the facilities. There were no hard-sleeper berths, and we had to sit up all night. The aisles were jammed with families eating food and playing games, and there was no way to pick one's way around them to get to the restroom. I don't know why people get so upset over water boarding, when Chinese trains exist. At least with water boarding you can tell your interrogator that you've had it, and that you'll talk, in order to end the agony.

For local transportation, I used the bus, three-wheeled vehicles, subways, and my privately owned bicycle, the latter being my favorite. The bus fare is very low, and as a result, the buses are often ludicrously crowded, depending on which city you are in. Shanghai is one of the most densely packed cities in the world, and the buses there reflect that. I remember trying to board a bus at the North

Railway Station in Shanghai, in the mid-nineties. Space was at a premium, of course, and little old Chinese ladies, students, adults, and I congregated at the bus door, and proceeded to imitate a rugby scrum. Those old ladies and their fellow Chinese citizens abandoned whatever Confucian dignity they may have once possessed, and violently pushed and shoved and banged me in several contradictory directions at once. I had to get on, because I was lost, and the only way I knew back to the apartment was by taking that particular bus. So, I took advantage of my height. I placed my hands on the left and right doorframes, placing them above the swirling mob below, and used the doorjambs as a base from which to push off, in order to leverage my hips, which I used as a battering ram to push bodies out of the way. The locals apparently had not seen such a tactic before, and relaxed their pushing for just a moment, which allowed me to shove myself onto the bus.

I wish I could describe what it was like on the bus, after I got on. Let me relate three scenes of Chinese crowding to give you an idea. Once, I was sitting on the right front seat, next to the exitway. Mobs were pushing their way in, and the sardines inside were pushing their way out. I couldn't move, so I just sat. Suddenly, a young mother pushes her baby over my head, and hands the baby through the window at my right, to a relative outside. Another time, I was on a bus to the Shanghai 2010 World Expo, trying very diligently to expand my lungs just enough to get sufficient air in order to survive. Suddenly, the water bottle in my pocket, whose top had been screwed on properly, popped loudly from the pressure. The subways are often just as crowded as the buses. At one time, I was on the light rail north of Beijing, and a young man tried to board. There was absolutely no room. A young woman on the train gently pushed him back out the door. He tried again. She pushed him back out. The third time he charged onto the train, just as the door closed behind him scraping his posterior. He was extremely angry, as he stood nose to nose with his antagonist. He started screaming at her. Because of the crowd, she couldn't get out of the way. She couldn't avert his gaze. She was intimately stuck to him. He attempted to punch her with balled-up fists, but his hands were pinned by the crowd, so he began giving her quite ineffective one-inch uppercuts at about waist level. After he ran out of nasty things to say to her, he stopped, but they couldn't turn their heads away from each other because of the crowd. They silently stared at each other, nose-to-nose, in intimate communion, all the way into town.

Because of the difficulties presented by trains, subways, and buses, I decided to take taxis as much as I could, in spite of the added expense. Talking with taxi drivers is delightful. Although some are close-mouthed, most love to talk, and many love to talk about politics. I would often ask them what they thought of Mao Zedong. Some hated him, and some loved him. I remember fondly a taxi driver in Yinchuan who was very excited because we were the first American fares he had ever had. He immediately asked me why America liked to start wars all over the world (which I thought was a little cheeky), and then he gushed that he would like to ask us over to his house to eat. As we left his taxi, he stood outside by the driver's door, repeatedly bowing to us at the waist, his arms extended, palms face down, fingers shaking as he gave us homage.

In my humble opinion, the best way to negotiate the streets of a city is to ride a bicycle equipped with multiple gears. The major streets of Chinese cities are two to three lanes wide in one direction. In addition, there are often wide bicycle paths on each side of the street. I used to ride my bicycle in the bike paths, but soon learned that parked cars, pedestrians, cars and motorcycles coming at you in the opposite direction, shopkeepers throwing dirty water into the path, and people playing chess, were all obstacles which could be avoided by riding in the street. I figured if cars can ride in my bike lane, I would ride where the cars drove. In negotiating the streets of a Chinese city on a bicycle, there are several important points worth remembering. The first is that, if anyone hits you, it's always the driver's fault. This causes car drivers to be very careful. Once they get within two or three centimeters of you, they will diligently apply their brakes. If you reciprocate, you live. If you miscalculate and die, your heirs will collect, assuming they can come to China and get a Chinese court to hear their case. The second thing to remember is that all traffic regulations are not really laws – they are rather rules of thumb. Red lights are run often and with impunity. I have many times found myself facing several lanes of oncoming cars, motorcycles, bicycles, and even buses, because somebody had decided to go up the left lane. I am ashamed to say that it wasn't long before I was riding up the left lane just like the natives. It just seems to be a necessary thing to do, sometimes. The best thing to do, if one becomes stuck in such situations, is to freeze, so the oncoming traffic will not be forced to miss a moving target. The third thing to remember is that, in many situations, there simply are no rules. If you are on the leftmost bicycle lane, moving opposite to the direction of the car lanes, should you stay on the right side of the bike lane, or the left, when faced with oncoming vehicles? The practice in different cities differs. Therefore, the first few days of riding a bicycle in a particular city should be done with great care. When faced with oncoming two-wheeled traffic, one should slow down, and watch for a telltale wiggle in the front wheel. This is the driver signaling to you which way he will go. Another good rule is to aim at the heels of crossing pedestrians, not their toes. Pedestrians know how to stop in the midst of flowing bike traffic, so the bicyclists can go behind their heels. Bicycle riding in China is as fun as any video game you have ever played. You have to keep your field of vision wide, because at any minute, some object will come flying from any direction into your path (and sometimes from above, if tree limbs extend over the road). The big difference from riding a bicycle in a Chinese city and playing video games is that, when you get hit in a video game, you get to play again.

THE CHINESE CONCEPT OF PRIVACY

When a foreigner lives his daily life in China, he will inevitably one day feel himself aggrieved by a perceived invasion of his privacy. I recall sitting on the steps of a public building, reading an English book, as I waited for someone to meet me, when, to my discomfort, I realized that a curious Chinese man was squatting on his heels on the next step above me. He had his head at my ear, curiously examining the English text, of which he did not understand a word. When I looked at him in astonishment, he just smiled, and kept on reading, and so I continued to read with him. On another occasion, a student was visiting us in our apartment, saw my checkbook on my desk, opened it, and began examining all the entries. On still another occasion, during a party in my apartment, a student grabbed a deodorant stick which was resting on my TV, pointed it towards me, and asked me what it was. I had to explain to him that foreigners smell bad when they sweat, unlike most Chinese, and we have to use deodorant. And all during my years in China, I have constantly been asked how much my salary was, although that practice is on the wane as Chinese become more familiar with the prickly habits of Westerners. All of these examples illustrate a very interesting point of Chinese culture: the Chinese concept of privacy is much less developed than the West, and much less valued. The Chinese character for "private" is si (私). I have been told that it is very hard to squeeze positive connotations out of that character, that it mostly means sordid, secretive practices, or selfishness. The Chinese have been living in close quarters with each other for millennia, and it is not surprising that they have become accustomed to not having privacy. Doctors examine them within a few feet of their fellow citizens. They watch their fellow Chinese walk the streets in their pajamas, and squat down to brush their teeth over a street drain. They have a hard time being alone with their girlfriends, so they kiss standing up in the parks. They often live with grandparents and children in small quarters. They get used to doing things in public, and pretending the public isn't there.

The following incident will also illustrate the Chinese ability to find privacy in the midst of a crowd. I recall being at a party at Shanghai Foreign Language University, standing in front of a urinal, when the door to the restroom opened, and, to my horror, I saw several of my women students standing in a group chatting at the door. Chinese restrooms are very often not designed to cut off the line of sight into the restroom, using baffles and corners. To save the situation, I thought to hurry myself, but that was impossible. But to my surprise, not one of those girls turned their heads to look into the restroom. I was told later that Chinese are trained early on never to look into open doors and windows where people would desire privacy.

One of the most interesting days I have ever spent in China was early, in 1995. I took my family to a public park in Shanghai in the morning, which is the traditional time for the carrying on of all sorts of activity: sword dances, taiqi, etc. I saw several things that day that illustrate the unique Chinese notion of privacy, or perhaps I should say, the lack of it. We saw a man with a microphone and amplifier belting out Western opera over the lake. He was surrounded by activity: people doing their own thing and paying him no mind. For instance, there was a woman dancing with an imaginary partner, using her own amplification system, and using her own music, which clashed discordantly with the music of the opera singer. Standing nearby was a girl, concentrating with her eyes closed, and slashing the air with her sword. In another place in the park, a woman was standing transfixed, staring at a tree, as the park visitors strolled past her, ignoring her as if what she was doing was perfectly normal. She stood there for over half-an-hour, I suppose to balance her inward qi. Meanwhile, on a nearby terrace, a young man lay down on the ground, parallel to the slope, and rolled down it. At the bottom, he picked himself up, walked to the top of the terrace, and rolled back down it, repeating his actions over and over. Once I began to realize that I was not inside some sort of crazy dream, and once I got over the wackiness of each individual activity, I was struck with how secure and carefree everyone was doing his own private thing in public. At another time, I experienced an instance of a lunatic doing his own thing in public, while his neighbors ignored him. At Ningbo University, in the apartments reserved for foreigners, an insane man greeted us every morning by standing on his balcony and unleashing a stream of murderous curses. It was rumored that years ago, he had been fired by the University, and was cursing them in retribution. It was more than slightly annoying. When I inquired if there was anything that could be done about it, I was told that no, there wasn't, and so my peaceful privacy was invaded daily for one entire semester.

Usually, the little invasions of the foreigner's privacy are minor nuisances. However, there is one place where the lack of privacy can cause grave discomfort to the foreigner, and that is in public restrooms. I remember well the first time I entered a public restroom, and to my dismay saw no stalls, but rather a long row of squatting men, separated from each other by nothing but a little bit of air, happily doing their business while ignoring each other. Some were even reading a newspaper. They ignore each other OK, but it's hard for them to ignore the rare foreigner who shows up, and can't figure out what in the world he's supposed to do, but he needs to do it quickly, because the train is about to leave. The good news for foreigners is that more and more public restrooms are installing stalls, equipped with Western throne toilets, which is Sir Thomas Crapper's most wonderful contribution to China's developing harmonious society.

CHINESE RESTAURANTS

There are three basic categories of Chinese restaurants: noodle shops, family-style, and high-class. Many foreigners are afraid of the first two categories. They fear they will be poisoned due to the lack of sanitation. These fears are groundless. For sixteen years I have eaten in these restaurants, and I am still here. I have only been poisoned once in such a restaurant, and the pain, though excruciating, did not compare to the time that I was poisoned at a high-class restaurant in Shanghai. That probably happened because I ate raw lettuce, a violation of a fundamental rule of survival for foreigners in China. All vegetables should be cooked before eating. The reason, I have been told, is that vegetables are grown in "night soil," which is a euphemism for human feces. Foreigners will look at the smelly restrooms in these little restaurants, see a few flies on the wall, and become unglued. They ignore the wonderfully delicious food that can be found in these eateries. One reason the food is so good is that the Chinese are not hung up about MSG. I ate in one restaurant where MSG was provided in saltshakers on the table. The Chinese should be proud of MSG. That chemical's inventor, a Ningbo man, obtained the first patent in modern China for inventing it. At least that is what a business museum in Ningbo claimed.

Foreigners who are working in China are usually treated to meals in high-class restaurants, often in five-star hotels. In my opinion, the fancy food is not nearly as good as what can be found in an average family style restaurant, unless you have a taste for squid, eel, Cuban bull frog, scorpions, monkey brains, or snake with the red blood and green bile colorfully served in separate shot glasses. And, by the way, despite the stereotype, most Chinese people don't eat dogs and cats. The folks in Guangdong province, however, have quite a reputation for eating dogs and cats, and a lot of other things, as well. There is a proverb in China that says "if it flies and it isn't an airplane, if it moves through water and it's not a boat, if it has four legs and it is not a table, Guangdong folks will eat it." That is no exaggeration. Several Guangdong residents have recently told me that, of course, they do not eat dogs and cats, but I think they doth protest too much. Recently a newspaper in Shantou, a city in Guandong province, reported that the city government had made it illegal to eat cats, in an effort to protect the feline population. An enterprising journalism student at Shantou University figured that if such a law was passed, somebody must be eating cats. She ran down a woman who enjoyed dining on cats and asked her why she did it. The woman responded that cats were good for the health of some parts of her body. This does not surprise me, as every particle of food a Chinese person eats is good for some part of their body. I feel like I'm at a doctor's office, every time I eat out, with the Chinese, because every time I eat something, I am informed which internal organ is being blessed. The Guangdong citizens are not so reticent about admitting that they eat snakes. I remember eating at a Guangdong-style restaurant in the north of China, when a waiter brought a very large five- or six-foot snake to the guests at the table next to us. The waiter had the snake in a two-handed chokehold, one hand on the snake's rear portion, and one hand just behind the snake's head. The snake was facing forward, enjoying the view, his forked tongue shaking happily.

One has to become accustomed to the decibel level in a Chinese restaurant. The noise is just below the threshhold of pain. Therefore, when a patron in a Chinese restaurant desires to call the waitress, he bellows at the top of his lungs to make himself heard: "FU WU YUAN!!!!!" (Waiter/Waitress!!!!!). The waitresses take this verbal abuse very calmly. They come to the table; they smile, and are often rudely ignored and treated like a part of the furniture. They often line up in their uniforms on the street outside, where the boss harangues them, and where sometimes they do calisthenics together. And for all that, they receive no tips, tipping not having become a custom in China.

CHINESE UNDERWEAR

It's best to bring enough underwear with you when you come to China. If you have to buy any, you are faced with several problems. For men, there is no fly in the front of underpants. I have been told that you can now find slotted underwear, but I have yet to see any. This can create certain problems, as you may see below in this extract from one of my emails home, in which I discuss preparations for a TV interview.

> Eight months of no diet and eating Chinese restaurant food every day has had an unfortunate effect on the size of my gut. I have expanded from a 34 to a 38-inch waistline. So, the morning of the TV interview, I discovered to my horror, that I could not button my only pair of long pants. I struggled and struggled, holding my gut in, changing the angle of the pants, you name it, to get it buttoned. I finally did, after about 20 minutes. Then, to my chagrin, I realize I had Chinese underwear on. Apparently Chinese men don't ever need to go to the bathroom, because there is no slit in the front of the underwear. I realized that if I went to a public restroom at any time during the long day ahead, I could never come out in public again. So, I was going to have to hold it for a whole day. This was very depressing, but my host said, no problem, he would buy me some other pants.

> We went to a market, and the cubicle-owner showed me some pants I liked, but I wanted to try them on first before I bought them. I asked the shopkeeper if there was anywhere to try them on, and the lady who owned the shop strung a waist-high sheet up across the corner of the cubicle, and I undressed behind the sheet while talking to the shop owner

and my host. I always wondered how those actresses in old movies felt when they did that sort of thing. I put the new pants on, and we went to a new cubicle to buy another pair. There were three ladies in this cubicle, and my host, having decided he wanted a pair of pants too, dropped his shorts in the cubicle, in front of the ladies, and tried on a pair. I thought, my gosh, that other lady must have thought I was awful prudish to have to stand behind a sheet. So, to continue my ever-persistent efforts to do as the Romans do when in Rome, I determined to imitate my host. I was sweating with embarrassment, but I unbuckled my pants, and started pulling them down, when to my horror, outside of the corner of my eye, I saw my host taking off his newly examined long pants. I saw that he had tried those long pants on over his shorts, that he had NOT indeed stripped to his skivvies in front of the ladies, as I was within a microsecond of doing.

But women are going to have even worse problems then men, as you will see as I now try to describe the Chinese bra. The Chinese bra is an engineering marvel. Tectonic plates, ridges, layers, ruffles, and wires are all pieced together to form the cups in a mysterious way with a view to support, not at all to exhibit feminine beauty. There are no curves, only angles. Underneath the cups is a thick band of elastic and wire, to hold the cups up, in case the cups themselves don't do the job. What is so strange about this, is that it is really unnecessary, since the average Chinese woman is usually not possessed of anything that might need support. The whole thing is reminiscent of an erector set. Chinese bras are on display everywhere from Walmart to street stalls on the side of the road. The interested shopper can choose bras in colors that include pink, brown, chartreuse, indigo, orchid, orange, and all sorts of combinations thereof. Various patterns are available for the bras, including hearts, teddy bears, stars, stripes, circles, random English letters, the names of American universities, whatever suits your fancy. In 1996, I heard that a store in the fashionable embassy district in Shanghai had decided to offer ladies Western-style bras. Since the customers didn't know how the strange bras were sized, the store hired old women, who cupped the customers' breasts, and expertly told the customer which size she should be buying.

My wife and I used to speculate on whether women in Yinchuan, and women students at Jimei University near Xiamen, were wearing only their underwear in the winter, with no pants or skirts on top.

The fashion in those two towns gave rise to this interesting intellectual exercise. An email extract will explain the situation.

Being in high schools and middle schools has been interesting. Think of your high school days, and think of the women teachers. Would they wear sweaters that go down to the top of their thighs, with no discernible pants or skirt underneath the sweater, tight black tights coming out from under the sweater, which then go down into calf-high (sometimes knee-high) high-heeled boots? I don't think so. Here, where the women are famous for being prudish, the women wear stuff that makes them look like a Huddle House hooker, and nobody even notices it.

CHINESE RESTROOMS

The traditional Chinese toilet is an Asian squatty potty. A squatty potty is essentially a hole in the ground. There are many foreigners who can adapt easily to chopsticks, but are struck dumb at the sight of a squatty potty. Let me try to dispel some of the negative feelings you may have toward the squatty potty. It is said that this form of toilet aids much in the digestion/elimination process. There may be some other alleged advantages, but I cannot think of them right now. All I can tell you is that more and more owners of restrooms in the Middle Kingdom are installing modern Western thrones, and may God bless them for it. Nowadays, if one is careful, one can go for months without having to use one of those accursed holes in the ground.

People will tell you how to use Chinese chopsticks, but they won't tell you how to use Chinese toilets. I guess they feel it's too embarrassing. Well, I'm not embarrassed, and I'll tell you in just a minute how to use one, to save you the suffering I have endured. There are so many things that can go wrong. Your clothing can dip too low, with disastrous results. Your aim can be off, with equally disastrous results. Your legs can cramp, and you can't stand up after you finish. You can be congratulating yourself on your successful use of the facility, and then realize you forgot to bring toilet paper with you, because most of the restrooms don't have toilet paper. You may finish everything successfully, and then discover there is no button to push or handle to pull in order to flush the squatty potty. Locals understand that one has to go to the proprietor to get a bucket of water to finish the job, but you aren't a local, and you might not speak Chinese, and so you just walk away mystified, leaving the toilet in a condition that, once it's discovered, is sure to occasion comment about the barbaric state of foreign culture.

Let's start with the toilet paper problem. The foreigner should always carry toilet paper with him, unless he can regulate himself to only go in the morning, before he leaves his apartment. This latter option is not as difficult as it might seem. For some reason, Chinese food makes every foreigner with whom I have ever discussed the subject to become rather, shall we say, unconstipated. But newbies, or anyone still irregular due to the effects of jet lag, better have the toilet paper with him upon leaving his lodgings.

To save you the discomfort of soiled garments, there is one simple rule that should be religiously obeyed. You must squat ALL THE WAY DOWN to your heels, and then relax. This procedure runs counter to your instinct that tells you are about to plop yourself down in a pile of doodley squat, which lurks just beneath the edge of the hole. It is true, you will come close, but you won't hit it. And, if you squat all the way down, upon completion of the elimination procedure, you will never miss the hole. I know one foreigner, whose name shall not be mentioned here, who, after a trip to the countryside, was so delirious upon seeing a clean, tiled bathroom in a Hard Rock Café, that he joyously began to begin the elimination process. He had not learned the all-important rule of squatting all the way down. He squatted halfway down, and soon realized his legs were too tired to hold him in the unnatural position in which he found himself. The walls of the stall, though narrow enough to press his palms into, had no handhold. Unfortunately, for some unknown reason, there was a lot of steam in the restroom. His hands slowly began to slide down the slippery wall. He couldn't stand back up to restart what he had started. In addition, the elimination process had begun, and could not be terminated. If the foreigner had slid all the way down to his heels, he would have been horrified, but he would have hit the hole. Alas, he fought the slippery walls just enough to only be halfway down when elimination began, and scored a direct hit on his underwear. This made the rest of the evening with his dinner hosts quite uncomfortable.

This incident also illustrates another problem with squatty potties, which is, how does one stand up after one is finished? If your legs are young and springy, there is no problem. If you are not young, and you are lucky, there is a handhold on the wall that you can grab.

If you are not so young and lucky, you are, if you will excuse the expression, in deep doo-doo. There is only one option now, and that is to enlist every molecule of your body in the concentrated effort of standing up. Otherwise, you will have to call for help. This will teach you the Chinese concept of losing face.

There are other potential problems. I recall one evening in a substandard Chinese hotel staring at the environs of a squatty potty that had unfortunately just been used. I could not find a button to push, or a lever to pull, that would clear the toilet of its contents. I figured I could not be dumb enough as to not be able to flush a toilet, even though it was a Chinese toilet. I was wrong. I just couldn't figure it out. So I sheepishly went to the front desk and told them that the dumb foreigner didn't know how to flush the toilet. The lady at the desk smiled, handed me a plastic bucket, told me to go back to the bathroom, fill the bucket up with water, and pour it down the toilet.

Before we leave this subject, I should mention one other unpleasant aspect of many Chinese rest rooms, which is the powerful odor that one often encounters within. This is changing, as many establishments are modernizing by installing very advanced bathroom fixtures, and are using chemicals to disperse the odor. They are also installing Western throne toilets with toilet tissue dispensers. But, there are many other restrooms that will take aback the unprepared Westerner. I have a friend who sticks toilet paper in his nose before entering a public restroom. I have learned how to go in and hold my breath and not breathe again till I re-emerge. But there has been remarkable progress since 1995, when I first arrived. Either that, or I have become hardened.

CHINESE MASSAGES

Sometimes I wonder: if there was only one reason to come to China, and that was to obtain a Chinese massage, would I go? The answer to that is, of course I would. Chinese massages teach you how hamburger meat feels when it is tenderized. They will make you feel at least one toke over the line, except that it is all legal. And cheap. One full hour will cost about 8.00 USD.

Cynics will often connect massages to prostitution, not medicine. There is good reason for this, because there are many establishments where one can find sex worker services coupled with a massage. However, if one asks whether the establishment is a zhenggui (regular, standard) business, it is possible to keep one's morals intact, while enjoying some of the best massages on the planet. If you can't find a zhenggui massage parlor, you can go to the other kind, and refuse "overtime," as one non-standard masseuse put it to me one time. Then you relax, get your massage, and pretend you are not in a whorehouse.

The connection between Chinese massages and medicine is this: Chinese medical theory states that there are many xuewei (acupressure points) on the outside of the body that connect directly to the internal organs. Therefore, if the masseuse manipulates the xuewei properly, the bodily organs are positively influenced. The theory arose, I have been told, because when doctors were called to treat the empress, they were not allowed to gaze upon her august feminine body. The empress hid herself behind a cloth, and extended her hand along to the doctor. The doctor, being under extreme pressure to cure the royal patient, had no choice but to discern the connection between the hand and the internal organs. Should you doubt the practicality of such a procedure, let me relate to you the following story concerning a masseuse in Yinchuan, who was in love with traditional Chinese medicine. I carried a young American gentleman to her for a massage. She grabbed one part of his palm, squeezed, and when the foreigner yelled in pain, the masseuse informed us that the foreigner had been smoking a lot (true). She then grabbed another part of the foreigner's hand, he yelled again, and the masseuse told us that the foreigner had been drinking too much (true). Upon repeating the procedure, and hearing the foreigner's third yell, she informed us that the foreigner had not been eating regular meals (true). I suspect skeptics will think this: "All foreigners smoke, drink, and eat irregularly, and she knew that." Please, do not be skeptical. After she finished with my foreign friend, she grabbed my hand in the same three places, squeezed hard, and I hardly felt a thing. The masseuse told me that I didn't smoke (true), didn't drink much (true), and had been eating regular meals (true). I have a friend in the USA whose wife walked into a Chinese doctor's office, without having met the doctor before, and who, after handing her hand to the doctor, was told where fibroid tumors were, and where her breast cancer was, and what her mother's medical history had been. There are Chinese doctors by the side of the road, or in certain pharmacies, who will grab your wrist, and feel the blood rushing past the xuewei. Depending on the characteristics of the blood flow, they can tell you whether you are pregnant, whether you have a urinary tract infection, or whatever other condition you may have. I know you don't believe this. But consider this. A Fulbright scholar, a Chinese man, was a visiting professor at my American college. Professors' salaries were top secret. I had been teaching there for about ten years, and never knew anyone's salary but my own. One day, this Chinese professor grabbed my wrist, looked off in the distance and concentrated a little bit, and then told me my salary to the penny. Apparently the xuewei in the wrist are connected to the brain, and with the proper traditional Chinese medical knowledge, a Chinese practitioner can do a core dump on it. I was informed of my salary just before my Chinese professor friend told me of an ejaculation contest in Taiwan, in which the participants competed to see who could shoot sperm the farthest.

There are many different types of Chinese massages, including full-body massages, foot massages, gua sha massages, oil massages, "walk-on-the-back" massages, medical massages, blind man massages, aromatherapy massages. Many foreigners like foot massages. The feet are washed in perfumed water first, after which they are worked over thoroughly by the masseuse. I have only had one, finding it rather painful. Of course, all Chinese massages can be painful, if you turn the masseuse loose. Most of my massages were full-body massages, and I would tell the masseuse "the harder the better." At first, I figured there was nothing to worry about, because many masseuses are young, tiny Chinese girls in their late teens or early twenties, and they don't look like they could swat a flea. But, as with most things in China, appearances deceive. Those young ladies could bring an elephant to their knees. They are especially leveraged when they do "walk-on-the-back" massages. They grab rails that are hanging from the ceiling over the massage cot, and they proceed to walk and jump on your spine. They are always polite, and ask, "Is this too heavy," but because it is hard to speak Chinese when you are crying, the masseuses are rarely restrained. The purpose of a Chinese massage is not to feel good during the massage; rather, it is to feel good after the massage. There are specialty massages available for those who desire them. After a massage you can have bahuoguan ("draw-out-the-fire-cup") done on you. A lighted alcohol swab is put into a wooden or glass cup, after which the swab is removed, and the cup is placed on your back, lip down. As the heated air inside the cup shrinks, it contracts, pulling your skin into the cup. Since cups are placed all over your back, when you leave, your back is covered with gigantic bright-red hickies that take several days to disappear. The purpose of this is to suck poisons out of your body. Finally, no connoisseur of Chinese massages would ever skip a blind-man massage. These unsighted masseuses don't rely on force, but on pinpoint control, as they attack the xuewei.

I had the pleasure to meet a Chinese masseuse who was extremely interested in Chinese medicine. It was through her that I realized the intimate connection between massages and the healing arts. I wondered for years why almost every massage parlor I went to had a standard chart of a human figure showing the nerve connections between xuewei in the outside of the skin and the internal organs. There is a reason for that. Below is part of an email that illustrates the nexus between healing and massage.

> Now I have a regular masseuse, which is a real luxury. This one is a frustrated acupuncturist and herbal doctor. She is throwing medical terms at me in Chinese, while she's boxing my ears. The pop-popping sound makes for a very challenging Chinese lesson. She told me today that each ear has about 200 acupressure points, and each foot has 600 or 700 or so. She informed me that various regions of the ears (and tongue, and eyes) change colors, depending on how each of the region's corresponding internal organs is doing. Once, she discovered a bump on my back. That bump had been on my back for decades. She went downstairs into her friend's hair stylist shop, came back with some scissors, and without further ado, started cutting. She cut a one-quarter-inch-in-diameter, shiny black ball that looked like obsidian out of my back. I felt no pain, and it was free of charge. Can you imagine what a

dermatologist in the States would have charged for that? She told me that if I would have told her about Linda's cataracts soon enough, she would have sold me some Chinese herbal medicine that would have dissolved them without the necessity of surgery. She also told me there was an old woman in her family whose ability to concentrate her qi (vital energy) was so pronounced that she could point at a candle in the distance and light it. I don't know if I believe in Chinese medicine quite that much. She told me all this while she was abusing my acupressure points along my sternum and ribcage (there are a ton of acupressure points there). Many Chinese masseuses are tiny 18-year-old girls who look like the wind would blow them away. Nevertheless, if you let them, they can just about break you in half. My masseuse, however, is not a tiny 18 year old, but a portly 35 year old. Ai ya. I never dreamed I'd be worrying about my ribs crashing into my heart and liver. It is experiences like this that continue to force me to have ambivalent opinions about Chinese medicine. The feeling of relaxation after the massage is over is heavenly: your muscles feel like liquid flowing around your bones. However, I have trouble when I see Linda, after her cataract surgery, putting into her eyes drops containing "Deproteinized calf-blood". It doesn't help that the instructions are all in Chinese. I often think when using Chinese medicine that a bad translation could do us in.

Just as there are many different types of Chinese massages, there are also many different techniques used by different masseuses, which provides much variety. Some like to do the "elbow-in-the-butt" maneuver. Some like to get you to grab your hands behind your back, forming a bracket through which they can entwine their arms and jerk you around like they were a mad chiropractor. A common technique, which is done for tourists, involves pushing a lot of the blood out of one's hand, holding the wrist firmly to keep the blood out, then dropping the tips of their hair on the fingers of the customer's hand, releasing the wrist slowly to let the blood run back into the hand, producing a pleasant, tingling sensation. Some masseuses rub oil on your back, which is at first very cold. The reduced friction allows them to rub the oil in your back faster and faster, as the movement heats the oil on your back. Some like to clap your ears repeatedly, producing a popping sound, making it all but impossible for the poor foreigner to understand their Chinese, as they merrily chatter away while they work. Once I had a masseuse give free training to a friend, and both the master and the novice began working on me at the same time. I then learned what women mean when they use that new word "objectify." The masseuses calmly discussed any blemish, the amount of hair, and any amount of fat that exceeded Chinese standards, which is to say, every little bit of fat you have on you. I guess they figured I was so zoned out from the massage that I wouldn't care. Incidentally, many Chinese are fascinated by Western body hair. I was standing in line getting ready to get blood drawn at a medical clinic in Yinchuan, when a thirty-year old Hui minority girl sneaked up behind me and started rubbing the hair on my arm. I thought this was a little forward, as we had never been introduced. When I turned to look at her, she smiled and said, "Your arm is so hairy!" So I smiled at her, rubbed her arm, and said, "Your arm is so smooth!" Two emails written from Yinchuan describes this Chinese tendency to objectify the foreigner.

The Chinese are famous for their indirectness. Being indirect saves people's face, and that, of course, is one of the salient points of their culture. But inexplicably and paradoxically, Chinese will sweetly, and inoffensively tell you things about yourself, which, although true, are not flattering to your ego. One young Chinese woman, the wife of the newspaper photographer who took my picture to put it in the big newspaper in town, told me: "I know an American man in Yunnan province whose Chinese is better than yours." Well, big surprise, I thought, I have met hundreds of such foreigners, so was it really necessary to tell me? Another Chinese woman told me I had a "pijiu du" (direct translation: "beer gut"), and then said my boss had one, and then started discoursing on that's what happens to men when they get older. Several students told a staff worker at the school that I looked like Colonel Sanders, and also like Santa Claus. The students at both Jimei University in Xiamen and Ningbo University also thought I looked like the Colonel. I wonder how all this is saving my face…The Chinese are famous for their indirectness, and so I am always surprised when they say things that sort of pin your ears back. The doctor is about to start operating on Linda's cataracts. He pauses to let all those around observing how deep and beautiful Linda's eyes are. And then he said: "She must have been beautiful when she was young!" Ah, Mr. Sensitivity. A young 21-year old nurse intern who bounced and chattered like she was approximately

12 years old topped this. She hopped into Linda's room one night after she got off work, sat down next to Linda, and started to examine Linda's eyes, chin, ears, whatever, running her hands over facial features (you would do the same if you saw a puppy dog whose breed you were unfamiliar with). The first thing she did was to repeat the doctor's sentiments: "Your eyes are so pretty, you must have been very pretty when you were young." She says this as her fingers are moving all over Linda's eyes, nurse-like, to take care of them. She fingers one of Linda's "wine-nests" (dimples), and then her fingers dropped and traced a line on Linda's face, and she said: "Oh, an old wrinkle!" The doctor and the intern said this without one milligram of hostility meant. It reminds me when a student told me "You are not only a good teacher, you are a nice grandpa." They love old people over here.

When Chinese people objectify foreigners, or other Chinese people, they do not at all mean to be offensive. I saw an extremely thin Chinese professor introduced at a faculty banquet as "the one who was extremely thin." I know an American English instructor who watched as the medical staff examined her and her fellow teachers as a requirement to get a visa. She heard the doctors say, "Look how fat this one is!" Foreigners have no choice but to get used to this. After telling them what the doctor had said about Linda's eyes being beautiful when she was young, several Chinese people explained to me that the doctor had not meant that Linda's eyes were not beautiful now. It was explained to me that Chinese don't think things get worse as people get older. There was no implication of that at all. But Americans, who worship youth, just assume the worst when age sets in. The Chinese, on the contrary, think getting old is a good thing.

CHINESE MEDICINE

Traditional Chinese medicine, like ping-pong and firecrackers, is deep within the Chinese soul. I have encountered many Chinese students who tell me that they didn't want to major in Business Administration, but preferred to study traditional Chinese medicine, instead. The dried herbs can be found in many places, even in tourist traps. Like most Westerners, I was at first extremely skeptical of the claims often made by the Chinese concerning the efficacy of this medicine. I remember a student from one of the western provinces telling me about an herbal medicine that could be rubbed on one's stomach, absorbed into the skin, after which it would begin eating away a beer gut. I started to laugh, until I realized he was deadly serious. I also started to laugh when one of his classmates told me how she ate lots of dog, plus took some other sort of herb, for her crippling arthritis that prevented her from walking. The student was perfectly healthy, and walked perfectly straight. I now believe in Chinese traditional medicine, with the understanding that, just as is true with Western medicine, there is some quackery that exists. I remember buying bottled water that claimed it could cure cancer. Having been forced to take numerous medications, whose names were written in unintelligible Chinese with no English translation, and not having a clear idea of what I was putting into my body, I can now say with a great deal of assurance that Chinese medicine works. I remember a former student gave me a black ball to chew on and swallow, when I had fever, stopped sinuses, and crud in the lungs. My gag reflex attempted about four or five times to throw the half-chewed black ball back out. I used to think castor oil and Kaopectate were the two nastiest medicines on earth, but no longer. I was so happy to get the medicine down without throwing up; I didn't care any longer about being sick. But, about a half-hour later, my fever, sinuses, and crud were completely gone.

Chinese medicine mixes Western medicines in with the traditional approaches. Antibiotics of all sorts are sold over the counter. A five-tablet Z-Pac cost me USD 1.50, which in the USA I priced at about 75.00. However, not all Western medicines are as cheap. Below is an encounter that I had with a young Chinese woman selling drugs in an airport.

> Linda had developed diarrhea, and I went to buy her some medicine. The salesgirl pulls out a two-inch bottle of Cialis. I tell her that I didn't think that was going to do the trick for Linda. She then pulls out a small bottle of Viagra. I didn't know how to say "erectile dysfunction is not the problem" in Chinese, so I repeated, give me some diarrhea medicine for my wife. She then quotes me the price for the Cialis: "600 RMB" (90.00 USD). I said I didn't want it, please give me some diarrhea medicine. She then tells me that if I don't want it, I can buy some to give to my friends! I told her, why didn't she buy it and give it to her friends?

No discussion of Chinese medicine would be complete without a discussion of dental and eye-care. I have never gone to a Chinese dentist. I fear them like death. I once had a dental problem, asked a

Chinese man about where I should go to have it fixed, and he simply replied: "Don't." The Chinese themselves seem to fear dentists. They don't go until their teeth are hurting so unbearably that they have no choice. I had a nineteen-year old sophomore who missed my class, and told me she had just been to the dentist for the first time in her life. She had a cavity filled for the grand price of $1.45 USD. For fees like that, I should think the pain of the drilling would be overcome by the joy of paying the bill. After class, the student happily downed an ice-cold fruit smoothie, and was good to go the next day. This unwillingness to go to the dentist has its inevitable costs. One can see so many beautiful Chinese smiles marred by gaps and angles in the teeth. I can really understand the hesitation to go see the dentist. My American dentist told me he has a Chinese patient whose teeth had turned pink. He had never seen that before, and so he called a fellow dentist who had served many Chinese patients, and asked him whether could he help with the pink tooth problem? My dentist was informed that his patient had received a Chinese root canal. The Chinese dentist had hollowed out the canal, inserted into the canal a solid, cone-shaped paper tube that had previously been soaked in arsenic. The poisonous vapors from this arsenic paper cone then killed the remaining nerves in the canal. When arsenic kills a tooth, the tooth turns pink. I can only speculate about what happens when the arsenic vapors meander down the esophagus. I do now know into which color an internal organ will change when in the presence of gaseous arsenic. I do know this, though: I do not plan to have a root canal done in China.

On the other hand, when it comes to eye care, I am very impressed with the Chinese system. The following email extract tells why.

> I learned in Yinchuan that it is very common for nearsighted people under 18 years old in China to have acupuncture done, and it will invariably cure the nearsightedness, for a price of about $600.00 USD. In America, we just buy glasses for about that, I guess. I just bought some glasses here in the midst of our little village for $45.00, including the eye exam. For the first time in two years, I can see. The eye exam is free, done by the shopkeeper (they do have to take a government test to know what they are doing, and they do know what they are doing). Trying to communicate about whether you can see or not, or whether you can see when you walk down the steps or not, is a trip. But since I was so successful, Linda went back and bought a pair too, for 150.00 total. All within a five

minute walk of our place, where there is a tailor, bike repair shop, post office, pharmacy, hospital infirmary, and tons of great restaurants, fruit and vegetable markets, etc. I've attached a picture of the village to this email, to let you know that when you see these primitive looking villages on TV, they are not at all primitive, and in many ways probably better than in the USA.

CHINESE HOSPITALS

I have become a connoisseur of Chinese hospitals, having visited many of them. When I first came to China in 1995, I swore I would never go to one, but, after so many years in the country, it became inevitable. I still remember the first visit with fondness. It was an Air Force hospital. It was freezing cold inside, because no Chinese hospital heats the inside lobby area. Often, the nurses will smile at you, wrapped in thick green military gear, fit for the arctic. The nurse gave me a thermometer to take my temperature. I retired to a chair alongside a nearby wall, and just as I was about to stick the thermometer into my mouth, the Chinese school official in charge of taking care of me grabbed my arm, unbuttoned my coat, and started pulling my shirt tail out of my pockets. I was thinking that his behavior was quite unprofessional, when I realized he was trying to stick the thermometer under my shirt, so I could put it under my arm. The thought of putting the thermometer in my mouth amazed and horrified him. That task done, we proceeded to the elevator, where a gentleman with a hacking cough hocked up a big one to spit in the large cigarette ashtray besides the elevator doors. We moved on to the doctor's office. He had a long line of patients in front of his desk. Each patient is responsible to keep his own medical records, because they are not kept at the hospital. There is none of the sissy American concern for privacy. All those in line watch the male patients in front of the line pull up their shirts for examination, and listen to the patient tell the doctor what it is that he's afflicted with. If it's a woman patient in front of the line, she is instructed to step to the side a couple of feet, where she steps behind a sheet pulled diagonally across a corner of the room, so she can pull her shirt up to let the doctor examine her. We received a prescription from the doctor. Included were directions for me to get blood drawn. I went to a dark, dingy hallway, where over half the paint on each wall had peeled off. The nurse dutifully stabbed my finger, and sent the blood to have it analyzed. I have since discovered that Chinese doctors love to do two things, no matter what your sickness:

they draw blood, and they take stool samples, and chemically analyze them on the spot, print out the paper, and tell you what you've got. If it's something that can be taken care of with an IV, they send you to the hospital pharmacy to buy the drip, after which you go to the drip room, hand your IV up on the hook above your chair, and sit with a couple of hundred other patients who are watching TV and chatting. So, you see, one's blood vessels are not as sacrosanct in China as in the USA. They love to mainline drugs into their patients. I still remember sitting in the drip room in a Ningbo hospital and watching the nurse first attempt to get a stick into a three-month old infant's foot, and failing that, inserting the needle into the infant's temple.

I spent one Chinese New Year in a Ningbo hospital's neurological unit. This was a somewhat rare experience, and so I will give you the description of it that I made at the time.

> Chinese New Year's Eve, I was riding my bike for exercise at Ningbo University, and came upon the little system of concrete roads the Driving School uses to train its drivers. For some reason they had a hill, at the bottom of which was a Mt. Everest-sized speed bump, unmarked of course, on the other side of which was a concrete dip, which I observed carefully as I was about to crash into the bottom of it, to be the size of Death Valley, all to somehow train the Chinese driver. The hill increased my speed, and the bump sent me flying. I hit my head on the concrete, and I didn't feel I should move till I could get an ambulance there. That was an hour and a half later. The first hour of that was waiting for Linda and the Chinese university officials to locate me. There was a big problem: this driving track was out in the middle of nowhere. There were reeds all around the road, and no buildings, and no people. I called my Ningo University contacts using my cell phone. One was not there. One had punched her phone number in wrong. But fortunately her father was the gatekeeper at our apartment, and so I called Linda to ask the gatekeeper for his daughter's phone number. The daughter, Shelly, is one of the people in charge of foreigners. It was so ironic – it was at a get together for foreign students and teachers where we had met here the day before that I had asked her who I should call in case we had to go to the hospital or something. I knew everybody would be gone for Spring Festival. I knew I shouldn't have asked her that –

because, in China, people don't like to mention bad things like that, even when taking precautions. I was once told that I shouldn't ask about flight insurance when buying an air ticket, because it might make the flight go down. I thought that was superstition. Now, I know better.

The Chinese doctor, who knows about as much English as I know Russian, tried to explain what I had: "head trauma, with under the surface hematoma," which I think is "Subcutaneous hematoma," which I roughly guessed to mean is "you have a huge knot on your head, and you are going to spend the next few days in this hospital with a mother of a headache." I had two CT scans, and my brain was pronounced normal, thank God. With no nausea, they gave me anti-inflammation drugs, and watched to see if there was any internal bleeding in my brain. The first night I had bouts of vertigo, as the fireworks exploded for New Year's night. The doc said that was normal, and then gave me some Tian Ma, traditional Chinsese herbal medicine intraveneously, which I didn't know you could do. As a result, I am walking about the hospital floor now, thankful to be alive. I wasn't sure anybody could find me where I was laying after the accident, and so I don't feel too bad being in a hospital.

Besides, it's been worth the cultural experience. This is the head injury floor, the neurological unit, and there are some long-termers up here. Their families just move in. The hospital has no security; anybody just walks up to whomever they want to. They told me to watch my computer, because thieves from outside the city could get it. Shelly hired the mother of a young man who had a head injury in a car accident to take care of me. She's an old (and, what I mean is, she only looks old, but she is only 58) country woman who can't speak Mandarin, except on a very limited basis, so we have a hard time communicating. Since she has been hired, she has shadowed me like an alter ego, like a spirit from another world. I got up to go to the bathroom once, and the doctor (a man) modestly stood outside while the ayi (auntie) stood behind me, and held me up, while I did my business. At that point in time, I hardly cared, I was so glad to go. The ayi's family just walks into the room randomly. I have gotten to know her grandson, who comes in to punch buttons on my computer, her daughter in law, who has come in twice to chat, her husband, who took me for my first walk around the floor.

The second guy who took me around the floor held my hand like he was my girlfriend, a Chinese custom which I don't particularly like. He was just somebody who is living here for ten days, staying with his wife's younger brother, who had a stroke. He says he's bored, so he comes to talk with me. These are country people and workers, and so their Mandarin is hard for me to understand, but they are bored, and they spend a long time with me making sure I understand. They just make themselves at home. One guy came in with a whole skinned chicken; soaked in soy sauce, ready to cook. One lady, who was just a fellow hometowner with my ayi and her husband, pulled out some black hair dye, and dyed both the ayi's hair, and her husband's hair, right in my room. There is a special room at the end of the hall where there are two long bars with clothes hanging on them.

My bed is a Chinese bed, very hard, but not as hard as some I've known. It's also short, so my feet stick about 12 inches through the holes at the end. One country lady, whom I don't know, started tapping on them, pushing on them, to get them back in the bed. Most of the time they just commented on the fact that I was not positioned right. They couldn't seem to understand that I was just too tall for the bed. So, I would curl my feet up on the inside of the bed, just to quiet them down. Then, when they would leave, I would stick them back over the end. Last night in the middle of the night, a nurse saw them sticking out, and woke the ayi up (she was sleeping contentedly in the bed next to me), and told her to make the foreigner sleep better. So, the ayi jumped up and started cramming my feet in the bed again. But today, she just sticks them on the top of the end rail, and cushions the heels with a quilt. She's given up. I won.

One bad thing is the ayi snores, quite loudly. Once the doctor came in in the middle of the night to check on me, and I told him the ayi was snoring. He woke her up and told her not to snore. After the doctor left, she went back to sleep, and snored even louder.

As I write this, a country woman I've never seen before just walked into my room. She said something to me in Ningbo dialect, and then left. Things are pretty casual around here. But it grows on you. The head nurse, Yang Yanping by name, was trying to get me to teach her some English. I asked her how long she had been nursing, and she said 17 years. I said that was impossible, since she looked like she was about 25. She asked me to guess; I said 25, thinking maybe I had misunderstood her Mandarin. She said 39. I couldn't believe it. Later, I met her in the hall when she was fixing the "breathing machine", and she took time to explain to me that the numbers on the wall were to identify patients when their were too many to fit in the rooms, they put them in the halls. Later, when I was taking a walking tour, hand in hand with the young bored guy, he was puffing on a cigarette, and he ground it on the floor. I pointed to the no-smoking sign and asked him: what did the sign mean? Yang Yanping, the 39 year-old head nurse, just laughed. No big deal to her.

The bill was about 600.00 USD, after two CT scans, three nights, and parts of four days, in the neurological unit of the hospital. It almost makes you want to get sick and come back. Of course, there is no food, and there are no towels and toilet paper, and the bathroom floor had a ground-down cigarette butt and a cockroach, but heck, an American hospital would probably charge you about 100$ a roll for toilet paper, and 200$ for the towel, and deny that there were any cockroaches on the floor. The nurses do as little as possible. Linda gave me a sponge bath, and the nurses always get the ayi, or me, to put the thermometer under my arm, etc. But for this price, you can't beat it.

That hospital story ended nicely. But, here's another one that isn't quite so jolly. I had eaten some mutton and drunk some cold milk one winter's day in 2010 in Yinchuan, a northern city with a very cold climate. According to the locals, I had committed the unpardonable dietary sin, and so I justly deserved the agonizing pains that I was suffering in my belly. After hearing at least ten, probably more, local people tell me that I had screwed up my interior yin and yang by doing such a dumb thing, I am actually frightened to ever do it again. I went to the hospital. Below is what I wrote shortly after the experience.

I have discovered something that should never, ever be done. Don't ever eat lamb and drink cold milk at the same time. I did so, and was afflicted with severe gastroenteric disturbances that forced me to go to the hospital twice during the three days it took to recover. I was told by every doctor, nurse, and patient, as well as bystanders quick to give their learned opinions, that I had done a TERRIBLE THING, because I had screwed up the balance of the yin and the yang in my body. Too much yin, not enough yang. You can do that sort of thing outside of China, but by golly, you better not do it over here. The first doctor told me he needed a stool sample. My heart sank. I envisioned them giving me a five- or six-inch tupperware container for the sample, but unfortunately, I was supplied with a tiny cup made out of plastic film, the bottom the size of a quarter, the opening the size of a half-dollar. I entered the rest room. Remember, if you can, those restrooms you were forced to enter on the way to the beach in those decrepit old gas stations in Andrews and Greeleyville [small towns in South Carolina]. I would have given my right arm for such a rest room. There was dirt and pipes everywhere. There was no sink. The walls had plaster and Lord only knows what else falling off of them, or growing on them. You could have planted a crop in the dirt on the floor, and on the top of the ceramic petitions. The smell would buckle your knees. There was a raised platform, no doors, and a lateral trough running the length of the platform. A single petition divided the top of the platform, intersecting the trough in the middle. The trough passed under the petition. The trough, of course, was the communal toilet, over which, if one was to use it, one had to squat. My first attempt at obtaining a stool sample was a failure, as I was blown out from 24 hours of first-degree diarrhea. I thought, hot dog, I'm getting out of this, but unfortunately, after we went back and told him, the doctor said that the stool sample was very important. So, we leave the hospital, I eat some noodle soup, and an hour or so later, I find myself squatting again over that damnable trough, the bottom of which looked like the unprocessed raw matter of a failed sewage plant: dark, mysterious, noisome, and quite unfortunately, much too close to my face due to my squatting position. As I was trying to keep from gagging, keep my clothes from being soiled, keep my legs from cramping up, and trying to get the sample, a man comes in to use the restroom. Chinese culture loves to emphasize harmony, togetherness, and group activity, and so I unbegrudgingly shared a communal bathroom experience with my unknown neighbor, as he placed his liquid contribution into the communal trough, which passed about 18 inches in front of my nose, because the trough was unfortunately slanted my direction, and because my legs were so cramped I couldn't move. I still had not obtained the stool sample. All this time, my stomach is convoluting itself because I had too much yin and not enough yang in me, due to my consumption of lamb and cold milk. It was at this point that I began thinking, this is really too bad to actually be true. However, I finally obtained the sample, gave it to the nurse, who ran it through a machine, printed out some numbers, gave the paper to us, and we carried it back to the doctor. And, you know what the doctor said? He said I had diarrhea.

Before you start feeling sorry for me, you should realize that the bill for the above experience (including all sorts of wonderful drugs which I don't have a clue what they were), was about $7.00 USD. And you thought Obamacare was great!

Every foreigner who desires a student or work visa is required to get a medical checkup. These checkups are quite thorough. One can get an EKG, eye exam, blood- and urine chemical analyses, MRI's, X-Rays, and various other procedures done for about $30.00 USD. Most of these procedures are done with modern equipment from the west. I always felt good when I recognized the name on a medical machine. But every now and then, the inexplicable would occur. The following email extract describes one of my wife's trips to the hospital in Yinchuan to receive her examination. This experience has not been repeated in other cities, so perhaps the procedure is unique to that area.

I was sitting outside of the "Wu Guan Ke," which means "Five Organ Department," which we more prosaically call "ENT" (Ear, Nose and Throat). The Chinese five main organs are ear, nose, throat, lips, and tongue. I walked in with Linda to get checked, and a half dozen Muslim women, all wrapped up in headscarves, pointed to the door and asked me to leave. I figured it was because, to examine the five organs, they would have to unwrap the head, and that would be immodest, so I left. Linda stayed. She said that the doctor lined them all up to do an examination. He was in a hurry because of the crowd, and so he did the examination en masse. He told them all to lift their shirts, which they all did together. I have yet to figure how you check five sense organs that are on the head, by lifting one's shirt, but the Chinese are good at this sort of thing.

Admittedly, Chinese hospitals take some getting used to. But the quality of care is rapidly improving. In 1995, a fellow professor was treated for a mysterious, potentially life-threatening illness for which he could find no relief in the USA. The doctors at Shanghai's Number One Hospital cured him. The Beijing United Hospital handled successfully an African friend's sickle cell anemia crisis. This was remarkable, because sickle cell anemia predominately strikes black people, and there are few black people in China. Nonetheless, the doctor called his brother, also a doctor, in America, and figured out what to do. My wife Linda had two cataracts removed in Yinchuan in 2011, which is considered remote and backwards by many others in China, especially those in big cities, like Beijing and Shanghai. The surgery was perfectly successful. We were told that she was the first American to have such a surgery in the city of Yinchuan. At her first post-op eye check, the doctor, plus several assistant doctors, plus several nurses, plus the director of the clinic (who had observed the operation) all huddled around the machine that Linda was looking into, as a photographer flashed pictures over and over. The total cost (uninsured) was about USD 2000.00. Before the operations, she had her eyes checked four times, at a total cost of USD 0.60. While I was waiting for Linda, I got my eye pressure checked. They did it for free. About five nurses and interns all took turns oohing and ahhing as they looked at the back of my eyeball, which had been reconstructed with plastic in the USA to repair cataracts and a detached retina. Almost every doctor in China who has checked my eyeballs has commented favorably on the work the American doctors did. Another story which illustrates favorably the reputed expertise of Chinese hospitals, at least the hospitals in Shanghai, but which at the same time reflects unfavorably upon Chinese bureaucracy, was related to me by an American student in America, who had been assigned by his Fortune 500 company to work at a branch in Shanghai. One of his employees had inexpertly handled some equipment, and unfortunately, his finger had become sliced off. The worker was bundled off to the hospital, but the finger was left lying at the scene of the accident. The workers on the scene were faced with a dilemma. Should they put the finger on ice and send it to the hospital, or should they obey the bureaucratic regulations that required that, upon accidents, the scene of the accident should be left undisturbed, so that a proper investigation might be performed? My businessman informant told me that he later learned the Shanghai hospital could have easily re-attached the finger, which I don't doubt, given the quality of the big hospitals in Shanghai. But alas, we will never know, because the good workers of that company, I suppose imbued with the spirit of Confucianism - which exalts order, propriety, conformity to pattern, obedience, even if it means a man lives fingerless the rest of his life - decided that the scene of the accident should go untouched as the regulations required, and the finger should not be sent to the hospital.

How do Chinese hospitals keep rates so low? Of course, various governments subsidize the hospitals. But, there is something else: they charge cash, up front. Once I was in Beijing, holding a donation that someone in the States had given to a Beijing orphanage. I called the director of the orphanage, and I heard over her cell phone that she was crying. I asked her what was wrong, and she said that she was holding two babies deformed with spina bifida whose parents had left them in a trash dump. She had no money, and the Beijing Children's Hospital would not admit the babies, and the babies were dying, and would be dead by that afternoon. Nonetheless, the hospital would not admit the babies. I rushed to the hospital, and gave the orphanage director the money. She charged towards the pay counter and had the babies admitted. One of the babies survived.

The Chinese are deadly serious about education. Education is deeply entwined with thousands of years of Chinese history. For millennia, personal honor and vocational advancement depended upon performance in the imperial examination system. Scholars were everything in old China, and lawyers were nothing. The traditional Confucian reverence for the teacher has subsided somewhat in modern Chinese society. However, it was quite in evidence when I first arrived in China, in 1995. Students rushed to pick up my briefcase, before leaving class. They rushed to wipe chalk dust, real or imagined, from my seat, before I sat. A student would rush to the blackboard to keep me from erasing it. Like some grand pooh bah, I was escorted to elevators, where I stood at the door, waiting for the women students to enter, and where they refused to budge, unless I entered first. In an elementary school, the students bowed to me as I passed. The students, dressed neatly in their school uniforms, would listen quietly and attentively to the teacher, sitting on the edge of their seats, hands folded on the edge of their desks, barking out in unison answers to their laoshi's questions. Those were the days and I thought they would never end, but they have. Fifteen years after that experience in 1995 in Shanghai, my wife and I had the privilege of teaching in an English training school in Yinchuan. Our suspicion that Confucian dignity was breaking down in the student population was confirmed many times by the Chinese middle- and high-school teachers to whom we talked. This was especially evident in a Yinchuan middle school whose students were from wealthy families, and that school mirrored our experience in a private Beijing training school, one of whose students was a famous movie producer. However, let it be said that the most insensitive and rude Chinese class does not nearly approach the lack of respect that can be encountered in an American classroom. Chinese students, especially in the higher-level universities, are a joy to teach. I will now relate several incidents of the many my wife and I have experienced teaching in secondary schools and universities in several cities in China.

CHINESE SECONDARY SCHOOLS

Chinese middle- and high-school students are in many respects like their counterparts in the west. The middle-schoolers horseplay, shoot spitballs, and idolize Michael Jackson, Justin Bieber, and Lady Gaga. However, secondary school students are different in that they can converse with English-speaking foreigners in an extremely foreign language, and they study every waking minute. School hours and student habits vary somewhat, but typically a student arrives at school at 8:00, takes two hours off for lunch, leaves at 6:00, eats supper, then does homework till bedtime at around 11:00 or 12:00. On the weekend, they attend special private training school to work on subjects in which they are having trouble, such as math or physics or English. One high school student told me about a group of students in her high school who had mothers, relatives, and siblings do everything for them, such as cooking and cleaning and shopping, so the students would never have to put their books down. They stayed up to 2:00 a.m., every morning, and arose at 6:00 a.m. They took their books into the bathroom every time they had to go. As a teacher who has spent his life bemoaning the lack of time that students put in studying, I was surprised to find myself full of pity for these students. Parents put excruciating pressure on them to exceed on the gao kao, the national College Entrance Exam. One middle school student who, like many Chinese was afraid that the global apocalypse described in the movie 2012 would actually come to pass, told my wife she wished it would happen, so she wouldn't have any more homework. I think she was being overly optimistic, because I am quite sure her Tiger Mom would crawl out from under the rubble, put her finger on her daughter's nose, Chinese-style, and command her: "Study! Study! Study!"

One cannot help but be impressed by the discipline and order exhibited by Chinese secondary school students. They line up by the hundreds and do calisthenics every morning, in unison and without complaint. With no teacher in the room, they will do eye-exercise massages to their faces in rhythm to music piped over the public address system. Each class has a monitor and a vice-monitor, who are responsible for passing out items, taking up papers, unlocking the computer for the teacher before class. The monitor even takes the key home for safekeeping. At certain times of each day, bands of students armed with buckets of water and huge straw brooms, without teachers present, will clean the stairs and the classroom floors. Hundreds of them will play at break on the playground, with no teacher present. It brings tears to my eyes, as I recall this. I happened to see this order and discipline put to good effect during an earthquake I experienced while speaking to a Yinchuan high school class. Below is what I wrote home at the time.

I was on the fourth floor, and went to the front of a class of about 25 students to speak. I said: "Hi, I'm Dan Trotter, and I'm from America." Now what I am about to tell you, you might not believe, because I know I have a tendency to exaggerate. But if I'm lying, I'm dying, no sooner did I get the words out of my mouth, than there was an earthquake. I felt like Barack Obama - the power of my oratory moved the earth. It was a small earthquake, but an earthquake, nonetheless. After the bang, and after the building stopped swaying, the students looked at each other in fear. Nobody moved. Then one teacher said, no, it wasn't an earthquake, and she pointed upstairs, saying someone had dropped something. Then, all of a sudden, the students didn't believe her, and headed in fear en masse to the door. I thought I needed to exit, too, so I headed out. When I got to the hallway, a good portion of the 2000-3000 students was pouring down the stairwell, and I couldn't get through. I had to wait till they were all out of the building, before I got out. Chinese students are drilled to perfection. In just a few minutes, with no teacher's direction, all two to three thousand of them were standing in formation on the soccer field. Since they were already there, in about one half hour, the authorities asked me to address them. So I did.

The middle-schoolers sent a bunch of their representatives to the front to ask questions. One little girl asked me, did I like Kobe Bryant? This was a particularly painful question, as Bryant is one of my most unfavorite people, playing as he does for the Los Angeles Lakers, who just beat my favorite team, the Boston Celtics in Game 7 of the NBA finals, a game in which the Celtics were ahead until the final 6 and 1/2 minutes. So I answered "No." She asked me why? I said "Because he is a Los Angeles Laker." I expected this to be a very unpopular answer, because EVERYBODY (or at least every male) in China idolizes the Lakers and Bryant. She sweetly responded: "I don't like the Lakers, either." And then, much to my gratification, the whole audience started clapping! I couldn't believe it. I smiled, and shook the little girl's hand. The clapping intensified. It was a healing moment.

The students' dress also emphasized their discipline. They all wore uniforms, and it appears to me that they wanted to. A few students would be without their uniforms, and when I asked why, the response was that they didn't want to wear them that day. I asked if they would get in trouble, and was told, no, not at all. Interestingly, the teachers looked a little ragtag and out of place, because they didn't wear school uniforms, but normal clothes. I say normal, but perhaps that is exaggerated. The women teachers in Yinchuan in the winter wore miniskirts and one-molecule-thick tights so tight they made spandex look like sackcloth. Meanwhile, the high school girls were all dressed modestly in baggy uniforms. It was one more example of how many things are backwards in the Middle Kingdom.

Sometimes, I somewhat cynically speculate that the famous discipline of Chinese students may perhaps have been inculcated in them to keep them from thinking dangerous thoughts. Chinese students are notorious in their lack of ability to think, to analyze, to synthesize, to weigh and compare alternatives. College-educated Chinese students will tell you this is true, and almost every foreign teacher with a little experience teaching in China will tell you the same thing. High school students are drilled, drilled, drilled to the point that they could memorize a phone book, if China had phone books, which unfortunately, it doesn't. The following email excerpt describes an incident illustrating the tendency of high school students not to think for themselves. I had heard several times Chinese people claiming Americans looked down on black people, which I had thought quite ironic, given the notorious, outsized prejudice against black-skinned people in China. I suspect, although I can not prove, that this has been fed to them like a mantra, similar to the line everyone spouts about Mao Zedong, that he was "seventy percent right and thirty percent wrong." I suspect that the incident this email extract describes is an example of the regurgitation of rote learning.

> I had a student stand in front of a class to introduce himself with four questions, one of which was "What do you dislike?". He said my name is so-and-so, and I hate the Japanese. In a Q and A session, a student asked me what I thought of the Japanese. I have only known two Japanese people. One was a very pretty Coker College student who could drink any Coker student under the table. Another was a young Japanese woman who was a fellow student of Chinese in Beijing, who is now running a brothel in Beijing. I thought it politic not to mention my personal experiences with the Japanese, and so instead I told them governments are not people, and just because the Chinese government and the Japanese government are fighting over Diaoyu Island, and the Japanese

treated you terribly in WWII (and they really did), that is no reason to hate Japanese people individually. I told them that over most of my lifetime I have hated my own government, but I don't hate individual Americans, and they can hate the American government too, but that was no reason to hate me. They took this quite well. Another one asked me, I think in one of the same classes in which hatred of the Japanese was mentioned: "Did Americans look down on black people?" I responded, "We have a black president, who do you think voted for him?" They all laughed at that, and nodded affirmatively. I was amazed they hadn't thought of that on their own. I always have the deep impression that Chinese students are spouting the Party line. They are notorious to foreign teachers over here for not thinking on their own. Incidentally, some college students got so incensed over the recent fishing boat incident with the Japanese, that they were protesting all over the place, and the Chinese government became concerned about the protests, and made them go to class on Saturday and Sunday.

In cities containing few foreigners, one must become accustomed to being famous. Photographers walk backwards in front of you, snapping away. Middle school students mob you in the hallways, thrusting their notebooks in your face, screaming for autographs. Below is an account of an encounter with some elementary school children in the small town of Xiao Ba, in Ningxia Hui Autonomous Region, where I had gone to promote the English language training school for which I worked.

I was instructed to stand on the sidewalk and say or do nothing, but just be an attraction. My assistant, who was one of the larger Chinese women I have seen, became engulfed in a mob of elementary school kids, who were clutching and clawing at her stash of brochures held in her hand. I told her to hold them over her head, which she did, but to no avail. The kids kept charging and pushing, till the assistant was just about to go down to the sidewalk. I grabbed the brochures from her to take the heat away from her, and then I felt the panic that people must feel in soccer crowds when they are about to be trampled to death. My knees began to buckle, and I almost went down. I then decided it was no longer the time to play the part of the polite foreigner, and I began to push and shove back until I gained my equilibrium, and got the little hellions off of me. I'm not sure what Confucious would have thought of these kids.

The middle school students in Yinchuan were just as star-struck. Below is my contemporary account of our appearances in several middle schools there.

As we walk through the campuses and halls, the responses have been varied, but all a little overblown. I remember passing two students, rounding a corner, and hearing this giant sucking sound, as the students, gasping, contemplated the arrival of foreigners into their world. Many of the students here have never seen foreigners. So, they say "How are you?" in English, and then run off giggling. They clap for you as you walk down the halls. They surround you and back you up against the hallway wall, and just stare at you, while one of them musters the courage to say something in English. Several classes have mobbed both Linda and me for autographs, shoving their notebooks and pens in front of us, as they pushed and crowded around so close that it was hard to breathe. I thought to myself, what a pain it must be to be a sports star - your fingers get cramped, your pen keeps bumping up against somebody's notebook, which is thrust into the middle, and you can't figure out who to sign first. One day, as we walked along, paparazzi walked backwards, in front of us, snapping pictures crazily. And of course, all the students have mobile phones with cameras, and they consider it the greatest honor to have a picture of you with them in it. One middle school girl told me (in English) "I like you!". This was topped only by a high school boy, who screamed across the campus (in English) "I love you!" It was touching.

CHINESE UNIVERSITIES

I have taught in four different Chinese universities over a sixteen-year period, an experience just broad enough to keep me from making facile stereotypes. I have observed differences between students who study in top-tier universities and those who study in special programs for those who didn't make the bottom tier of the College Entrance Exam results. In addition, university students have changed over the sixteen years that I have. Sixteen years is a lifetime in China.

The Chinese themselves are dazzled by the dizzying speed of change in their country. They often tell you of momentous changes that happened five years ago in their city, and they often exclaim "China changes every day." I would imagine that this would be difficult for a citizen of a country whose cultural foundations are rooted in thousands of years of history and tradition. I have detected some resistance to the increasing globalization of Chinese culture amongst older Chinese, but not much. It seems to me that the Chinese look much more to the benefits of "opening and reform," than to their past, which includes thousands of years of obsolete feudalism, and most recently, the discredited excesses of the Cultural Revolution and hard-core communism. Incidentally, this near-lust for change, which almost directly translates into desire for all things Western, is curiously intermixed with a naïve nationalism, often anti-Western and anti-American, which dictates that university students mouth repetitive slogans they hear on the state-controlled CCTV TV network ("Mao was seventy-percent right and thirty-percent wrong"). Anti-American foreign policy is especially subject to reductionism. I have heard from different people on opposite diagonals of the country give me almost identical word-for-word rehashes of the evils of the American involvement in Iraq and Libya, which suspiciously tracked the scripts of CCTV broadcasts I had heard. When the American government accidentally bombed the Chinese embassy in Belgrade in 1999, an American friend teaching at a Shanghai university reported to me that he could not conduct class, because the students were all crying. Ah, such patriotism! Can you imagine American college students breaking down if China bombed the U.S. Embassy in some obscure foreign country? Yet, on the other hand, I have often heard students, as well as other Chinese, openly doubt that what they hear on CCTV is true. Despite diligent efforts by the government to censor the Internet, information is getting through to university students.

At any rate, the changes undergone over the sixteen years I have taught in Chinese universities make it difficult to generalize too much about Chinese universities and their students. With that caveat, let me proceed to give my reflections on college life in the People's Republic. First of all, the teaching styles of Chinese professors and their Western counterparts are remarkably different. The Chinese professor is oh-so-formal. I remember seeing Chinese women professors in Jimei University in Xiamen dressed to the nines as they lectured in the sweltering 95 degree Fahrenheit heat, even after the air conditioning was turned off to supposedly stop the spread of

43

H1N1 swine flu. They wore professional gray skirts, frilly, silky blouses, pearl necklaces, black high heel shoes, and lipstick. Meanwhile, I and the other Western professors wore shorts, sandals, and short-sleeve shirts, which I personally considered necessary for my comfort and survival. Chinese professors rigidly stand, or sit, in one place behind a microphone and lecture. Socratic dialogue with the students is not seen, because, I was told by one student, that would show disrespect to the teacher. Apparently, to question a professor would imply that the instructor might be wrong, and that would cause him to lose face. I remember, in 1995, sitting down in a windowsill to rest a bit while the students copied down what was on the board. The whole class burst out laughing. I discreetly checked my fly, I looked around, and I could see nothing that warranted laughter. Later, one of the students told my daughter that "Dr. Trotter and his funny movements" occasioned the laughter. Apparently, the students had never seen a professor sit in a windowsill. A Chinese student who has never had a Western professor before, and who is accustomed to listen passively to a Chinese lecturer, will be nonplussed when a Western professor walks down the aisle and asks him a question. They are not used to the mobile professor, and they certainly aren't used to being confronted in class. The reaction of the women students is especially noteworthy. First of all, they don't look like women, but more like schoolgirls in middle school or high school. Next, one watches them as they shyly and modestly bow their head, place their hand over their mouth, and start to giggle uncontrollably. Their faces then turn a bright red. They turn their heads from you, and show you the back of their neck. The first time I observed this phenomenon, I was shocked to see it, not knowing that it was possible for yellow skin to turn red. It is very hard to carry on any sort of intellectual discussion this way, but fortunately, as time goes on, the students become quite accustomed to the Western teaching style. I have never met a Chinese student who doesn't prefer Western teaching methods to the traditional Chinese style.

Chinese college students are often required to tolerate insufferable classroom conditions, although this is changing as the country develops. Almost every classroom in which I have taught in recent years is equipped with a computer, overhead projector, and an air conditioner that also heats. However, over the years, I have suffered through sub-freezing days teaching in unheated classrooms with two coats on, watching the frosty breaths of wrapped-up students whose fingertips protruded from the cut-off fingers of their gloves. The students never seemed to mind. They would twirl their pens around their fingertips in a way that I've never seen elsewhere, and which I cannot imitate. They would cheerfully open the windows for "fresh air," never mind that the temperature was below freezing. The chalk in a Chinese classroom is inevitably fifty percent air and fifty percent dust, and breaks if you look at it. In summertime conditions, I have watched students collapse their heads on their desks, because the air conditioning was turned off. My wife returned sweating from one class, looking like she had been swimming with her dress on. Some classrooms are not air conditioned, but have high ceilings with fans. The fans are so loud that they compete with the shouting in the halls, all of which makes it difficult for the instructor to be heard speaking a language foreign to the students. But the students are used to all this, and they never complain.

In general, Chinese university students are world-class cheaters. Cheating is a game to many of them, a part of the system that they have to negotiate in order to succeed. There is very little stigma attached to the practice. Ironically, the group-oriented nature of the Chinese culture apparently contributes to the practice. Chinese students join a class, and they stay with that class through every classroom session for four years. No matter what class they attend, they have the same classmates. As a result, strong, tight loyalties develop between them. If it turns out that slower members of the class are not performing academically, the whole class loses face. Therefore, the academic leaders feel the need to help the slower students along, by cheating. In addition, there is a different attitude to intellectual property in China. I remember hearing a story at one Chinese university where I taught, where an Ivy League professor had given a student an "F" for plagiarizing a paper. The university told him to stand down, the professor refused, and the professor ended up back in the U.S.A., his trip to China cut short. I remember how, at that same university, a student called me to her desk to ask me what the answer was to an exam question. Of course, I told her I couldn't answer the question. She then cheerfully turned and asked her neighbor on the opposite side, with me standing six inches away from her, on the other side. At another university, I caught a girl cheating and took her paper away from her. She just smiled cheerily and walked out of the classroom, with no hard feelings. What really drives the cheating is the pressure for good grades, and the desire to find a job. China has a very materialistic culture that is just a few years away from great poverty, and the desire to make it financially is close to the surface of every Chinese student. And, the cheating goes beyond the classroom. I helped a former Chinese student apply for entry to a Master's program in an American university. She asked me how many A's she should put on her Chinese college transcript. It seems that a former professor was now an administrator in her former college, and wanted to know how to properly doctor her transcript. Once in South Carolina, I received a call from a Beijing man who wanted me to help him apply for political asylum in the USA. He had formerly run a cram school in Beijing, was given access to advance copies of the College Entrance Exam, and had passed the information along to his students. The government was on his tail, and would I help him? (I didn't.) College students in China who want to go to graduate school in the west routinely pay RMB 1500 (USD 317.00) to RMB 3000 (USD 476.00) to websites that will write application letters and personal statements for the student. Corruption is a big problem, and it is not confined to the government.

As sixteen years have passed from the time I first arrived on a Chinese college campus, I have noticed a shift in the worldview of Chinese university students. They used to routinely ask philosophical and religious questions of their foreign professors, anxious for something new from the west. Now they seem to care mostly about how they can get a good job and make money. This is not universally true, however. College students are aware of government corruption, and sometimes complain, but most say there is nothing they can do about it, so why worry. In addition, Chinese university students can get ginned up over nationalistic issues, as they did recently when the Chinese government stoked Chinese nationalism in order to protest Japan's actions in a conflict over fishing boats. The students poured out into the streets to protest, and when the government thought they were getting overly rambunctious, the central authorities dictated that classes would be held on Saturday and Sunday, thus destroying the protests. I recently told a very intelligent Chinese university student that there were three kinds of Chinese college students: one, those who were forced to go to college by their parents; two, those who were very good students but whose education was merely a means to making money upon graduation; and three, a small minority who were interested in discovering truth. She immediately recognized the categories, and placed herself in the third category. Recently, in my experience, the third sort of student is rare, even as it is in the west.

I will close this section with two experiences obtained at a Chinese university whose strategic vision is to imitate the universities of the west. The first occurred in the classroom, and the second occurred in a faculty meeting.

Six of my students performed a role-play in my Business English class, using a PowerPoint background. They flashed up a young female-bodied person in an advanced state of undress. This person was supposed to be a competitor for the spokeswoman for the company in the role-play, "Sexy Underwear Co." I promptly got up and locked the classroom door, at which the students all laughed. I later found out prospect #1 was a famous Korean transsexual. The other competitor for the spokeswoman's job was Feng Jie, who was actually a woman, but whose picture drew jeers and laughter from the class. I later asked why. Turns out she was a "terrible, disgusting" person. Curious, I asked why she was disgusting. It was because she had advertised for a husband on the Internet, and had falsely claimed in the ad that she was working for a Fortune 500 company, when actually she was a clerk at Walmart. For these perversions, Feng Jie is now a proverb in China. I asked all these questions after the role-play, but during the role play I couldn't figure out what was going on. It was especially shocking when one of the girls in the role-play, wearing a miniskirt for the occasion, puts her leg up on a desk, pulls her short dress up even shorter, and starts running her hands up and down her leg, imitating one of the spokeswoman prospects. The whole class is now whooping and hollering. I just wonder whether Chairman Mao would have approved of this sort of thing.

Below I recount the most interesting faculty meeting I have ever attended.

I was the only foreigner, in there. A colleague, who has lived and taught for years in the USA and Canada, was explaining cross-cultural pitfalls to all the Chinese professors there. He mentioned that his Dean in his American college called him in one time and told him to never wear a T-shirt with "69" on it, that this could get him fired. Because I had not understood the Chinese, I asked the teaching affairs assistant (a young 25-year old Chinese girl) what was going on, and she said very solemnly that it was something about "69", which in the west is some sort of religious symbol. Then, to my horror, one of the Chinese professors, in front of the Dean, the Vice-Dean, and over fifty Business Administration professors, said he would like to ask Dr. Trotter what "69" meant. I indignantly told the assembled professors it was something HORRIBLE and I was not going to be able to tell him!

CHINESE ENGLISH LANGUAGE TRAINING SCHOOLS

China is mad for English. English, of greater or lesser quality, is on signboards, TV, Radio, the Internet, banners, T-shirts, everywhere. I have tried, and I emphasize tried, to learn some Chinese. I have a first-hand appreciation of how difficult it is for an English-speaker to learn Chinese, and so I suspect that the converse is also true. So then, how have so many Chinese people learned to speak English? I will include here some research I have done into English language training schools. The size of the market in 2008 was about 20 billion RMB (roughly 3.17 billion USD), an astounding figure. This will perhaps explain the pervasive use of English amongst educated Chinese. I include this information because it might be helpful to the many, many Westerners who desire to travel to China to teach English.

Introduction

There are countless firms serving the very large and growing EFL market in China. EFL stands "English as a Foreign Language," which should be distinguished from "English as a Second Language." English as a Second Language is taught to non-native English speakers living in an English speaking country, while English as a Foreign Language is taught to non-native English speakers in a country whose native language is not English. An umbrella term used to describe both ESL and EFL is TESOL: "Teachers of English to Speakers of Other Languages."

Some of the more prominent EFL firms in China include New Oriental Foreign Language School, Wall Street Institute, and Cambridge Oriental Education Group. New Oriental, established in 1993, has thirty-six schools in thirty-four cities in China, serving 5,000,000 learners. New Oriental is noted for being the first Chinese educational organization listed on the New York Stock Exchange. (China Easy Booking, 2011) Wall Street Institute invested 40 million yuan (US $4.84 million) to set up schools in Shanghai and very quickly attracted more than 1,000 trainees. (People's Daily Online,

2002) Cambridge Oriental Education Group, established in 1986, has eighteen various institutions and has taught 12 million people.[3] (China Easy Booking, 2011)

What has made EFL so popular in China? There are several factors. One, the government is extremely supportive of EFL. Various Chinese local governments mandate English learning at various levels of primary school, middle school, and high school. It was reported in the official government press that plans had been made in Beijing in the early 2000's to require English training in the Beijing primary schools, at first beginning in the third grade, and then later, beginning in the first grade. (People's Daily, 2001, a) During the same period of time, the Ministry of Education listed English as a compulsory subject for millions of primary school students. (People's Daily, 2001, b) By 2007, the government had even extended its support beyond government schools, having launched a series of laws and regulations to regulate and promote the development of non-public funded education. (China Market Intelligence Center, 2008) One of the major components of the government-sponsored College Entrance Exam is English. The government's motive for such support can be traced to China's growing involvement in the global economy, in which English is the lingua franca. (Market Avenue, 2009)

Another factor pushing the growth of EFL in China is private self-interest. Chinese citizens are spending much on tuition at English training schools, both for themselves, and their children, being very aware that English ability often directly impacts their income. (Market Avenue, 2009)

It is quite apparent that the English training market in China is huge. But just how big is it? It is impossible to obtain a precise estimate. The government-reported figures, some of which were provided above, are subject to some skepticism. English training is occurring everywhere in China, but how much of that training should be contained in the English-training "market" is problematic. For example, should the millions of school children in the government schools who are being trained in English be included? They are not paying for the training; rather, the government is. Another example: should those students who are involved in voluntary exchange programs be included? These programs facilitate language-training barter. For example, a Chinese-speaking student teaches Chinese to an English speaker, who in turn provides English instruction to the

Chinese speaker. No money ever changes hands. Should this be included in the EFL "market"? (Fons, 2002)

In addition, it is difficult to say whether certain substandard English training schools should be included in the EFL "market". There are many, many "mom and pop" English training schools all over the country, some operated illegally out of homes, some managed by retired Chinese English teachers whose English is substandard, some starting up in small rooms above storefront shops. One frequent visitor to China, reporting on the state of English training schools in the country, claims that many of the schools purporting to teach English are less than good. They hire people who are not qualified to teach, and pay them poorly, while charging students big bucks. There are frequent articles in English language Chinese papers pointing out the inadequacies of the teachers. One author said that he and his wife had met a "teacher" who was "teaching" to folks selling securities. He had absolutely no teaching experience and could not speak a word of Chinese. (Fons, 2002)

Even larger, well-established schools have come in for criticism concerning the quality of their educational offerings. According to one observer, "bigger companies, such as Wall Street English, often charge exorbitant fees for their training, are more concerned about their bottom line than they are about people, and commonly hire "backpackers" instead of professional trainers."[11] (Allison, 2010) While it may be easy to describe Wall Street Institute as a relevant player in the English training market, even if it were true that the quality of Wall Street English is substandard, it is difficult to say whether other less prominent schools operating at a substandard level should be included in the relevant market.

Size of the Chinese EFL Market

Despite the problems in measuring the size of the Chinese EFL market, there is enough data available to indicate clearly that the Chinese EFL market is very large. No matter how the market is measured, it is demonstrably clear that the Chinese English training market is huge. We shall examine the market from the aspect of profits, number of training schools, number of students enrolled, and number of English teachers hired.

Profits

Below are listed several examples of profits earned by English training schools in China.

• In 2001, the industry in Beijing made a gross profit of 700 million yuan (US$84.68 million)… (Xinhua News Agency, 2002)

• The oral English course of Beijing New Oriental Language School reported an income of over 90 million yuan (US$10.89 million) in 2001, while the Eastern English Services and Wall Street English schools all grew rapidly in the city at the same time. (Xinhua News Agency, 2002)

• Eastern English Services say that it has set up four schools in Beijing. Each has brought in 500,000 yuan (US$60,483.60) monthly. (Xinhua News Agency, 2002)

• The annual output value (2008) of the English training market in China is about 20 billion RMB. This market still has plenty of room to grow. The overall market value of English training in China in 2010 is expected to be 30 billion RMB.[15] (Market Avenue, 2009)

Number of Training Schools

Estimates vary on the number of English training schools in China. One expert reports a number between "hundreds" and "thousands" (Allison, 2010). This imprecision probably reflects the difficulty in defining exactly what is a training school, and perhaps, a lack of published data. Another professional marketing company reports more than 50,000 English training schools existed in China in 2007. (China Market Intelligence Center, 2008)

Number of Students Enrolled

Exact statistics are impossible to obtain. However, reports in the official Chinese prints hint at large numbers. For example, The People's Daily Online reported that the EFL training industry in Beijing trained nearly 200,000 people in 2001. (People's Daily Online, 2002) One school by itself, the Beijing New Oriental School, enrolled 30,000 students in July 2001. (People's Daily, 2001, b) This

Beijing institution also expanded into Shanghai in 2001, and by January 2002, 10,000 students had enrolled in the school. (People's Daily Online, 2002) In addition to Beijing, Shanghai is considered a prime-recruiting field for English EFL students. After the Wall Street Institute set up shop in Shanghai, they quickly attracted more than 1,000 trainees, mostly from foreign companies.(People's Daily Online, 2002)

In addition to the traditional EFL training market, the online English training market has served millions of English learners in China. According to the report of a professional marketing firm issued in 2009, there had been up until that time 300 million users of online English. (Market Avenue, 2009)

Number of English Teachers Hired

The State Administration of Foreign Expert Affairs (SAFEA), a Chinese government agency, offered 1,221 EFL jobs for native-speaking foreign English on its website in 2001, as reported by The People's Daily. Gao Pengfei, an official with this organization, said that tens of thousands of native English speakers have been hired to work at Chinese colleges as teachers of English during several decades before that. (People's Daily, 2001b)

Diversity of the Chinese EFL Market

The above statistics make it possible to grasp the large size of the Chinese EFL market. But a description of this market, indicating its wide diversity, will give further insight into the very large Chinese English training market. This market is not only diverse geographically, with English training schools being found in every region and district of China, but it is also diverse. This diversity is reflected in the different categories of English students, different tuition levels, and different subjects taught. There are many different kinds of students attending Chinese English language training schools. Students ranging from kindergarten age to adults diligently study in these schools, some of them studying in traditional classrooms and some of them studying online. For example, an international English training school in Guangdong province offers training to children aged from three to twelve years old. (Xinhua News Agency, 2002) Kindyroo, an Australian franchise operating in Beijing as well as other cities, enrolls children from three months to three-year olds. Charging a pricey tuition, this firm emphasizes "child development" as well as English training. (Kindyroo, 2011) The online English training market is enormous; 300 million Chinese having enrolled for online English learning by the end of 2008. (Xinhua News Agency, 2002) The range of fees charged for EFL services is quite broad. For example, a small startup school in China's Northwest with which I am familiar charges 2000 yuan per term, which contrasts with the 20,000 yuan per term tuition charged by Wall Street English in Beijing. (Xinhua News Agency, 2002)

Challenges in the Chinese EFL Market

The Chinese EFL market may be described as huge, growing, and diverse. Such a market will inevitably attract many players, especially when one considers that entry-level costs are low, and English training services are fairly scalable – it is comparatively easy to start with a very small school, and possibly expand the school's enrollment to thousands. However, there are many challenges facing potential market entrants. Among these challenges are: 1) recruiting quality teachers, 2) scheduling classes, 3) intense competition, 4) dealing with a good deal of government bureaucracy, and 5) maintaining good relationships with teachers.

Recruiting Quality Teachers

There are many placement organizations who act as a middleman, recruiting qualified teachers, and then placing them in English language training schools, whether in China alone, or in English training schools all over the world. There are also websites such as www.seriousteachers.com that act as a specialized employment agency for TESOL teachers. Although there are many credentialed and experienced TESOL teachers apparently available, my experience tells me that actually obtaining a teacher is a difficult process, for several reasons. For example, a teacher might have family issues, such as a trailing spouse who is not suitable for employment at the school. Or, perhaps a parent might suddenly become ill. Young married teachers will have trouble raising children in China, and also, housing and travel becomes more problematic for the school as it deals with caring for the children. Usually a teacher will sign a contract for a maximum term of one year, and often for only six months. This creates a built-in problem of turnover, which is especially damaging, because students often become attached to a special teacher, and become disappointed with the new one, and then quit the school.

Scheduling Classes

Scheduling classes in an enormous administrative difficulty for an English training school in China. Typically, during a school year, classes in the public schools operate Monday through Friday from about 7:00 a.m. to 6:00 p.m. Often, schools schedule more classes in evenings and weekends, in order to help students whose grades are not good. Many times, students who are contemplating an English training course are also taking physics and math training courses as well in their spare time. High school students, especially have difficulty scheduling classes, as almost all seniors completely devote their time to studying for the nationwide College Entrance Exam.

Intense Competition

There are plenty of English training schools in a typical Chinese city. I have observed that parents often choose to be very fastidious as they shop for a school for their children. Parents will carefully compare price, curriculum, location, scheduling, teachers, physically facilities and availability of supplemental grammar classes.

Dealing with Government Bureaucracy

The local city government must license each English training school. Often the required permits can take long periods of time. For example, I know of one permit that was held up for over a month, because a required signature could not be obtained from a vacationing official.

Additionally, in order to obtain visas for foreign teachers, the school must obtain an official Letter of Invitation and a Foreign Expert Certificate from the local government. At any time, in its discretion, the government can refuse to issue the requisite paperwork to obtain a visa. I knew of one teacher who lost his job at an English training school in Beijing that closed its doors right before the Olympics, because the government refused to allow visas to be issued to foreign teachers.

Finally, the government requires paperwork designed to prove that the school is delivering quality instruction. Lesson plans and curriculum outlines for each class must be forwarded to the relevant government regulatory agency.

Maintaining Good Relationships with Teachers

Keeping foreign teachers content is essential. Teacher turnover is expensive in terms of recruitment and training costs, and in terms of lost institutional memory. Such turnover also makes it difficult to maintain rapport with students over the relatively long period of time it takes to demonstrate improvement in the student's English abilities. There are many things that make it difficult for a foreigner to live in China, not the least of which is the language barrier. Daily living can become a difficult chore. Simple activities at home, like drinking water, turning on a hot shower, finding a snack, washing clothes, banking, and transportation can be almost impossible for a non-Chinese speaking teacher. Any English training school that wishes to be competitive in the market for hiring EFL teachers has no choice but to provide a quality assistant to the teacher.

CHAPTER REFERENCES

Allison, Michael. (2010, November 17). Five Mistakes To Avoid When Sourcing Business English Training, Retrieved April 5, 2011 from http://www.buzzle.com/articles/five-mistakes-to-avoid-when-sourcing-business-english-training.html.

China Easy Booking. Top 20 Foreign Language Training Organizations in China, Retrieved March 24, 2011 from http://booking.at0086.com/rank/Top-20-Foreign-Language-Training-Organizations-in-China.html

China Market Intelligence Center. (2008, March 24) Abstract of China Education & Training Industry Report, 2007-2008, Retrieved April 5, 2011 from http://chinamarket.ccidnet.com/report/content/3190/2008 03/40441.html

Fons. (2002, May 09). English language training in China [Question ID: 14057]. Message posted to http://answers.google.com/answers/threadview/id/14057.h tml

Kindyroo. Retrieved April 5, 2011 at http://www.kindyroo.com.au/ Market Avenue. (2009, April). 2009 Report on China's Online English Training (OET) Market, Retrieved April 5, 2011 from http://www.marketavenue.cn/upload/ChinaMarketReports/ REPORTS_1168.htm

People's Daily. English Classes to Start from Third Grade, Retrieved April 5, 2011 from http://www.china.org.cn/english/MATERIAL/14054.htm (July 6, 2001)

People's Daily. Olympic Bidding Success Spurs English Language Fever in China, Retrieved April 5, 2011 from http://english.peopledaily.com.cn/200107/29/eng20010729 _76042.html (Sunday, July 29, 2001)

People's Daily Online. English Language Training Profitable Industry in China, Retrieved April   5, 2011 from http://english.peopledaily.com.cn/200201/22/eng20020122 _89150.shtml (Last updated at: (Beijing Time) Wednesday,   January 23, 2002)

Xinhua News Agency. (2002, January 22). English Language Training Profitable Industry in China, Retrieved April 5, 2011 from http://www.china.org.cn/english/SO-e/25691.htm

FREEDOM OF THOUGHT IN MODERN CHINA

CHINESE POLITICS

While in China, I deliberately chose never to mention Chinese politics, domestic or international. The reasons were practical. One, it is very difficult to understand the politics of any foreign country. And, two, I didn't want to deported. I arrived in 1995 with the typical foreigner's fear of being bugged or tapped by big brother in Beijing. I expressed this fear to a Chinese student, who contemptuously dismantled my phone in front of me, asked me to look at the pieces, and show her where the bug was. However, this student, being pro-Communist, was biased. For fun, I used to ask her why in the world China would want to annex Taiwan, an independent country? I enjoyed watching her explode with a torrent of invective against "China-Taiwan." Taiwan is a very sensitive subject. I have only found one mainlander who felt like China should leave Taiwan be. This person, a professor, said he was glad the U.S. Seventh Fleet had stopped China from conquering Taiwan in the 1955 Taiwan Strait Crisis, because it gave the Chinese a chance to show the world that they could govern themselves democratically. This sort of thinking, I suspect, is in the minority.

My life in China has thoroughly destroyed many stereotypes I have had of the country, but one former stereotype has been confirmed in my mind as a reasonable generalization, and that is the brainwashing that has gone on. I have got to hand it to the Chinese government; they have done a remarkable job. One intelligent college sophomore told me she would refuse to orally recite Chinese history texts in high school, as required by the teachers. She was afraid that her mind would be trained to believe what she knew could not be true. She knew it could not be true that the Party was so exalted, beneficent, magnificent as betrayed in the Party-approved textbook. She then held her hand up in the air, lowered her voice, and said that she had to be careful, because there was "censorship" everywhere. She had good reason to be nervous. A student at her university recently spent a night in the hoosegow for criticizing the Party in class, having been turned in by a classmate. And it must be said that many, many students do not know how to think critically, as almost any foreign teacher in the country will attest.

Despite such off-putting offenses against freedom of thought, the Chinese are definitely much freer now than formerly. This is not Mao Ze Dong's China. Were he alive today, he would not recognize his own country. Letters to the editor of newspapers openly complain of corruption and other social ills. After I recently told a graduate class that in the west one should not mention politics or religion to new business acquaintances, a student in the class told me that in China, politics is talked about all the time, because "everybody knows the Party is corrupt." I cringed, pointed to the closed-circuit monitor, and exclaimed, "He said it, I didn't," which is my standard response when such offenses against Party unity occur. The TV cameras in the classroom are themselves a smelly symbol of the lack of freedom of thought. Of course, sometimes it is claimed that the cameras are turned on merely to monitor the professor's attendance and teaching methods. If you believe that, you will also believe the United States government can manage its debt. Despite these constant reminders that China is not a free country, demonstrations are a very common occurrence. For example, the city authorities in Xiamen decided to put a polluting chemical plant within the city limits, and the citizens raised hell about it. The plant was removed out of the city to the outskirts of town. Recently a student told me she had participated in a demonstration in Guangzhou, aimed at a Beijing decision to impose Mandarin too strictly upon the Cantonese-speaking province. And ironically, it is little trouble for me to hear about Chinese intellectuals complaining about their freedom being squelched. The internet and cable TV have no trouble getting that news to me, despite the government's block on YouTube, Facebook, and Twitter.

One can see from the above that, although China is freer than during the heyday of Maoism, the country is still not free intellectually. One still has to be very careful. Especially irritating is the government's selective blocks put on individual Internet accounts. I was told of one professor who lived next to a Taiwanese, and when the government blocked the Taiwanese professor's Internet account, making it worthless, the Western professor's Internet account was also made worthless. Not being able to access any American blog is aggravating. But there are leaks everywhere in the government's system of thought control. The "Great Firewall of China" can be tunneled under with software that is easily available and free, although the process is somewhat clumsy. Citizens can travel to Hong Kong, and buy a book (in English) that is one long, very satiric paean to Chairman Mao. George Orwell's classic antitotalitarian Animal Farm is freely available in stores and libraries and on the Internet. I heard of one student, a formerly committed pro-Party individual, who read the famous story of the rise of Snowball the pig, and the sign on the barn that said "Everyone is created equal, but some are created more equal than others," who is now bitterly anti-Party. I talked to another student who told me he was more interested in economic development than political freedom, but who then later said he was personally worried because, he said, the government could indict and convict him if he "might" be guilty of something. The lack of precision of Communist law, and the great deal of latitude given to Communist bureaucrats to enforce that law, is notorious, and worrisome.

One stereotype that I often encounter with Westerners is that China is a "communist" country. It should be noticed that only six percent of the Chinese people are members of the Party, and of those Party members, one would be very hard-pressed to find an ideological Marxist. As far as I can tell, in China, communism as an ideology is dead. The students endure their Wednesday-afternoon Marxist economic classes and their Party-indoctrination classes, but I have yet to find a student who claims to enjoy the sessions, much less believe in what is being taught. The Communist Party is like a glorified Kiwanis Club – something that upwardly mobile young people must join in order to advance their careers. I know one young member of the Communist Youth League who loves fashion magazines, and dreams of owning a Louis Vitton purse at one point in her life. It took me several years to realize this interesting fact, that China is no longer a communist country, but culturally, it is still at root a Confucian country, and economically, it is a crony capitalist country. Confucianism is still struggling with Western materialism, but it hasn't died, not by any means. Communism, however, has.

Remarkably, even that old villain, Chang Kai-Shek (Jiang Jieshi) has been somewhat rehabilitated. His home in Nanjing is a public museum. At the time I visited, the master bedroom (surprisingly) displayed an obviously Christian painting, reflecting the beliefs of Chang Kai-Shek's wife, one of the famous trio of Song sisters, who were educated at Toccoa Falls College in my neighboring state of Georgia, and who managed to end up marrying Sun Yat-Sen (Song Zhongshan), Chang Kai-Shek, and T.V. Song, the chief financial official of the new government begun in Taiwan after the Communists defeated the Nationalists in 1949. All of China knows of these famous women, but they don't realize that they spent their formative years like I did, in southern America. Chang Kai-Shek's home town (Xikou, Zhejiang province) has restored the Generalissimo's family residences, and turned the town into a first rate tourist attraction, to which 300,000 people every year visit. Below is an account I wrote shortly after my trip to Xikou in 2010.

We went on a day trip to Xikou, which is Chiang Kai-Shek's home town. A guy from Shanghai on the bus on the way there told me that his parents' generation hated Chiang Kai-Shek, but that the current younger generation doesn't hate him at all, and in fact, many admire him. It was an interesting experience to be walking through the town, and hearing in a clear, loud, English voice the words of Jefferson's Declaration of Independence, spoken by Song Mei Ling (Chang Kai-Shek's Georgia-educated, American-born wife) on a TV which was showing a movie to a about forty or so tourists sitting down watching the film. Soong Mei Ling was beautiful, fluent in English, sophisticated, charming, and politically astute. She knew Eleanor Roosevelt and other high-placed types, and was more than twice on the cover of Time magazine. She displaced Chiang Kai-Shek's first wife (Mao Fumei), whom he divorced. The first wife was fat, ugly, a simple village woman. The exhibit of her kitchen had a sign that said that the first wife very happily fixed "delicious dishes" for Chiang Kai-Shek and his new beautiful wife, when they came back to town. In back of the kitchen, they had left the twisted bars on the window, which resulted from a Japanese bomb that landed in the alleyway behind the kitchen in 1939, killing Mao Fumei. The next day, back in Ningbo, I remarked to a university worker (Chinese) who was accompanying us to an old library, what a tragic and demeaning life Mao Fumei had, to be thrown out by her husband, to serve her husband's new sophisticated wife, and then to get prematurely killed. My counterpart quickly responded by saying, no, she was better off than Song Mei Ling, because Song Mei Ling never had a son like the first wife did! I told the university worker that she had just given me a clear peek into the Chinese mind. This thing about Chinese and having sons is just about the deepest thing I've ever seen in anybody ever.

While we were in Xikou, we went to the tomb of Chiang Kai-Shek's mother. At the entrance to the steps I saw this tall ball-headed man in a black robe, very sophisticated looking. I realized he was the spitting image of Chiang Kai-Shek. So I went up to him, shook his hand, and joked: are you Chiang Kai-Shek? He didn't laugh, and I thought to myself, you should never try to joke in Chinese, because going across cultures with jokes is nigh unto impossible. But the reason he didn't laugh is because he was, as he told me, a descendant of Chiang Kai-Shek, his "wai sheng", Chiang Kai-Shek's nephew on his sister's side. We had to leave before we saw "Breast Mountain" nearby, about which our Internet printout (in English) said: "there is a stone cave under the 'Breast Peak' which can expel the spring, like latex and snow."

CHINESE RELIGION

Often Chinese people will tell you that there is freedom of religion in officially-atheist China. This was surprising to me, the first time I heard it. A student was hired by the police in Shanghai to translate city ordinances dealing with religion, asked me for help, and confidently assured me that there was freedom of religion in the country, even as he showed me the ordinances which prohibited anyone from talking about religion freely. I realized that "freedom of religion" to the average Chinese means "the freedom to believe anything you want, as long as it does not intrude into the public square, and as long as you don't tell anyone else about it," which, come to think about it, is exactly the same idea that secularist progressives have in America. This subtlety is lost on many Americans. One may find many erroneous statements such as one I saw in a book written by an investment counselor cruising China on a motorcycle, in which the author confidently proclaimed that religious freedom had arrived in the country. The Chinese government, masters at propaganda as they are, have convinced many, many people that freedom of religion exists in the country. The tactic usually involves taking prominent people like Billy Graham to a Communist Party-controlled official church, and then aggressively publicizing the event. Once, the government gave free airtime on CCTV for the now-disgraced American televangelist Benny Hinn. Not long after that, while I was in the USA, someone approached me and asked me what I thought about the new freedom of religion in China, citing to me Benny Hinn's televised services in China. I assured him that, using normal definitions of the word freedom, religious freedom definitely does not exist in China.

The three religions that have impacted China the most in modern times are Buddhism, Christianity, and Isalm. Buddhism has greatly affected Chinese culture, ever since the famous monk Xuan Zang braved the wild, wild west of China to go to India in the seventh century, and whose adventures inspired the Chinese literary classic Journey to the West. That famous novel has made its hero, the Monkey King, famous to all Chinese, and has inspired dozens of movies and TV shows, both in China and abroad. (See http://www.imdb.com/character/ch0074135/ for a comprehensive list). Buddhism is now what I would call a "cultural religion." Its philosophy is, if somewhat vaguely, known to the educated public. Its temples are everywhere, showcasing backwards (backwards from the way Herr Hitler displayed them) swastikas, each having much the same floor plan and contents, through which walk saffron-robed monks happily collecting tourist dollars, who contribute to the monks, and who hold burning incense sticks, and knock their foreheads on the ground as they kneel in front of the tall golden Buddhist statues. While teaching at Shanghai Foreign Language University (SISU), I was offhandedly informed that a bodhisattva was enrolled there. That a living Buddhist worthy of nirvana, but who had postponed his trip there in order to help others, was living amongst the students did not seem to engender a whole lot of excitement. Many Buddhist cultural relics have survived the Cultural Revolution, such as the beautiful Thousand Buddha Cave near Tulefan (Turpan) in Western China, the mammoth, gargantuan Buddhist statues in the caves near Datong, and the 233-foot tall outdoor Buddhist statue at Leshan. There are an estimated 100 million Buddhists in modern China, which matches a common estimate for the number of Christians in today's China, and there are 20,000 Buddhist temples. (Xie 2006) One can see Buddhist monks in bright orange saffron robes talking on their cell phones as they wait in line at McDonald's. The government seems to have a very pacific attitude towards mainstream Buddhism. Buddhist monks and intellectuals are often seen on Chinese state-controlled television, and Buddhist cultural attractions can be seen there, too. The government supports Buddhist institutes because they contribute to world peace and a "harmonious society." (Xie 2006)

The impact of Islam is felt mainly in the western part of the country. There are large minority populations, such as the Hui minority, who are sincere practicing Muslims, and who have built mosques in very many places in the Western provinces. The Cultural Revolution was rough on the Muslims. Mosques were defaced, destroyed, or closed, and copies of the Quran were destroyed. Muslims were accused of "anti-socialist trends" and "superstitious behavior." (Wikipedia, 2012) I tried to visit a mosque in Tianjin, only to be told that the Cultural Revolution had turned the mosque into a public restroom. However, in today's China there has been a modest upsurge in the practice of Isalm. (Wikipedia, 2012) There is a huge Hui museum and mosque in Yongning, Ningxia Hui Autonomous region, which seems to operate freely without government interference. One university in the East at which I taught even offered pork-free alternative meals for the Muslim students, most of whom were from the West. It appeared to me that the sort of Islam you find in China is not quite as committed as the various versions of the religion in the Middle East, and thus, does not pose any perceived threat to the central government, despite the fact that there have been radical Islamist terrorist activities in Xinjiang province, in the far west of China. The following account of my encounter with a Muslim high school principal is perhaps illustrative.

I was being coerced to get drunk at a business banquet with a particular high school principal. Yinchuan still has a lot of old Chinese culture in it, and part of that culture is to get business associates drunk in front of each other, to show trust. When I resisted chugging a whole glass of wine like I was supposed to after he beat me at dice for the umpteenth time, he asked me: "Do Americans only drink one glass of wine at a meal?" I answered him, "This one does." And then I went after him. "Didn't you tell me this afternoon you were a Muslim Hui minority?" "Yes," he replied. "And do Muslims drink wine and liquor?" I innocently asked. Everybody at the table laughed. He seriously informed me that after retirement, he was going on a pilgrimage to Mecca, at which time he would receive "redemption" for drinking all the liquor he had drunk. This guy has got an obsession with making people drink. His English teacher, a married Chinese woman, like me refused to chug her glass after losing at dice to him. He asked her, "Are you pregnant?" Meaning, is that why you aren't drinking? She replies that no, she wasn't pregnant. The principal then suggests to her, "Perhaps it's your husband's fault!" During the meal, he pulled out a cell phone with a risqué Chinese joke on it, asked me to read it. I read it, and surprisingly understood what I was reading, but I didn't get the punch line, because it was based on pronouncing a word with different tones. He then explains it, I get it, and we all laugh heartily. This was some Muslim.

Christianity is the fastest growing religion and the one with the greatest impact on modern China. In fact, Christianity has grown faster and larger than anywhere else in the world in history. Estimates very, but a reasonable estimate places the Christian population at about 100,000,000 people. A group of people so large, and so fast-growing, is bound to invite the watchful eye of an officially atheist regime. The government is aware of the long millennia of Chinese history, during which many emperors were overthrown through organized conspiracies. The *guanxi* (relationship)-type networks which are everywhere seen among Christians (as everywhere else in Chinese society) makes the government nervous. But the government seems to be entirely unaware that the Chinese Christians are overwhelmingly pacific, rural people, roughly seventy-percent women, good, patriotic citizens who have not one thought in the world of overthrowing the current government for a new one, their dreams being directed towards a heavenly kingdom, not an earthly one. While the government does not harass most of the millions of Christians in the country, it has brutally persecuted the top Christian leaders. One of these young leaders was on the run right before he was captured, and used his cell phone to call an elderly Chinese man, a spiritual leader with whom I was spending a weekend at a Christian establishment. The old Christian man gave us updates until he lost contact with the younger leader. Later, we heard the fugitive had been arrested and jailed. I never heard whether he was released. I knew a businessman in a large city who was arrested and jailed for three years for the shocking crime of printing Bibles and sending them to poor rural Christians. His lawyer was disbarred merely for representing him. I remember all too vividly a terrifying night ride I had in a taxi, escaping a rural farm where Christian meetings had taken place. I had been awakened in the middle of the night by a young woman who broke into the bedroom where I and three other men were sleeping, turned on the light, and hissed, "Pack now!" She watched as we staggered and groped around, trying to get oriented as we packed. No clothes hanging on the wall, no gum wrapper on the floor escaped her notice as she barked orders to us. As we awaited the taxi, the rural Christians who usually slept in the fields at night before sifting into the cities in the morning in order to evangelize, all stood calmly and patiently as they prepared to walk out into the night. They were quite used to this sort of thing.

Treatment varies for those jailed for spreading Christianity. Shan gao huangdi yuan is a Chinese saying which means that the mountains are high and the emperor is far away, illustrating the common occurrence in public administration which sees the local authorities not carrying out the policies of the central government. Sometimes, local officials develop favorable attitudes towards the Christian church, but are then told to crack down by Beijing. Sometimes, the crackdown is half-hearted, superficial. On the other hand, sometimes the Beijing government wants to ease its policy towards the Christians, but the local officials persecute them, instead. Some local provincial and municipal authorities are on very good terms with the Christian leaders. I heard of one top leader who was given a private room in the jail complex, with an Internet connection so he could continue his work. In one province, the local church there had rebuilt homes and other buildings destroyed by flood and fires. The local authorities were so impressed, that they became annual visitors to the church's annual Christmas play. The church actually had a building, which is the only time I have ever heard of an unregistered church openly operating in public view. However, the leader of this church was later arrested for entertaining foreigners. He was interrogated once a month, and was told that his family members would face serious consequences if he didn't rat out who the people were that visited him. Another leader to whom I talked, after having been arrested, was discovered to have been a former high-level member of Taiwan's intelligence services. At the time of his arrest, the Beijing government was trying to thaw relations with Taiwan, and the local police were scared to interfere with that, and so they put the arrested Christian leader in the top-floor penthouse suite of a five-star luxury hotel.

However, savage persecutions of Christian leaders are well known, and well documented. I remember sharing a hotel room with a young man from the east whose mother hosted church meetings in her house. The police raided a meeting one night, and forced everyone on the floor while they searched the house. My companion was jailed. He described to me his time in prison. There was one room, which held about a dozen men, who sat elbow-to-elbow along the walls. Along one wall was a hole, used for a toilet, which was never cleaned nor flushed. The toilet stank insufferably in the summer heat. There was no furniture at all. My companion's cellmates were hard core criminals, including rapists and murders. As hard-hearted as these characters were, they nevertheless felt sympathy towards my informant, and often criticized the guards for the way they were treating the religious prisoner. The guards would force him to assume a squatted kung fu position in an open courtyard under the sun for hours at a time, denying him water. His throat swelled with thirst, and he thought he was going to die. He told me this was worse than making him break rocks without food, worse than being beaten with a telephone swung at the end of its cord, worse even than being prodded in the genitals with an electric cattle prod. One day he almost collapsed from weakness, and prayed that he would die, because it had become clear that he could no longer continue. He told me shortly thereafter that he miraculously no longer felt pain from his routine beatings, and that he was given a job to cook for the guards, allowing him a chance to eat much better food, and so he survived. After he was released, he was arrested again. After two prison terms, he thought it the better part of valor to escape to the far western province of Xinjiang, where he was living with his wife and son, cut off from physical contact with his mother and other family members in the east. I remember being struck very strongly at how happy, contented, and smiling this young man was. When I told him I admired him, he flashed a big smile, and pointed his hand heavenward.

Interestingly, there are very many ordinary Chinese Christians who do not know how top Christian leaders are being treated. The government only persecutes about one hundred or so leaders. And there are many church activities the government supports or winks an eye at, such as the operation of orphanages, aiding the rural poor with agricultural advice, hygiene, etc. Those in the church who don't know the persecuted leaders often don't know about the persecution. Many Chinese Christians who do know about the persecutions today paradoxically desire the persecutions to continue, to steel the faith of the believers, and to cause the church to grow. They are worried about the increasing dangers of materialism, which has seduced many younger Christians from the faith.

The Christian church is demographically unbalanced: there are many more women than men, many more rural folks than urban, and many more young people than old. I have heard estimates of the percentage of Chinese women believers ranging from 70 percent to 80 percent. The usual Chinese Christian explanation of this is that women are tenderhearted, and much more open to the Christian message, where as men are more interested in making money. Another theory suggested to me by a foreigner is that since there are so many women, Chinese men look upon the church as a "sissy" religion, not worthy of their time. Perhaps if Chinese men were more aware of the bravery exhibited by Chinese Christians under torture, they might shed themselves of those feelings, if they do indeed exist.

The church is also overwhelmingly rural. This leads to a lot of unsophisticated beliefs, such as when one baptizes someone in water, one should hold his head under until he drowns, after which God will raise him up again. Sometimes, it is felt that baptism should be practiced in the nude (with gender segregation). Despite the strong presence of Christians in the rural areas, there are many, many house churches meeting every week in every major Chinese city. There are also many Christian intellectuals. I have personally encountered Christian university professors whose expertise included international law, Western civilization and history, computer science, game theory, and accounting. Song of a Wanderer is a very popular apologetic book written by a graduate of Beijing University and the Chinese Academy of Sciences, which castigates secular unbelief, communist dogma, and which defends orthodox Christianity. However, if numbers is the metric of interest, the overwhelming majority of Christians is in the countryside.

Finally, the Chinese church is very young. Oftentimes, one may meet top leaders who are in their early thirties, with small children. They long for "spiritual fathers" to help them with their many burdens and responsibilities. They are so zealous for the propagation of the gospel that they will often neglect their families. I heard of one young rural mother who was left to handle the harvest alone while her husband was out evangelizing. When asked how she felt about that, she replied, "It's for the gospel, it's my duty!" As a result of this widespread martyr-like attitude, many Chinese Christian families are suffering, and their longing for marriage seminars is near universal.

Despite the persecution, or perhaps because of it, Chinese Christianity has pervaded Chinese society and culture, infiltrating even to the top levels of the Communist Party (Aikman 2003, p. 10). I recall listening to a Scottish Christian speaking to a group of foreigners in the "Foreign Expert" dormitory at a Shanghai university in 1996. He had just been to Beijing, speaking to university students about Christianity, when a son of a high-level member of the Communist Party started asking very pointed questions about how could he become a Christian, and about how the Party was corrupt and nobody believed in communism, anymore. In America, sons and daughters rebel against the Christian faith of their parents, but in China, the situation is reversed. It is an amusing irony to think of young people rebelling their way away from communism and towards orthodox Christianity.

Although the great majority of Christians reside in the countryside, there are plenty of urban Christians who are affecting Chinese society and culture. There are Christian orphanages everywhere. I even had the pleasure of making several visits to an "artists' church" in the countryside. I went with two friends who were staying in my apartment with me. One of those friends was an artist, and the other was a friend who had intermittently spent a weekend or so criticizing a print on my bedroom wall as one that "incited to lust." It was a Greek pastoral painting featuring a Greek shepherd girl carrying a vase on her head, with a sarong diagonally draped across her chest in such a way that one breast was exposed. Upon arriving at the very large farmhouse that served as the artists' church headquarters, my artist friend examined the cluttered array of statues that stood in the atrium. He pointed to one fully nude feminine statue, and asked impishly, and loudly, "Hey! Does this statue tend to incite lust?" The artists showed us around their colony, showing us their artwork, which included paintings containing Christian heroes such as Hudson Taylor (Dai Desheng) and Watchman Nee (Ni Tuo Sheng]. My favorite painting was one of The Forbidden City in Beijing, containing the front gate facing Tiananmen, which is seen everywhere, all over the world, on newscasts, and in films, and which has Mao Zedong's huge painting on the wall over the arched entranceway. The artists had replaced Mao's picture with one of Jesus Christ.

The painting of Jesus overlooking Tiananmen Square was, I am sure, painted with conscious symbolism in mind. It is interesting to speculate on the impact of Christianity on the future of China. Will Christianity officially replace the discredited ideology of communism, and the outworn philosophy of Confucianism? Or will galloping materialism fill the void? David Aikman, a former Beijing Bureau Chief for Time magazine, thinks there is a Christian future for China. He relates a telling story in which Jiang Zemin, the former General Secretary of the Communist Party of China, was asked at a dinner party, "Comrade Jiang, if, before leaving office, you could make one decree that you knew would be obeyed in China, what would it be?" Jiang Zemin replied," I would make Christianity the official religion of China." (Aikman 2003, p17) I suppose that Comrade Jiang was longing for the morality and social control that would be provided by Chinese Christians. Even more interesting than this anecdote is the opinion expressed by a scholar at the Chinese Academy of Social Sciences (CASS), the very prestigious academic research institute in Beijing. This scholar, whose name had to be withheld by Mr. Aikman for reasons of security, was looking for reasons which might explain the success of the West all over the world. Said he:

> One of the things we were asked to look into was what accounted for the success, in fact, the pre-eminence of the West all over the world. We studied everything we could from the historical, political, economic, and cultural perspective. At first, we thought it was because you had more powerful guns than we had. Then we thought it was because you had the best political system. Next, we focused on your economic system. But in the past twenty years, we have realized that the heart of your culture is your religion: Christianity. That is why the West has been so powerful. The Christian moral foundation of social and cultural life was what made possible the emergence of capitalism and then the successful transition to democratic politics. We don't have any doubt about this. (Aikman, 2003, p.5)

I have always felt a little disoriented in China, because so many things are backwards from what I'm used to. But, as the West heads for its post-Christian, or rather I should say, its anti-Christian future, in the eyes of one prominent observer, we are told that China is morphing into an effectively Christian country. Opines David Aikman: if present growth rates continue, China will be 20 to 30 percent Christian within three decades. If that occurs, writes Aikman, then "it is almost certain that a Christian view of the world will be the dominant worldview within China's political and cultural establishment, and possibly also within senior military circles." Perhaps one day a professor will feel free to express his humble opinion concerning religion and morality in a Chinese classroom, the way he cannot in a Western one.

CHAPTER REFERENCES

Aikman, David (2003). Jesus in Beijing: How Christianity is Transforming China and Changing the Global Balance of Power. Washington, D.C.: Regnery Publishing, Inc.

The Monkey King. International Movie Data Basee.
http://www.imdb.com/character/ch0074135/. Retrieved
February 16, 2012.

Wikipedia (2012). Islam in China.
http://en.wikipedia.org/wiki/Islam_in_China. Retrieved
February 21, 2012.

Xie, Chuanjiao (December 22, 2006). Buddhists Praised for
Contributions. China Daily.
http://www.chinadaily.com.cn/china/2006-
12/22/content_765071.htm. Retrieved Feb 21, 2011.

SINGLE WOMEN AND CHINESE ROMANCE

Chinese tradition and culture subordinates romantic, married love to the prime directive of having children. In order to have children, the family unit must have finance. All through China's long and troubled history, Chinese parents and their daughters have been driven to find an oasis of financial security for the unmarried girls in the family. This attitude has not died. The modern Chinese woman's desire for money is almost frightening to behold. A movie star recently became a sensation by proclaiming that she would rather cry in the back seat of a Mercedes then laugh on a bicycle. I remember seeing a survey taken in the 1990s by a professor at Beijing University that asked young unmarried women to rank the top ten things they looked for in a potential mate. "Love" didn't make the top ten. "Money" was at the top of the list, along with "Education" and "Parental Status." The young Chinese girl marrying an aging foreigner in order to get a green card for emigration purposes has become a stock figure in modern China. I saw a TV report in Shanghai which informed viewers that a new government office had opened in the city in order to assist couples in a Chinese-foreign mixed marriage, necessary because there were now so many of these unions.

Therefore, from a traditional aspect, Chinese romance is an oxymoronic term. In the eyes of a young Chinese girl, there was nothing romantic about watching her parents haggle with matchmakers as they tried to locate a suitable match for her with a man she would never see till her wedding day. Traditional China must have produced a tremendous romance deficit, because there is syrupy romantic goo now everywhere in China. Phrases containing the English word "Love" are plastered all over T-shirts and dresses. TV shows match girls up with dream dates, or at least they did until the government decided the shows were too tacky, and restricted them. Speed dating clubs are everywhere in the cities. "Chinese MTV" has been showing for years and years the same old tear jerking, schlocky music videos displaying sobbing, crying, shouting, abandoned girls longing for the man they lost. Girls have college boyfriends who most likely they will not marry, but whom they enjoy during their time at the university, till their boyfriends go off, live and work in different cities, find other girlfriends to marry, and disappear. Many of the parties involved in these temporary romances know that they won't last, that the practical imperatives of finance, family approval, and job location will win in the end. But the young women will enjoy the romantic interlude while they can, on college campuses far away from their parents' prying eyes. In 1995, the movie and book Bridges of Madison County was wildly popular in China. The feminine protagonist in that movie was trapped in a pedestrian marriage with a good, but decidedly unromantic farmer. One day, a dashing photographer (Clint Eastwood) showed up in the area to photograph old-fashioned covered bridges, and one thing led to another. After her romantic passion had cooled off enough for her to realize her responsibilities, the farmer's wife went back to her husband, to nurse him during a serious illness. This wife could have been the poster girl for Chinese women, which is what I believe explains the outsized popularity of that book amongst the fairer sex in China. Their romantic options are so constrained, I think that they long for a chance to enjoy true romance, even if they all know they will eventually have to return to reality, reality usually being tied very much to their parents' wishes. Once I taught a married student whose parents broke up her relationship with the young man she loved. She dutifully obeyed her parents, as most Chinese young people do. She ended up marrying her ex-lover's good friend. The ex-lover's good friend and the ex-lover settled down to become next-door neighbors. My student, now living next door to the man she used to love, often baby-sat for the children of the woman who had supplanted her. The only woman I have met who crossed her father, at first dutifully obeyed him and married a man she didn't love. The man she didn't love one day discovered her in bed with the young man she wanted to marry in the first place. She was disgraced and divorced. The single girls in her university class treated her as somewhat of a pariah. Her father would have nothing to do with her for years, until happily father and daughter were reconciled. Sad stories like this abound in China. Of course, there are many parentally influenced marriages that turn out for the good, but even in these marriages, the parents' control is everywhere to be seen. Once a young single man in Beijing showed me a picture of his fiancé, and I responded by noting that she was pretty. The young man responded yes, she was pretty, but he didn't love her. I asked why then did he intend to marry her. His response was that his father had commanded him to marry by the age of thirty; he was almost thirty, and so he had agreed to marry a friend whom he didn't love. The absolute moral imperative to marry by thirty is pandemic. It seems to me that every young single girl in China has a death warrant waiting to be executed on her thirtieth birthday, which can only be rescinded by marriage. One married woman in her thirties said that she had friends whose parents told her just to marry anyone before she reached thirty, have a baby, and then divorce the husband. Apparently the desire by these Chinese parents to have a child trumpted their desire for their daughter to have a happy marriage.

In 2011, I asked two university students, one man and one woman, to give an impromptu presentation in class, listing their top requirements for a future spouse. I was struck by the young people's desire to please their parents. The man's first requirement was that his wife be aotu. The Chinese characters for aotu are illustrative of what he meant: 凹凸 – concave-convex, which is to say, "curvy." His second requirement was that his parents approve of the girl. The woman's first requirement was that her future husband be a plastic surgeon, so that he would have lots of money. The second requirement was that her parents approve of her choice. I couldn't help but notice that "love" did not top "parents' desires," although the student's did mention, "love" in their top five. In 2010, I interviewed a forty-something Filipino-Chinese man for a job in Yinchuan. I asked him why he wanted to come so far to China's northwest, and he responded that his Chinese grandmother was putting pressure on him to find a Chinese wife. I told him Chinese women could be charming, but he had better be careful, because Chinese women could also be very complicated. The man responded by saying that, actually, Chinese women were quite simple to make happy. For the first two years of marriage, you buy your Chinese wife everything they want, and after two years, you hand over your credit card.

The often-contradictory requirements of romance and finance create a certain tension in young Chinese women. They will read romantic novels, watch soap operas, and listen to Chinese pop singers endlessly sing of romance (usually romance gone awry). But in my studied opinion, the prime directive of the young modern Chinese woman is to obtain financial security. Traditional Chinese women found economic security through good marriages. The modern Chinese single woman looks for her security in education and a good job. I have never heard a Chinese university student say she wants her future husband to support her. The drive for education and financial independence has created a modern Chinese phenomenon, the shengnu (left-over woman). These are women who are approaching, or who have passed, the magic age of thirty, but who have not yet found a husband. They are so educated, their English is so good, their job is so good, that very few potential husbands want to marry them, regardless of how charming or pretty they are. I have discovered that Chinese men love to be in charge, which I presume to be a legacy of the traditional Confucian principle that the wife should always be submissive to her husband and her son. Chinese men no doubt find it hard to be in charge of highly educated, professional women. The shengnu is usually not opposed to marriage and family, but her drive for economic security has hurt her marketability in the eyes of potential husbands. I have suggested to one bright and promising senior university student that she try for a Ph.D., and she told me that she didn't want to because it would hurt her marriage prospects.

Hong Yan Zhi Ji

A relationship has developed in China that seems to split the difference between the financial and kinship complexities of Chinese marriage and family arrangements, and romantic, but illicit, adulterous adventures. There seem to be a good number of people, both men and women, who crave "soulmates," but can't find them in their spouse. At the same time, they don't want to offend Chinese morality by finding paramours. One university student speculated that it is very difficult for a husband, caught in the dangerous no-man's land that often exists between his mother and his wife, to talk to his wife about conflicts involving his immediate family and his birth family. He therefore is tempted to find solace by opening his heart to a woman who is a friend. This friend is generally single. Their friendship develops until their friends recognize her as the man's *hong yan zhi ji*. Nothing sexual occurs between the man and the *hong yan zhi ji*, either in word or deed. If things cross the line, the woman is no longer a *hong yan zhi ji*, but is rather a mistress. The man and his *hong yan zhi ji* never mention the word – outsiders, not the man and the woman, define the status themselves. Oftentimes, the relationship applies to men who are still single, but who have a girlfriend and a *hong yan zhi ji* at the same time. Sometimes, the wife or girlfriend knows about the *hong yan zhi ji*, oftentimes they don't. This sympathetic woman, the *hong yan zhi ji* knows all about the man. She often knows more than his wife does. But she is not granted nuptial privileges, and she is not burdened with family obligations.

Hong yan zhi ji's spring from the soil of Chinese history and literature. In feudal times, the path to riches and fame passed through the imperial bureaucracy. Many aspiring government bureaucrats trained themselves in classical Chinese literature and philosophy in order to prepare for the famous imperial examination system. Many men failed to advance, gave up on their ambition, and wasted their time in leisurely pursuits, including cultural and literary ones. They enjoyed going to a qinglou, which is rudely translated whorehouse. In the qinglou, there worked two types of girls. One was the ordinary prostitute; the other was a *hong yan zhi ji*. The *hong yan zhi ji* did not provide sex for the clientele. Rather, she sang, she danced; she discussed literature and poetry with the customers. She rouged her face in order to perform. She talked about deep and profound things with her male customer. Hence the name *hong yan zhi ji*, which is literally translated "red face know yourself," ie., "the red faced girl will help you know yourself." She was a girl who had intimate conversations with a (usually married) man, but who did not have sex with him, and who painted her face red in order to perform for him. In modern times, a new term was invented for the male counterpart of a *hong yan zhi ji*. *Lan yan zhi ji*, literally translated, means "blue face know yourself." Blue is opposite to red like male is opposite to female, thus the term. There are two types of *lan yan zhi ji*. The first is a man, married to another woman, or boyfriend to another girl, who has a *hong yan zhi ji*. The second can theoretically be a single man who has become a soulmate with a girl who is already involved romantically with another man, or is married to another man. This is rare. I have yet to hear of the latter type of *lan yan zhi ji*.

The skeptical Westerner may be tempted to say that a *hong yan zhi ji* is nothing but an adulteress on the make. While it is true that the situation is unstable, and sometimes the *hong yan zhi ji* stumbles into adultery, it is quite amazing to me how often the relationship endures, and indeed, how often the wife or girlfriend becomes friends with the *hong yan zhi ji*. The first time I noticed something odd about Chinese opposite sex relationships was on a bus in Shanghai. In 1995, two young graduate assistants, one a man and one a woman, accompanied me on a visit to a model Shanghai high school. The man and woman were so comfortable with each other, laughing and joking, talking, that I just assumed they were boyfriend and girlfriend, especially because I saw them together all the time. I asked the young man when he intended to marry his girlfriend, and with a shocked laugh, he responded, "Oh no! She is not my girlfriend; she is just a friend. My fiancée is in another town." I think he was as shocked at my reaction as I was at his statement. She must have been his *hong yan zhi ji*. There is no way that a boy and girl can be so palsy-walsy, comfortable with each others as old shoes, engaging in no flirtation, and be "just friends." They seemed to me like they had been married for ten years.

The first time that I ever talked to someone I knew certainly was a *hong yan zhi ji* occurred in Yinchuan in 2010. A young 22-year old woman worked in my school and she had a boyfriend. This girl liked to talk, and I soon discovered that she had been matched up by her father while she was at college. An unwelcome suitor was pursuing her; she decided marrying her father's choice would take the heat off, so she married the man her father wanted her to marry. When I say, "marry," I mean she got a marriage certificate from a government bureau. I have yet to discover whether "marry" means to live together and have sex, have a ceremony at a restaurant, or to get the marriage incense, or some combinations of the three. My young coworker didn't live with her new husband after she graduated and she returned home to Yinchuan. She lived at home with her family, and he lived at home with his family. She got along with her husband famously. She then showed me a present she had gotten from a "friend," with whom she was eating out that night. I assumed it was her husband, and she said no, it was her *lan yan zhi ji*. It transpired that my young coworker and her *lan yan zhi ji* went out to eat about once a month. Each time he brought her flowers or a present. "Does your husband care?" I asked with eyebrows raised. "Of course not, he is good friends with the *lan yan zhi ji*," she responds. "Well, he does care if I and the *lan yan zhi ji* go out more than about once a month," she added as an afterthought. What a possessive husband, I thought.

My wife Linda discussed the romantic situations of two *hong yan zhi ji*'s she encountered. The first spent much time empathizing with her *lan yan zhi ji*, who had several girlfriends during the time that he was the *lan yan zhi ji*. The *hong yan zhi ji* finally decided to end the relationship with the *lan yan zhi ji* because he had moved to England, and had become "loose" morally (but not with her, of course). The second *hong yan zhi ji* who discussed her status with my wife counseled her *lan yan zhi ji* through approximately three girlfriend relationships. Finally, one day, it dawned on the two that perhaps they themselves should become boyfriend and girlfriend. The young girl was beaming, stating that now she didn't have to wonder at all about her new boyfriend's romantic past, because she herself already knew all the intimate details.

I talked to a *hong yan zhi ji*, a college junior whose *lan yan zhi ji*'s girlfriend was an unknown girl living far away in a different city. The *hong yan zhi ji* was tiring of the relationship, and wanted to get out of it. I told her, "You aren't married to him, you aren't even dating him, for crying out loud, just tell him!" "Oh, I can't," she replied. "It would break his heart." Suspicious when I heard this, I asked, "Has this boy ever kissed you?" "Only once on the cheek," she replied.

The strangest *hong yan zhi ji* story I heard involved the uncle of a very serious, very bright university student of journalism. It seems that this student's uncle, a man of about sixty years of age, developed an online relationship with a young girl in her twenties. The man lived in Guangzhou, the girl in Shenyang, a city a long way away in the north. The two had never personally met. The man's wife discovered the relationship and was quite upset. Now, if this had happened in the United States, you know what would have happened next: quarrels, violence, broken glass, bloodshed, lawyers. But oh, no! Not in China. The man showed his wife the transcripts of the chats, in which there was nothing sexual or inappropriate. The man and his wife then bought a gift, hopped a train to Shenyang, and together took the young girl out to eat. The young girl and the wife are now fast friends.

For all of you imbued with the spirit of chivalry, and who are warmed in the heart by stories of Jeb Stuart sitting on his charger, handing flowers to the ladies in Richmond while quoting poetry to them, I must pause here and announce to you: chivalry is not dead in China.

Cross Cultural Romance

Let me conclude this section with some observations on Chinese romance with foreigners. For reasons I have yet to fully fathom, it rarely happens that a Western woman finds her soul mate with a Chinese man. But the contrary happens all the time. Cynics will note that often a young Chinese woman will match herself up with a Western man, often a good deal older than she is, for pecuniary reasons alone. I cannot judge the heart of a Chinese woman. But I must say, the number of young, pretty Chinese women accompanying fat, bald, and comparatively wealthy Western men is somewhat suspicious. However, as King Solomon once said, the way of a man with a maid is a wondrous and incomprehensible thing.

Far be it from me to cast aspersions on the motives of Chinese women. Instead, let me give you a learned explanation of why international Chinese unions make for the best marriages, by citing an email home concerning the subject.

Linda has discovered in a text written by a Chinese man in order to teach foreigners, that Chinese kiss with their heads straight up, we are informed, that non-Chinese foreigners must tilt their heads, because of their oversized noses. Therefore, international unions are the best, because a straight-up head and a tilted head create more "roundness," like the yin and the yang symbol. The learned Chinese professor went on to say that white people liked to fight wars more than Chinese people. I don't know how he explained the Warring States period, not to mention all the dynastic struggles and revolutions over the years.

Second, an opinion columnist in the English-language Chinese daily has set off a furor, by attacking laowai's (foreigners). It seems that laowai's are always trying to impress the mother's of their Chinese girlfriends by eating chicken feet, and while they do so, they don't understand they are supposed to spit out the bones, thus causing their Chinese hosts a great deal of anxiety, because they fear the laowai will choke to death. I suppose the anxiety derives from the fear of losing a rich foreign husband and a visa for their daughter. At any rate, the author, a genteel Chinese woman, went on to say that laowai just could never understand the Chinese thing for firecrackers. They had been setting them off for 5000 years, and nothing was going to change that. The author went on to say that on one night of the year, Chinese could burn down a fully furnished building, and no one would even criticize them for it. That if a laowai ever tried to burn down a building, however, a Chinese would "kill him." I must confess, I fail to understand this point of Chinese culture. She went on to attack China's foreign guests as "barbarians." There's one thing I especially love about China - there is not a smidgin of politically corret hyper sensitive don't-say-that-you-might hurt-someone's-feelings mentality over here.

CHINESE PROSTITUTES

I have had a good deal of interaction with Chinese prostitutes. Not as their customer, you understand, but as an objective observer with anthropological interest. I have not sought out these encounters, but as most foreign men fast discover, they are marked men for Chinese "little sisters." They see the foreigner walking down the street, and they become enraptured with the thought of financial gain, believing as they do in that ubiquitous Chinese stereotype, that "all foreigners are rich." I recall fondly an occasion when I was walking down the famous Nanjing Dong Lu in Shanghai with a Shanghai born American accountant, a married man. Two young women in their twenties started walking with us. At the time I knew almost no Chinese, and so I could not understand what they were talking about with my Mandarin-speaking friend. I gradually became suspicious. I asked, "What do they want?" My friend responded that they wanted us to eat a meal with them at a nearby restaurant. I thought, well maybe that's innocent enough. But we kept walking, and the girls kept talking, and my friend neither accepted nor refused their kind offer. But, apparently because he was Chinese and couldn't force himself to be direct, he kept putting off the girls' appeals. Finally, I looked at my friend (who was appropriately named "Hou," pronounced "Hoe"), and I seriously inquired of him, "Hou, are these girls prostitutes?" Hou responded that he didn't know. I thought, OK, if you don't know, either tell them to scram, or let's go eat with them, but this promenade can't go on forever. I finally realized that hell would freeze over before Hou would tell the girls to leave. I therefore took it upon myself to get rid of them myself, using as much chivalry as possible given the circumstances. The girls spoke halting English. I told the one next to me, "We have enjoyed this walk together. We appreciate you asking Hou and me to eat. But both Hou and I are married men, and we are not sure our wives would approve of us eating with two pretty girls like you." I was seriously lying about the "pretty girls" part, but rationalized it by thinking I was in China, and I needed to save the girl's face, which was frightfully ugly. The girl to whom I had addressed myself, whose English was quite poor, misunderstood me, and responded: "Pretty girls? Pretty girls? We can find you many pretty girls."

Actually, it is totally unnecessary for a foreigner who desires illicit pleasures to engage the services of a broker. One time, I placed a wager with a former student. She was raised very conservatively. She wouldn't let men help her get the wash off the line, and she wouldn't tell anyone the name of her mother, because that offended traditional Chinese proprieties. I told this student that I would bet her whatever amount she wanted that I could stand on the Bund in Shanghai and a prostitute would approach me within five minutes. My student was skeptical, but she dutifully walked away to set me up as a lone male target. I pushed the button on my wristwatch stopwatch, and before the digit counter got to two-and-a-half minutes, up walked a little sister. My student saw her coming before I did, and had stormed back to protect me. As we walked off, she fumed that how could I do such a thing in China, I was a professor! She apparently did not understand the research ethic with which professors are imbued.

Chinese prostitutes are called "little sisters" (xiaojie). I don't know the origin of the term, but it is descriptive, because Chinese ladies of the night don't look like your typical whore. They are modestly dressed, often with bangs. Often they look like cute high school girls, and the unsuspecting foreigner who is asked "drink Chinese tea?" or who is given a paper cut-out by one of these young ladies is completely unaware of what sort of person he is talking to. The foreigner should be highly suspicious of phone calls to the hotel at night, during which young girls offer to provide in-room massages. Prostitution rings wlll make deals with the staff at the hotel desk, who will feed the prostitutes the phone number of prime targets. I used to receive these calls every night while on a trip. I would use them to practice my Chinese. I tried to aggravate them by telling them I had already eaten if they invited me to eat, or asking them if they would give a massage to my wife who was in the room with me. I have discovered that Chinese prostitutes in search of a trick are implacable. No matter how many times I mention that my wife is with me, the ladies of the night just keep right on offering their services. In fact, one of the most unpleasant confrontations I had with Chinese harlotry occurred while my wife and I were traveling together. We were on a trip to San Ya, the Hawaii of China, located on Hainan Island in the far south. On the way, we stopped at Haikou, the capital of Hainan, and registered in a four-star hotel. I asked our Chinese tour guide, a university student who had accompanied us, to check out the hotel's massage parlor to see if it was zhenggui, i.e., whoreless. She reported back, and gave me the green light. I entered a small room with a cot, and waited. I double-clutched when the masseuse entered. She was dressed in a skin-tight solid red silk dress, which nicely matched her dark red lipstick. A pearl necklace contrasted beautifully with her long dark hair. She looked too high-class and beautiful to be a whore, but I was nevertheless suspicious, because I was quite aware that Chinese prostitutes don't look like American ones. I knew she sure didn't look like a masseuse on duty in the middle of the afternoon. My suspicions were further aroused when she asked me to change into some print silk shorts, which may or may not have been Chinese underwear. I told her I didn't want to, because I was already wearing shorts. But she wouldn't continue unless I changed, and so I figured it must be house policy to wear standard silk shorts. Since I was still relying on the (false) assurances from my student tour guide that the place was reputable, I agreed to change into the silk shorts. I assumed the masseuse would leave to give me the opportunity to change, but to my discomfiture, she remained in place. So I hopped off the table, and modestly hid myself behind it, and changed, while she stood on the other side of the table. I was beginning to feel just a bit tense. The massage commenced as they all do, one-half hour on your back, and one-half hour on your stomach. The masseuse had been working for about fifteen minutes, when I noticed that her hands were wandering a little close to forbidden territory. Massages are supposed to relax you, but this one wasn't doing the job. But then I figured, I was being overly suspicious, because, after all, my student tour guide had checked this place out, and it was in a nice four-star hotel. I tried to relax, but then when the masseuse performed a maneuver that in the United States would be considered sexual harassment, I objected loudly, and turned away slightly. The masseuse went back to being legitimate. The red flags were up everywhere now, though. But I still couldn't quite believe she was a whore, because of my student tour guide's seal of approval on this place. I decided to test her. I asked her if she would give my wife a massage, my wife who was right here in this hotel with me. She didn't miss a beat. She said she would be glad to. So, I began to think that maybe she was straight. At the half hour mark, I turned over. She asked me if I had eaten yet. I said yes, I had. Then suddenly she climbed up on the table, and with only one foot on the ground, she lay face down on my back, stuck her ruby-red lips in my ear, and gave me the universal call-sign for Chinese hookers, except that it was in Chinese: "Drink Chinese tea?" I told her I wasn't thirsty. The massage ended unpleasantly. It was only supposed to cost 15 RMB, but the masseuse cum whore insisted I pay her more for extra services. I said, "You didn't give me any extra services, I don't owe you anything." I finally paid her 50 RMB just to get out of there. It really doesn't pay to get a Chinese prostitute angry with you. I know of one immoral foreigner who, while negotiating a price with a Chinese hooker, offered a price that the prostitute considered beneath her dignity. Angered, she stole the foreigner's glasses. The foreigner, who perhaps did not understand the value of Chinese money, fought hard to retain his glasses, but the hooker was not about to give in. The altercation excited the attention of the local constabulary, who consigned the foreigner to jail for the evening. After my adventure in Haikou, I later found out from an elderly friend in Shanghai that Haikou had more hookers per citizen than any other place in China. In fact, a group of professors from a university that shall go unnamed attended a conference at Haikou, only to have it cancelled because the academicians' extracurricular activities had caused the spread of "disease." I thought that reflected poorly on the profession. The academic one, I mean.

The prevalence of prostitution illustrates another subtle point about life in China. Prostitution is said to be illegal. You will often hear that something or the other is illegal. The people, or the signs, which tell you that something is illegal should be taken with a large dose of skepticism. One can see a dozen swimmers swimming in a reservoir posted with a sign warning of the danger to swim there, and forbidding it. Hockers on the pavement will surround a "No Spitting" sign. Every hour, two or three thousand motorcycles will pass a "No Motorcycles in This Lane" sign. A water tank full of thousands of coins, besides which a sign is posted: "Don't throw coins into the fountain." Huge eight-foot high, ten-foot long signs saying college cheaters are bums, and they will pay. This country is in love with signs and banners and slogans telling you that something is illegal. But reality is not to be found on those signs and banners. Reality rests with whom you know, or whom you have paid off going through the "back door." There is a huge multi-story brothel/massage parlor located in a small university city located right next to the municipal authorities, to better serve the needs of the city officials. I used to regularly get massages at this establishment before I discovered its true nature. The owner was a very nice woman in her late thirties or so who had a little schoolgirl who did her homework at the desk. All the masseuses wore official-looking white robes with badges. I found out the truth when a lady barber cutting my hair expressed her distaste for the place. She told me it had been picketed, and was the subject of a TV report. Another professor told me that this enterprise offered all sorts of non-traditional services, such as a "happy-ending massage." Nonetheless, this establishment, located right next to the city officials, was "illegal." I should note, incidentally, that the owner and her employees were very professional with me, never once offering extra services.

Once, I went to get a haircut at a barbershop with pink curtains. My experiences there, plus information later obtained from Chinese friends, taught me that barbershops with pink curtains are barbershops with whores. A Chinese hair stylist typically has her customer lay on a cot, placing his head into the sink at the end of the cot, and having her assistant wash the customer's hair. After the hair is washed, the hair is cut, after which the hair is washed again. I was getting my first hair wash, when the young twenty-something assistant pulls out two paper cones, and sticks them into my ears. I thought that was strange, since it had nothing to do with washing hair. As she was blowing air into my ears with a machine in order to clean them out, and while I was wondering whether I would have any hearing left after the pain subsided, she persistently asked me, did I want a massage? I just as persistently responded that no, I did not want a massage; I had just had one. All of a sudden this pony-tailed darling grabbed my yinjing and started wagging it. I yelled in pain, shame, and discomfort, and jumped up. (I will leave it to you to find a Chinese dictionary and look up yinjing.) Two other sweet high-school age girls who I suspected were there to get a glimpse of the strange foreigner accompanied the young hairwasher. All three of these charming little girls just laughed and giggled. My anger perturbed them not in the least. Peeved, I headed for the door through the barbershop, when the owner-stylist/madame stopped me and insisted that she finish off the haircut. She might have been managing a brothel, but that in no way going to interfere with her professional hair-cutting duties.

Whores can pop up when you least expect them. One could guess eternally the background of those innocent-looking little girls, and never once suspect that they were sex workers. I met two other such young girls in what I thought was a zhenggui massage parlor operating right across the street from my apartment in Beijing. I learned from the young masseuse that she grew up poor in the country, in the south of China, had graduated from high school, and had come to the big city to find employment. Her employer, the fat, ugly, jolly middle-aged proprietor of the massage parlor, had enticed her to come to Beijing and had "trained" her. The fat lady came in to the very tiny massage room, and asked me, did I want two masseuses to do my massage instead of just one? I had never heard of that, so I agreed. Another young teen-age girl appears, and starts massaging. Suddenly, without warning, the first young lady hopped up on the massage cot, and continued the massage. I tensed, thinking this was highly irregular, having never experienced this before in a massage parlor. Both of the girls then began opportuning me for "overtime," which convinced me of the truth of my situation. I told the girls that my WIFE just across the street had rented a movie, and we were going to watch it at 9:00. As I mentioned earlier, the word "wife" does not seem to faze a Chinese prostitute. Then the fat lady proprietor reentered, and starting soliciting me for "overtime." I refused, and then she asked me to sit up on the end of the bed, and put my arms behind my back. I did so, and she then proceeded to play the role of an unlicensed chiropractor, as she somehow lashed my arms with hers, grabbed my neck, twisting it violently till I heard my bones snap, crackling, and popping like Rice Crispies. I suspected she was taking it out on me because I had refused her services. As I protested, she just cackled happily. I got up to leave, and the fat harridan blocked the door. I tried to push past, and she started playing middle linebacker. I finally pushed her out of the way, staggered into the street, only to find that I had left my wallet and watch in the room. I returned, but they ignored me, all three of them having latched their mercenary eyes on another potential customer who had just arrived. I grabbed my valuables and exited.

It turns out that these two young girls, refugees from the countryside, prostituting themselves in the big city, were part of quite an interesting, but tragic, phenomenon. Most of the xiaojies in China come from small towns or rural parts of China, and are part of the overall grand migration of villagers to the city, which has followed upon the heels of "opening" and "reform," the turn to market capitalism away from socialism. Why do they do what they do? It is entirely superficial to dismiss these young women as gold-digging tramps. A few anthropologists have studied these women with a view to plumbing their inner emotions, although most scholarly work has focused on the sex workers merely as immoral women or a public health problem. (Yu 2011) What motivates them to leave their rural villages to market their bodies in the city? Money, of course, is a motivation, but the motivation is not simply money. The money is often viewed as a means to an end. And very ironically, the end that many Chinese prostitutes seek is romantic love, and sometimes even marriage. Yu Ding, an anthropologist at Sun Zhongshan University in Guangzhou, after spending two years interviewing in depth 23 Chinese sex workers in the Pearl River Delta, concluded that marriage and love were important issues for the xiaojies. "Our conversations would often slip into the topic of love and relations, no matter what we were talking about. Most of the women would mention their husbands, boyfriends or ex-boyfriends in the interviews and conversations, although they may have brought them more pain than happiness... From the data I realized that love and intimate relations are important to explore if I want to understand these xiaojies' lives." (Yu 2011)

Oftentimes, it is an intimate relationship gone sour in the countryside that drives the little sister to the city to become a sex worker. Six of the 23 prostitutes interviewed by Yu Ding were married women who had left their rural husbands to work in the cities. Says Professor Yu: "For these married women, marriage seems to be a thing to escape from, to confuse (sic) about, to struggle for, and perhaps to discard as a whole...The sweetness of marriage may disappear soon when they [the husband and wife] have to face the brutal reality of rural poverty, child rearing, unsatisfactory marital relation (sic) and in in-law family relations." (Yu 2011)

However negative the xiaojie's marital situation may have been back in the rural countryside, or how negative were her marital prospects in case of the single xiaojie, she nevertheless has aspirations of love and romance, even as she plies her trade in illicit sex. Professor Yu relates the story of a little sister who was prostituting herself in order to earn money to support her boyfriend's drug habit. The professor tells of a married xiaojie in Shenzhen who lived together in the city with her young boyfriend, with no intention of moving back to the countryside to live with her husband. Her boyfriend fulfilled her dream of being young and free. Professor Yu tells us that some of the xiaojies left home not because of bad marital experiences, but rather in order to "fulfill sexual needs, to explore new forms of intimacy." The little sisters dream of "having several boyfriends and lovers, [and] having multiple relations." (Yu 2011)

A final example from Professor Yu illustrates the common desire of Chinese prostitutes to find marital happiness. He relates what a 26-year old sex worker told him:

> This 26-year-old woman has a hierarchy of intimate relationship in her mind. She puts "communication with the heart" at the top of the hierarchy and says that spiritual communication is the best thing between two persons of the opposite sex. Her dream marriage is between two people who have such communication. Sexual relationship is in a low position in this hierarchy and is regarded as "merely sex"...She puts the relationship between herself and her

current boyfriend in the middle. When she faces her boyfriend, she can feel affection. However, their relationship is not good enough to convince her to marry. She believes that there are still good men available around and that one day she may be able to marry well, and she "just hasn't met the one yet. (Yu 2011)

Of course, not all prostitutes have adapted marriage and family values. Some prostitutes, says Dr. Yu, "realize that marriage is not necessarily the beginning of a good life, not their ultimate aims, not the only choice, and perhaps not a good choice at all. Their sexual values are thus changed and opened up, making them more aware of what a woman can do with her own body and sexuality." (Yu 2011)

One last motivation that impels xiojies to migrate to the city is something that in my view motivates just about every Chinese, and that is to appear "modern" and "open" and "urban." In the case of the little sisters, "the xiaojies think it worthwhile to see the urban world and experience its life even in the most superficial way. Taking on urban appearances, developing personal networks, living an urban lifestyle, alternative intimate relations, etc., are their urban dreams reified in material or affective forms." (Yu 2011)

CHAPTER REFERENCES

Yu, D. (2011) Negotiating Intimacies in an Eroticized Environment: Xiaojies and South China Entertainment Business. International Journal of Business Anthropology, 3(1):121-133.

Guanxi is everywhere in China. I heard about it as soon as I arrived in the country, I experienced its power shortly thereafter, and I have been befuddled by it ever since. The English definition of *guanxi* is quite simple: it means relationships or network. However, that definition is next to worthless as an aid to understanding the concept. In this chapter, I'll probe fairly deeply into *guanxi's* complexities, probably just about as deep as it is possible for a foreigner to go. I'll start out the discussion by giving you two personal experiences of the wonder of *guanxi*.

Around 1996, my wife and I found ourselves stranded in an overloaded train station in Qingdao, trying to make our way back to Shanghai. A student tour guide about 21 years of age accompanied us, who had never traveled outside of the city of Shanghai, and who was just about as flummoxed as we were about how to get back home. The three of us were huddled in the Qingdao train station, looking at some papers we thought might help us, when a stranger cheerfully joined our huddle and started reading with us. We experienced this phenomenon many times. We were told that since the Chinese do not hold the same sense of privacy that Westerners do, this sort of thing would happen. I recall a student in Shanghai who was visiting our apartment, who in my presence picked up my bank statements and began to cheerfully call out the numbers to all present. I recall waiting to be picked up by someone, sitting on some public steps in Shanghai reading an English book, becoming suddenly aware of breath in my ear, as a stranger leaned over to see if he could decipher the English. It is hard to overcome one's cultural biases concerning privacy and personal space, and, in addition, I was aggravated about being stranded in the train station, and so I began to become somewhat agitated. Meanwhile, our young student tour guide picked up her phone, dialed a number, and in about one half-hour we are standing at the outside front entrance to the train station in a crush of travelers, facing a man who had magically appeared with three train tickets to Shanghai. I asked our student guide who this man was. She said she had no idea. I remember thinking this would never happen in the U.S.A., and was I in the Twilight Zone? So how did it happen? *Guanxi* is what happened. The student called her brother in Shanghai. The brother called a workmate. The workmate called a friend or a workmate in Qingdao. The Qingdao man was unknown to at least our student guide, and probably was unknown to her brother in Shanghai. The

Qingdao man stopped what he was doing, and brought three tickets to three perfect strangers. You can see that "relationships" or "networking" is involved, but, even though we have relationships and networking in the West, what happened to us at the Qingdao train station would never happen in the West.

The second *Guanxi* experience I enjoyed occurred when my wife and I were planning to spend several months traveling all over China. I called my old boss at Shanghai Foreign Languages University and asked him: did he know someone who could serve as a tour guide? He procured the services of a student whom we did not know. We told her we wanted to go to Xinjiang, among other places, and we wanted to see the Taklamakan desert, the second largest desert in the world, which was extremely remote and difficult to get to. The student was young, and had never traveled much beyond her local Hangzhou-Shanghai area. She called her mother, who worked in Hangzhou. Her mother contacted a workmate at her place of employment in Hangzhou. The workmate called a friend in Wulumuqi, the capital city of Xinjiang, in the far west of China. When we arrived in Wulumuqi, we were put up in the newly constructed four-star hotel, the first such hotel in Wulumuqi, at half-price. The hotel owner called a friend who drove a taxi in a small remote town called Kuerle. The hotel owner put us on a bus to Kuerle, and after we had left the major highway and bounced through several rocky, dirt roads, we ended at the bus station in Kuerle. The taxi-driver who was friends with the hotel-owner in Wulumuqi met us, and took us to a small hotel. The next day, he picked us up before the sun rose (in order to avoid the summer heat), and drove us into the desert. After we enjoyed looking at the desert, which was an experience I will always treasure even more than having stood on the Great Wall, the taxi driver returned us to Kuerle. The taxi driver had a friend who was the librarian in Kuerle. The librarian had a key to a special room containing historical artifacts. The room was hot and without air conditioning, and it was also unheated in the winter. Inside the room were several corpses of teenaged girls who had died in the desert about 1000 A.D. They were perfectly preserved, if blackened by the sun, looking as if they had fallen asleep the night before. The air was so dry that the primitive, un-air-conditioned room continued to preserve these girls as well as any Western museum could have done. Such corpses existed in Wulumuqi, and in fact were advertised in the travel literature, but we had somehow missed them. But nobody to my knowledge had ever advertised about these mummies in Wulumqi.

No tourists knew about this place. Seeing those corpses was the closest thing to a time machine that I will ever experience, and it was because of *Guanxi* that I was able to see them. And incidentally, the librarian/curator, the taxi driver in Kuerle, and the hotel owner in Wulumuqi were all unknown to our student tour guide's mother.

GENERAL DESCRIPTION

I will quote a standard scholarly definition of *guanxi* to get us beyond the one-word definition "network" or "relationships." *Guanxi* "refers to the concept of drawing on a web of connections to secure favors in personal and organizational relations... *Guanxi* is an intricate and pervasive relational network that contains implicit mutual obligations, assurances, and understanding." (Park & Luo, 2001) If you are like me, you will think that there is no difference in that definition and those social networks that are seen in the West. However, as we probe deeper, you will see that there are subtle, yet profound differences between Chinese *guanxi* and Western networks.

Guanxi, like so much else in Chinese modern life, springs from the soil of Confucianism. Confucianism's essence was relationships, five of them foundational, namely ruler-subject, father-son, elder brother-younger brother, husband-wife, friend-friend. Because all relationships entail obligations, duties and obligations of the parties within these relationships were paramount to Confucianism. So, at root, a *guanxi* relationship is one that "contains mutual obligations," as the definition I quoted above states. It runs very deep in the Chinese soul that one must always be prepared to give back, if something is done for him. Once, I had a very above-average, superior teaching assistant. I told her I really appreciated her making my job so much easier, and I wanted to reward her in some way. When I would mention this to her, she was always saying no, and changing the subject. I was almost feeling a little offended about it, when one day it hit me: she was worried about coming under a *guanxi* obligation. I directly asked her if this was so, and she quickly responded that it was. I told her to not worry about owing me anything, because Americans don't do *guanxi*. She responded, "I can't help it." I am willing to bet there's not a Chinese person alive who can help it. *Guanxi* has been pervasive for centuries in every aspect of Chinese life. It "reflects delicate fibers woven into every person's social life and every aspect of Chinese society. It is deeply embedded in China's culture, with a history of more than 5000 years." (Park & Luo, 2001)

As my two personal examples of *guanxi* experience at the first of this chapter indicate, one party usually uses *guanxi* to get something that he couldn't otherwise obtain on his own. Since economics by definition involves dealing with shortages, and since shortages were especially acute during the pre-reform Maoist era, *guanxi* was particularly alive and well during that period. Some thinkers on this subject suspect that *guanxi* will diminish as shortages diminish during the market-driven modern era. Others, however, believe that *guanxi* is so deeply embedded in the Chinese soul that it will endure through all ages and all political systems. (Chang 2011) I suspect the latter is the correct view.

We need to move from one-word definitions of *guanxi* and the short definition of *guanxi* I gave above in order to delve deeper into the subject, but first I will give an example of *guanxi* in business that is very typical of how business is carried on in China. This example will foreshadow our further discussions of *guanxi*. You will see how *guanxi* can come close to looking like bribery. You will see how *guanxi* might appear to violate rational norms of business behavior. In this one simple example, you will see how personal *guanxi* obligations could very well interfere with legal norms established for all members of society.

> The tax auditor just showed up one day and wanted to see the company books. There are no standardized rules on how to keep books in China, especially for private companies like ours. If they want to find fault with your income tax, they will always find something wrong . . . I call my administrative assistant, X, into my office and told him the situation. He smiled and said, Give me a 2,500 yuan allowance [equivalent to a middle managers' six-month salary] and I will take care of everything." . . . By noon, my phone rang, X asked me to go to lunch with the auditors, at the best restaurant in the city… After expensive drinks and Peking duck, the head auditor started to praise our accounting system, saying how good and efficient it looked . . . Later, I found out that X's father is a good friend of the head auditor . . . I hired X, a high school graduate, with his father's connections in mind. It does not sound right but everyone does it; you have to be open-minded. (Chang 2011)

DIFFERENT FORMS OF *GUANXI*

There are many relationships and status situations out of which *guanxi* may arise; for example, family members, relatives outside the immediate family, friends, common hometown, common school, common social club, workmates, supervisors, subordinates, neighbors, teacher-student, or fellow soldiers. (Ai 2006; Chou et al. 2006) Some of these relationships create strong *guanxi*, whereas others create weak *guanxi*. Categorizing from strong to weak, there are three general types of *guanxi* networks: core *guanxi* circles, intermediary *guanxi* circles, and periphery *guanxi* circles. The strongest of *guanxi* networks is the core *guanxi* network, which derives from family relationships, and the relationship of close friends. Individuals in these relationships are burdened with the obligation to sacrifice, give, and to manifest unconditional loyalty to their counterparts. Those who give in a strong-*guanxi* relationship do so with little or no expectation of repayment or material compensation, which is quite different from the weaker forms of *guanxi*. If, for example, a family member suffers a disaster or from financial difficulty, the other family members will share resources with him, not expecting to be repaid. The obligation owed to the counterparts in a strong core *guanxi* relationship is called ganqing (literally, "feelings and love"). (Guo and Miller 2010)   Below, is an example of this. As a Westerner, ask yourself, would you have done what these two Chinese family members did? With strong *guanxi*, who needs lawyers?

When I had an idea to start my own business in plastic product manufacturing, I had to ask my relatives if they could provide me with financial support, because the local bank refused to loan money to me. I had two family members who, with no hesitation, generously offered me the help so I could build up the plant, purchase equipment, and hire employees to pursue the opportunity. They did not even ask me to sign a letter to acknowledge the debt or give me a payback deadline, because we are qinren (family members) and these documents are completely unnecessary when we have such a strong ganqing jichu (base). If it was not for their support, I would not have been able to start the business at all. (Guo and Miller 2010)

There is *guanxi* that is weaker than strong *guanxi*. An example of this is that which exists in an intermediary *guanxi* circle, such as the relationship that exists between non-kinfolks: business partners, investment banks, major clients, or government officials. These players are in an intermediate *guanxi* relationship, halfway between a strong *guanxi* relationship with family and close friends, and an even weaker *guanxi* relationship which may be called a periphery *guanxi* circle, which is a network of strangers who are cultivated for the possibility of unknown future benefits, such as an unknown seatmate on an airplane flight with whom a business card is exchanged. The obligations that are owed between the parties of an intermediary *guanxi* circle are called renqing ("benevolence and love"). The relationships in an intermediary *guanxi* circle are frankly instrumental, unlike those of a core *guanxi* circle – the parties in an intermediary *guanxi* circle expect to possibly get something out of the relationship, and if one gets, he is expected to reciprocate. Below is the report of a businessman describing this sort of *guanxi*. Notice the reference to "banquets," "offering gifts," and "sending constant greetings."

In the stage of growth, it is of paramount importance to have renqing based *guanxi*, especially with governmental officials in business-related bureaus . . . Even though you have done everything in a legal way in China, if you do not cultivate renqing with governmental officials in these bureaus, they will think you don't know renqing shigu (social etiquette), and they may not trust you when you need their help for certain things. Nowadays, offering hongbao (red envelopes with money enclosed) to governmental officials is definitely illegal, and no one would accept it. But renqing could be cultivated through, for example, inviting them out for banquets, offering gifts on special occasions, such as national holidays, and sending constant greetings. These social activities, although they may look trivial, are essential for building long-lasting harmonious relationships. Through these ongoing social interactions, the governmental officials will know you and your business better, and more importantly, they know they are well respected. Over time, a certain degree of trust and affection will be cultivated . . . I know if I need their assistance and advice some day in the future, they will help me without question. (Guo and Miller 2010)

I mentioned banquets, offering gifts, and sending constant greetings. I have often thought that if the word "respect" were removed from the Chinese language, the whole Chinese civilization would fall to the ground. Even when business cards or money or exams are handed to you, it's always with two hands, because that shows respect. So much respect is required to be generated in order for Chinese society to function; it is necessary for banquets, gift giving, and greetings to be multiplied in a dizzying fashion. There are not enough numbers in the universe to count the number of banquets I have attended, and gifts I have been given, and greetings sent to me at holidays. The gift giving is particularly noticeable. Jin Ping Mei is a famous old Chinese novel set in the Ming dynasty. The Chinese government bans it because it is peppered with some really salacious material. I found an English translation that translated the dirty parts into Latin. There was a Roman Catholic priest serving as a visiting professor at my college in America. I asked him to translate one Latin paragraph. He got half way through, and I told him, never mind. I never thought I would end up agreeing with a Communist government's decision to ban the publication of anything. However, Jin Ping Mei, while unfortunately remembered by so many Chinese as just a dirty novel, is chock full of Chinese history and culture, and is useful to read in order to understand that culture. It is a four-volume work describing the life of a man and his wife and concubines. It seemed to me that about two full volumes were occupied with describing the rolls of silk given and received as presents: who gave the silk, what was their status and location, what was their current value on the market, what was the color, the texture, how long was the roll of silk, which present was sent back to the giver of the silk, how much money was given to accompany the silk, and on and on and on. It made Jane Austen's descriptions of wallpaper in her living room seem exciting by comparison. The novel reflects the Chinese compunction to give gifts, which still exists. If you go to a meal, you bring a gift. I regularly receive emails from my university's administration, asking me to come pick up gifts. The administration randomly puts money into the professor's accounts, just as a gift! I would ask all college professors in the West reading this book to ask yourself: when was the last time that happened in your college? Students give Christmas gifts to professors, at Christmas. I remember unwrapping so many presents at Christmas time, that I felt like a kid on Christmas morning. Of course, I have been offered gifts as a professor in the United States. I recall with special fondness one fourteen-layer caramel chocolate cake presented to me along with a gift-wrapped book, right at exam time. The offeror was an adult student taking a college course for the first time, and who told me my exams were making her break out into hives on her neck. This, of course, was a shameless, transparent attempt at a bribe. But when Chinese students do it, I know they don't consider it a bribe. However, I still get that *guanxi* feeling that I owe them. And you jolly well can't refuse the gift in China, not if you don't want to cause the gift-giving student's face to be destroyed. At any rate, it took me many years of living in China to realize that all the banquets were deadly serious, on the surface a mere meal, but underneath, something deeply vital to Chinese life and culture, something which has endured for millennia, and something which the foreigner must respect, even though he may not understand it.

We are left now with the task of describing the weakest form of *guanxi*, the type that exists in a periphery *guanxi* circle. This category of *guanxi* is described as yiban ("ordinary") *guanxi*. These ordinary *guanxi* ties are established with people previously unknown, and with people who do not have a family or business relationship with the person seeking the relationship. The purpose of the relationship is to keep open the possibility of future benefit. This contrasts with the intermediary *guanxi* relationship, which is usually designed to get an immediate benefit, such as a governmental permission, or information of some kind. Examples of this form of *guanxi* contact are contacts made at college alumni associations or at academic conferences. (Guo and Miller 2010) Below, is a businessman's testimonial describing this sort of weak *guanxi*.

I got to know one of my business associates because we were on a business trip, same flight, and we sat next to each other. At a certain point, we started talking. We talked about our hometowns and the kind of business we were engaged in. Although I did not disclose too much detailed information about my business because I didn't even know this person, we did exchange business cards before we got off the plane and promised we would contact each other in the future if an opportunity arises to do business together. Two months later, I received a phone call from this person asking me if I would be interested in establishing a joint venture with his company. If I didn't jianli (establish) some jiaoqing (acquaintance) with him beforehand, I wouldn't have this business opportunity at all. (Guo and Miller 2010)

This last example illustrates the common Chinese practice of exchanging phone and address information with so many people of even the most casual acquaintance, in a way that is foreign to the West. These Chinese are cultivating ordinary *guanxi*. They remind me somewhat of all those non-Buddhists who burn incense (joss sticks) at Buddhist altars. They are not committed to the Buddha at all, but they are hedging their bets for the future.

SALIENT CHARACTERISTICS OF *GUANXI*

There are certain prominent features of *guanxi*, some of which will help you distinguish the ordinary Western social network from the Chinese form. For the sake of discussion, I have labeled these attributes of *guanxi* as transferability, reciprocity, intangibility, the utilitarian nature of *guanxi*, (Park and Luo, 2001) and longevity.

We'll start first with transferability. If A has *guanxi* with B, and B has *guanxi* with C, and A has never seen nor heard of C, nevertheless, A has *guanxi* with C. This means that if B tells his friend C that A needs something, then C is obligated to deliver to A, even though C does not know A. If C does not deliver, he will suffer loss of face, which of course, is extremely painful to Chinese. As a Westerner, I can't imagine a friend asking me, in a manner in which I could not refuse, to help an unknown friend of my friend. But it's different in China. This attribute of transferability explains how I could get travel help all the way from Shanghai, in the far East, to the Taklamakan desert, in the far West, from people who didn't know each other.

Reciprocity is that feature of *guanxi* that states that if someone has scratched your back, you must in return scratch theirs. That, of course, is nothing new to Westerners. But *guanxi* reciprocity is different than Western reciprocity. In the west, folks generally feel that they should give back approximately what they have received. But in China, weaker parties often call for special favors without having the ability to reciprocate in kind. Chinese *guanxi* networks thus often stretch across unequal hierarchical ranks. I recall a Chinese professor telling me that on certain holidays, he would sit all day by the phone, individually answering calls from old students. It seems that he owed it to them to spend as much time with each of them as they spent giving him greetings. Whether or not the reciprocity is exercised between different social or organizational ranks, the time and effort required to reciprocate favors can in fact be quite burdensome. I recall a Chinese professor who taught at my American campus as an exchange professor tell me how much she loved teaching in the West. I asked her why. Her response was that her time was her own, whereas in China, hours out of every day were consumed with doing favors for people she owed *guanxi* to.

Intangibility is that characteristic of *guanxi* which states that the amount of favors, or the frequency of favors owed, is not spelled out so that the parties know exactly what they owe each other. A party cannot grossly ignore his obligations without a serious loss of face, but on the other hand, the parties don't keep the books tightly balanced in the short term. Someone with a *guanxi* deficit may not be called on to satisfy it until long after he has received his favor, and the parties are happy with that. It would seem that in order for all parties to feel satisfied, there must be prerequisite advanced social skills, in order for all concerned to nimbly negotiate the subtle, unstated, shadowy requirements of personal relationships which can extend far off into networks of people who often are not even known. But the Chinese, who are essentially Confucian, even though modern, are noted for their ability to maintain social harmony. I don't really believe individualistic Westerners could pull *guanxi* off.

Utilitarian is an apt descriptor of *guanxi*, at least *guanxi* of the intermediary and peripheral kind. These kinds of *guanxi* are based entirely on the exchange of favors, and not on emotional attachment. This explains how perfect strangers can provide one with train tickets, cheap hotels, and travel assistance. It is because they expect one day to possibly receive something in return. They don't know who you are, nor do they really care.

Longevity is that feature of *guanxi* which describes the very interesting fact that *guanxi* networks survive beyond the grave. I recall a Chinese professor telling me that his father was a well-known Chinese intellectual and scholar, a very respected man who had accumulated a lot of *guanxi*. This professor's father had died before the son took his College Entrance Exam. The son's scores on the exam were subpar and not to his liking. The colleagues of the deceased father, who felt they had much *guanxi* obligation to the deceased father and therefore also to the son, managed to get the authorities to look into the grading of the entrance exam, and found that indeed, there was an error. The son went on to go to the college of his choice, and became a university professor. It never would have happened without *guanxi*.

PROBING EVEN DEEPER INTO *GUANXI*

Comparisons with the West

There have been efforts to find similarities with *guanxi* relationships and certain relationships found in the West. Most of the comparisons, however, between *guanxi* in China and relationships in the West have highlighted the differences, not the similarities. We'll look at the similarities, first.

Relationship marketing, recently emphasized in the West, on the surface bears a resemblance to *guanxi*. Relationship marketing is supposed to reduce transaction costs, facilitate cooperation of marketing channel members and is supposed to retain customers. (Ai 2006) *Guanxi* is supposed to do all of that, too. Relationship marketing is described as "a purposeful form of marketing effort aiming at an enhanced exchange process." *Guanxi* could easily be described in the same manner. Relationship marketing is characterized by "satisfaction, trust, commitment and mutual exchange with profit," which of course precisely describes *guanxi*. (Fok and Woo 1998)

However, having noted the similarities, it is necessary now that we inspect the difference between Western business relationships and *guanxi*. First, the *guanxi* relationship is not necessarily equal: reciprocity often runs up and down a social or organizational hierarchy, and in fact the exchanges tend to favor the weaker party. Second, relationship marketing consists of relationships which are purposively constructed in a business context, whereas *guanxi* often arises from family ties, or ties of close friendship. Third, and most interesting to me, *guanxi* relationships are personal and not organizational, and indeed often run counter to organizational and societal (legal) interests. It is common to hear of stories concerning judges who have *guanxi* ties to the fathers of defendants, and who will not execute the laws with impartiality. In China, personal loyalty is often more important than organizational affiliation or legal status. (Fok and Woo 1998) It is this characteristic which sometimes gives *guanxi* a bad odor to Westerners, who have been raised on the axiom that all are equal before the law. In fact, *Guanxi* sometimes runs very close to bribery and corruption, at least as seen through Western eyes.

Let's stop here and examine *guanxi* from the aspect of bribery and ethics, a point that originates from the personal, non-organizational nature of *guanxi* relationships. For example, a mother of a college-age daughter who had not scored high enough to get into her chosen university had *guanxi* with the university officials. The officials changed the girl's exam score in order to allow her to matriculate. (Riley 1994) To the Western eye, this is simple corruption. However, from a Chinese viewpoint, it could very well be viewed as a positive thing. A college official was doing something personal to help a friend, he was performing his *guanxi* obligations, and he was a good man. The individual obligation triumphed over the organizational one. Gift giving can often approach the line that separates appreciation and corruption. The famous hongbao, red envelopes with money enclosed as a gift, according to one Chinese businessman, is now definitely illegal and would not be accepted. But there are other things Chinese businessmen can do for government officials, such as inviting them out to banquets, giving gifts on special occasions, and sending greetings. (Guo and Miller 2010) As China moves towards a rational legal and regulatory system, this sort of *guanxi* that is really bribery apparently is becoming less popular, as more and more Chinese come to see it as bribery and corruption, and as more and more Chinese see bribery and corruption as immoral. (Guthrie 1998, cited in Chang 2011) Often, the Chinese will use this sort of *guanxi* privately (Yang 2002, cited in Chang 2011), but they are more and more publicly distancing themselves from this sort of behavior. (Guthrie 1998, cited in Chang 2011)

A fourth difference between Western and Chinese thinking about *Guanxi* is that Westerners and Chinese tend to view equality through different lenses. Westerners tend to think that laws and ethics universally apply to all peoples regardless of their status, and that, when people get special favors, when they jump the queue, it is a moral affront. (McComb 1999, cited in Ai 2006) Insider trading laws are reflective of this sort of thinking – all investors should have an equal shot at obtaining information to trade securities. Chinese people, however, when they see some getting an advantage because of their *guanxi* connections, are much less likely to view the transaction as corrupt.

A fifth difference between Western and Chinese concepts of *guanxi* has to do with the order of priority of law (fa), reason (li), and affection (qing). To order their business relationships, Western businessmen typically look to the law first (the contract must be legal), and then reason next (it is reasonable that our business deal will be profitable), and finally affection (our business relationship worked out so well that we can be friends now). The Chinese order is reversed. Chinese take care of the relationship first, and then see if it's reasonable to enter into a business deal, and finally, they worry about where the activities springing from their relationship are legal or not. (Guo and Miller, 2010) It is a staple of cross-cultural literature dealing with China that the Chinese don't regard contracts too highly, that having signed one, a Chinese will shortly thereafter try to change it. There are deep cultural reasons for this, and the Westerner will ignore this at his peril. To put it somewhat differently, in China, the relationship comes first, and the business transaction comes last. In the West, the opposite tends to be true. The Chinese believe that if a successful relationship is constructed, business deals will follow. A signed contract is merely an indication of the beginning of a successful relationship, adjustments to which will have to be made as time goes on, even as husbands and wives in a successful marriage have to adjust. The parties in this successful relationship will honor their promises, not because of the contract, but because of the relationship. For Westerners, however, the tendency is to keep promises based upon respect for the contractual agreement, not respect for the business partner. (Ai 2005, cited in Ai 2006; Park and Luo 2001)

Relationship with Face

Face is a concept about which most Westerners are aware, probably being more familiar with the idea of face than the concept of *guanxi*. The two notions are related. Face is something that all cultures have, including Western ones. Nobody likes to be shamed in the presence of his significant others. The difference between the West and China is probably in the extreme sensitivity Chinese (and other Asian) cultures feel towards the loss of face. Traditionally, the Chinese have compared losing face to the pain experienced when one's eye, nose, or mouth is physically mutilated. (Park and Luo 2001) How is face inter-related with *guanxi*? First of all, the loss of face is the sanction that gets people to reciprocally perform once they have been benefited through a *guanxi* network. If it weren't for the fear of loss of face, I would imagine it would be very difficult to tear yourself away from whatever you are doing to procure train tickets for perfect strangers. Secondly, the more face (prestige) one has, the easier it is to get the favors flowing through the *guanxi* network. (Park and Luo 2000)

How to Initiate and Maintain *Guanxi*

One research study asked some senior Chinese managers how *guanxi* should be initially created. The methods, given with the percentage of managers who felt the method should be employed placed in parentheses to the right, are listed here: introduced by others, not by approaching directly (100%), mutual help (75%), trust (83%), friendship (67%), help in bad situations (67%), and social acceptance (67%). Other methods reported in this research used to maintain *guanxi* once it has been initiated included sharing profits from *guanxi*, frequent mutual help, and keeping in contact. (Ai 2006) It is important to note that *guanxi*, once established, does not by default stay established. Continuous cultivation is required to maintain, or strengthen, the *guanxi* relationship that has been established. (Morgan and Hunt 1994, cited in Fok and Woo 1998)

The Downside to *Guanxi*

Before even considering the costs of maintaining a *guanxi* network, it is important to remember that *guanxi* is not a panacea. Sometimes market or regulatory forces will win out over someone playing a strong *guanxi* hand. Li Ka-shing is reputed to be the "richest man in Asia," as the taxi drivers in his home city of Shantou, Guangdong Province, will be happy to tell you. Mr. Li, a Hong Kong businessman, had powerful *guanxi* with top Chinese officials in Beijing. He used that *guanxi* to get McDonald's booted out of one of its stores in Beijing to make room for one of Li Ka-shing's real estate developments. Nonetheless, local government authorities suspended Mr. Li's real estate project twice thereafter. (Business Week, Feb. 24, 1997, cited in Fok and Woo 1998) It is not only regulatory forces that can beat *guanxi*; even *guanxi* itself can beat *guanxi*. Sometimes, someone else's stronger *guanxi* might supersede one's own *guanxi*. And if regulatory forces or other *guanxi* don't beat one's *guanxi*, sometimes modern market forces might do so. One research survey reported that 38% of its respondents felt that traditional marketing mix strategies were more effective than *guanxi*, contrasted with only 23% who felt that *guanxi* was more effective. One research paper indicated that although *guanxi* contributes to firm growth in terms of market expansion, nevertheless *guanxi* did not improve a firm's net profit. (Park and Luo 2001) In any case, *guanxi* is expensive, time consuming, and often perceived as corruption. (Fok and Woo 1998)

The Importance of *Guanxi* to Business

Despite the above-mentioned skepticism towards the value of *guanxi* in business, and despite some scholarly speculation that the practice of *guanxi* will shrink before the onslaught of Western market forces (Chang 2011), nevertheless *guanxi* is said to be critical for businesses, whether foreign or local. *Guanxi* is a critical factor in firm performance in China, affecting firms' access to resources. *Guanxi* is important for the management of uncertainty and external dependency. (Park and Luo 2001) *Guanxi* can affect a firm's financial outcomes (Luo and Chen 1996, cited in Park and Luo 2001), and can affect market benefits (Davies et al. 1995, cited in Park and Luo 2001). *Guanxi* can bring competitive advantages (Tsang 1998, Yeung and Tung 1996, both cited in Park and Luo 2001), and can contribute to the sales growth of organizations by minimizing transaction costs and business uncertainties (but at the cost of low prices or liberal terms of payments offered to the buyer). *Guanxi* with suppliers helps firms obtain quality materials, good service, and timely deliveries. *Guanxi* with competitors mitigates costs and standardizes inter-firm processes, and facilitates resource sharing. *Guanxi* can cut through the opaque maze of bureaucracy, which often is not based on reason, but rather personal interpretation of vague, inchoate rules. (Park and Luo 2001) There is a good deal of research showing an association between the practice of *Guanxi* and entrepreneurial success. (Batjargal 2007, Batjargal and Liu 2004, Carlisle and Flynn 2005, Wu and Leung 2005; all cited in Guo and Miller 2010)

It should be noted that the amount of *Guanxi* used in one firm may well be different than that used in another. For example, firms with strong managerial capabilities will tend to use marketing strategies which are free of *Guanxi*, such as advertising, research and development, and product/service quality, whereas firms without those managerial strengths will tend to rely on *guanxi* in order to perform marketing tasks. (Park and Luo 2001)

Not only is *guanxi* important to firms operating in China; it also affects individuals within those firms. If a subordinate develops *guanxi* with his organizational superior, the subordinate is likely to see his career enhanced. (Wei et al. 2010) The better *guanxi* with a boss that is owned by a subordinate, the more likely the boss will overlook and forgive mistakes. It has been argued that Chinese employers value loyalty more than competence. In that situation, it is not surprising that *guanxi* is highly important to individual career development. (Daniels, et al.1985, cited in Wei et al. 2010) Better *guanxi* with superiors allows subordinates to obtain resources for the firm, thus pleasing the supervisor, and it gives the subordinate an opportunity to perform in the sunshine, where his boss can see it. (Wei et al 2010) Many subordinates have been rewarded with commissions, bonuses, and promotions, as a result of leveraging their personal *guanxi* for the benefit of their superior's firm. (Park and Luo 2001)

A CONCLUDING OBSERVATION

Now that we have pulled apart the concept of *guanxi* and examined it sideways and forwards, let's go back to the simple one word definition: relationships. The Chinese prize relationships probably even more than they prize money, were that possible. Even the concept of the self in Chinese thought is only envisioned as the self in relationship to others. The shorthand definition of Confucianism that is ubiquitously given is the five basic relationships of Confucianism. Because they prize relationships so much, harmony is a derivative good. Instead of the phrase "good society," English-speaking Chinese constantly say "harmonious society," which is a phrase I don't remember hearing in the West. Like anyone else, I have seen some unpleasant human confrontations, but I don't recall ever seeing them end in smiles, as I did in the incident I am about to relate. In this story, you will see the operation of the related concepts of *guanxi*, face, and harmony.

But before I relate the story, I am going to give jarring counterexamples to the Chinese ideal of relationship and harmony. I have never understood, given Chinese cultural imperatives, why the Chinese like to scream at each other in public. This is one of the strange paradoxes of modern China that I cannot begin to explain. I can speculate that the public berating that occurs is because of the breakdown of traditional Confucian society, and thus is not a paradox at all. But I really don't know, and I list this as one of the many unresolved mysteries about China still lingering in my mind. On numerous occasions, I have seen seen "lovers" yelling at the top of their lungs in the street. For reasons unbeknownst to me, it is usually the woman who yells at the man. I remember riding a bicycle in Shanghai when my pedal came off, and as I looked down to attend to it, I continued my forward motion and accidentally hit an elderly woman, who proceeded to address me in most un-Confucian like terms. My Chinese friend who was accompanying me refused to translate until later at a restaurant, after I begged him ten or eleven times. I must say the obscenities were such as I've never heard in the West. The old lady was extraordinarily unconcerned about my face. I recall another occasion in a Shanghai Carrefour (the French version of Walmart), when I was engulfed in one of the typical mobs swirling around the twenty-something check out lines. An old man broke in front of me as I paused to examine something in my shopping cart. It was no big deal. However, the student (a woman) who accompanied me exploded and began to hysterically scream at the old man (who gave it back as good as he got). As I pushed the student away from the scene, and as she kept turning her head to eyeball the old man, to scream at him some more, I asked myself what had happened to the traditional relationship and respect between the young and the old?

Back to my story of *guanxi*, face, and harmony. An American friend and his wife had come to visit my wife and me in Beijing. We had befriended a young Tangshan girl in her mid-twenties, and my friend had spoken to several college-age friends of the Tangshan girl who were visiting Beijing from Tangshan, and who were impressed with my friend, and who wanted to hear some more. We arranged a bus trip to Tangshan to visit the college students, who were loosely organized into a group that informally met at a bookstore in Tangshan. The Tangshan girl we had befriended in Beijing operated the bookstore. This girl had some sort of (non-romantic) *guanxi* relationship with a middle-aged college professor, an instructor in international law, who somehow felt like he needed to protect the innocent minds of these college students. He had no organizational relationship with the college, or with the bookstore. After my friend and I and our two wives, plus the Tangshan girl, arrived in Tangshan, the professor met us. He took us to a room in a local business, served us all tea, and began to visit with us. The visit was going on about two hours or so, and I was getting antsy. The smiling professor, as he sipped tea with us, used his excellent English to ask us all sorts of questions about America and about our lives. It finally dawned on me that this man was stalling us, and had absolutely no intention of letting us visit with those college students, despite our trouble and effort to make the long bus trip to Tangshan. I observed my American friend. He was blissfully unaware that we were about to get shot down. Our host, the smiling law professor, then escorted us to a five-star hotel, where we sat down in a private dining room overlooking a pretty garden, and ate all sorts of expensive local delicacies, and talked for the usual eternity of time that Chinese banquets require. Then, at the end of the meal, he explained to us in a very soft voice that we were not to be allowed to talk to the college students. We got on a bus and went back to Beijing. I told my friend that only in China can you get shafted and feel good about it later. We had just had our face saved. Our relationships were preserved. I could probably go back to that professor's university today and eat jiaozi with him with not a bit of discomfort.

CHAPTER REFERENCES

Ai, Jin (2006). *Guanxi* Networks in China: Its Importance and Future Trends. China & World Economy 14(5):105-118.

Batjargal, B. (2007). Internet Entrepreneurship: Social Capital, Human Capital, And Performance Of Internet Ventures In China. Research Policy, 36(5):605-618.

Batjargal, B. & Liu, M. (2004). Entrepreneurs' Access To Private Equity In China: The Role Of Social Capital. Organization Science 15(2):159-172.

Business Week, Feb. 24, 1997.

Carlisle, E. & Flynn, D. (2005). Small Business Survival In China: *Guanxi*, Legitimacy, And Social Capital. Journal of Developmental Entrepreneurship 10(1): 79-96.

Chang, Kuang-Chi (2011). A Path to Understanding *Guanxi* in China's Transitional Economy: Variations on Network Behavior. Sociological Theory 29(4):315-339.

Chou, Li-Fang; Cheng, Bor-Shiuan; Huang, Min-Ping; Cheng, Hung-Yueh (2006). *Guanxi* Networks and Members' Effectiveness in Chinese Work Teams: Mediating Effects of Trust Networks. Asian Journal of Social Psychology 9:79-95.

Daniels, J.D.; Krug, K.; and Neigh, D. (1985). US Joint Ventures In China: Motivation And Management Of Political Risk. California Management Review 27:46-58.

Davies, H.; Leung, TK; Luk, S.; and Wong, Y. (1995). The Benefits Of *Guanxi*: The Value Of Relationships In Developing The Chinese Market. Industrial Marketing Management 24:207-214.

Fock, Henry K.Y. and Woo, Ka-shing (1998). The China Market: Strategic Implications of *Guanxi*. Business Strategy Review 9(3):33-43.

Guthrie, Douglas 1998. The Declining Significance of *Guanxi* in China's Economic Transition. China Quarterly 154:254-82.

Guo, Chun and Miller, Jane K. (2010). *Guanxi* Dynamics and Entrepreneurial Firm Creation and Development in China. Management and Organization Review 6(2):267-291.

Luo, Y. and Chen, M. (1996). Managerial Implications Of *Guanxi*-Based Business Strategies. Journal of International Management 2:193-316.

McComb, Robert (1999). 2009: China's Human Resources Odyssey. The China Business Review 5:27-29.

Morgan, R. M. and Hunt, S. D. (1994). The Commitment-Trust Theory of Relationship Marketing. Journal of Marketing 56:20-38.

Park, Seung Ho and Luo, Yadong (2001). *Guanxi* and Organizational Dynamics: Organizational Networking in Chinese Firms. Strategic Management Journal 22:455-477.

Riley, Nancy E. (1994). Interwoven Lives: Parents, Marriage, and *Guanxi* in China. Journal of Marriage and Family 56(4):791-803.

Tsang, W.K. (1998). Can *Guanxi* Be A Source Of Sustained Competitive Advantage For Doing Business In China? Academy of Management Executive 12:64-73.

Wei, Li-Qun; Liu, Jun; Chen Yuan-Yi; and Wu, Long-Zeng (2010). Political Skill, Supervisor–Subordinate *Guanxi* and Career Prospects in Chinese Firms. Journal of Management Studies 47(3):437-454.

Wu, W. & Leung, A. (2005). Does A Micro-Macro Link Exist Between Managerial Value Of Reciprocity, Social Capital And Firm Performance? The Case Of Smes In China. Asia Pacific Journal of Management 22(4):445-463.

Yang, Mayfair (2002). The Resilience of *Guanxi* and its New Deployments: A Critique of Some New *Guanxi* Scholarship. China Quarterly 170:459-76.

Yeung, I.Y. and Tung, R.L. (1996). Achieving Business Success In Confucian Societies: The Importance Of *Guanxi*. Organizational Dynamics 3:54-65.

The attitude of Chinese prostitutes who migrate to the city in order to feel "modern" and "open" and "urban" is merely one example of the attitude of just about every Chinese I have met. Rural is bad, poor, "uncivilized," not "open," not "modern." Urban is sophisticated, wealthy, educated, powerful, and good. I have been surprised to find several examples of young Chinese who grew up relatively poor in the country but who were able to escape out of it, without having to resort to prostitution. I know one young Chinese woman who grew up poor in the countryside of Harbin with a disabled father, but who was nevertheless able to learn fluent English, and who read Gone with the Wind (in Chinese) in middle school. She later became a nurse. On a bus near Nanjing (a small town in Zhejiang province], I sat next to a young woman about thirty years old, who told me of her life in the country. Her parents were too poor to send her to high school. Nevertheless, she managed to get her high school degree at 26, and later on her college degree, and she was preparing to work on her Master's degree. Her brother had obtained a Ph.D. from Beijing University, China's top-ranked university. Another sibling stayed on the farm. She said that when she went back home, the conversation completely centered on the price of pigs and chickens, the weather, etc. She said her parents and the brother still on the farm were perfectly happy living there. Once, she had brought her parents to stay with her in Beijing for a visit. The parents couldn't read road signs, were afraid to go outside, sat home and watched TV all day, and finally asked to be taken back home to the country. I asked this young woman: was her Ph.D. brother happier or was the brother who stayed on the farm happier? She couldn't say one way or the other. I have talked to another Master's student who excitedly recalled her happy childhood during which she had no toys. She would, for fun, flip paper chips in the depressions of the earthen floor, and who would fly paper airplanes. She also played a marble game with rules which were exactly like a marble game I played as an elementary school child, a game we called "Roly Poly." It amazed me to think that a poor rural girl with no contact with the West would be playing the same game I did on the other side of the globe three decades earlier. She firmly insisted that she still didn't like toys.

It is my impression that there is a huge social divide between city folk and rural people. I talked to a Beijing girl who claimed that she could tell a waidi ren (a person from outside the city) merely by looking at them, without even hearing their country accents. It was obvious to me she held them somewhat in disdain. I asked her if her father would let her marry a waidi ren and the answer was an immediate "No!" She told me that it was more than just prejudice against waidi ren that caused her father to say that. He was concerned that she not marry anyone that was poor. But I thought it interesting that no matter how looked-down upon a country person was, every country person I talked to was not only unashamed of her origins, but rather nostalgic about her childhood in the country.

The prejudice against rural poverty that exists in the cities exists parallel with the prejudice against those living in the more undeveloped cities, especially those in the western part of the country. A Beijing resident expressed great concern for me because I was going to live in Yinchuan, a city of a mere two million population in China's northwest, because it was so "undeveloped." Yinchuan residents who had gone to colleges in the east told me that fellow students there in the east asked them, with a straight face and with no intention to joke, whether Yinchuan high school students rode to school on camels! Pizza Hut just opened up a restaurant in Yinchuan, and I never saw any camels tied up, out front. There was also several KFC's in the city, although the city had not developed enough to have a McDonald's. This is how most foreigners judge how developed a city is: does it have a KFC (beginning to develop), a McDonald's (partially developed), and a Pizza Hut (fully developed). I have come to believe that the Chinese word fazhan ("develop") is the most fashionable word in the language. One hears it all the time. Chinese are mad for development, and development essentially means foreign companies coming in and establishing themselves in a city. Development is proceeding at a dizzying pace. I have talked to taxi drivers in Xining (a small provincial capital in the west of the country) and Yinchuan (another provincial capital in the west of the country), who both clearly demarcated a time when their respective cities were "undeveloped" and "developed," about five years before the time I talked to them. They said their cities were almost unrecognizable from the city that was there five years before. Since the turn of the current century, the Chinese economy has quadrupled in size. (BBC television broadcast, November 27, 2011) It is interesting to see this incredibly rapid change juxtaposed with a conservative, traditional culture. The Chinese language is changing, sexual mores, living arrangements, dining etiquette, tastes in music, just about everything is undergoing a transformation. One often hears of the "generation gap" in China. Chinese students love to talk about it. I suspect it's the largest generation gap in history.

CHAPTER REFERENCES

BBC television broadcast, November 27, 2011

CHINESE BUSINESS DINNERS

A banquet in a fancy Chinese hotel restaurant is a sine qua non for doing business with the Chinese. I have endured hundreds of these banquets, and it is only relatively recently that I have begun to enjoy them. In my view, eating is second only to language as a cultural barrier between foreigners and Chinese. The language is more difficult to master, but eating properly comes just behind. I have realized that, as time has gone on, I have breached many, many rules of Chinese etiquette; however, the nice thing is, the Chinese knew I was a dumb foreigner who didn't know what I was doing, and more often expressed admiration for my ability to pick up a peanut with chopsticks, than they showed scorn when I dropped food on the tablecloth.

When one enters a relatively higher-class Chinese restaurant, he first walks through two facing lines of pretty girls dressed in traditional Chinese costume, like football players leaving the tunnel for the playing field. The girls, as soon as they see you, pipe out in a perfectly coordinated chorus "huanying guanglin!" (Welcome!) I have yet to determine if these girls have any other duties. They seem to have been rented for cosmetic effect. The job seems easy enough, yet they and the other restaurant staff during off hours are lined up on the sidewalk in front of the restaurant, in full view of the public, where they are given rah-rah pep talks by the restaurant owner, and where they do calisthenics together, and where they receive such other instruction as is needed. I do not yet understand why they need to be in shape to say "huanying guang lin" over and over. After one passes the huanying guanglin girls, one is confronted with a wall of sound. Talking in a Chinese restaurant is like talking at the Southern 500, or trying to converse in the midst of Hurricane Hugo. One sees one's partner's lips move, but no sound comes out. I have left a Chinese restaurant with a bad sore throat after trying to converse with a colleague. Chinese are generally very gentle and refined people, but there is something about a restaurant that brings out the gregarious side in them. The more bottles of beer are piled up on the floor around the table, the louder it gets. This is especially true in the ordinary family-style restaurants. It is usually a little quieter in the fancy restaurants in which the foreign businessman will find himself; however, it is still noisy enough that the businessman's host will have reserved a private room for the dinner party, usually upstairs, apart from the hubbub.

The center of the private room is occupied by a huge round table. The standard table will seat about 12 people comfortably. The round table is much more sociable then a square Western one, and facilitates the Chinese desire for togetherness and group harmony. In the middle is a very large lazy Susan. Where one sits is dictated by hoary Chinese rules of etiquette. The guest of honor, which would be you, is led to sit at the far seat of the table facing the doorway, which is the seat of honor. The guest of honor's wife is seated to his immediate left. The Chinese host is seated to the guest of honor's right. The chauffeur who drove the party to the restaurant is seated across from the guest of honor and the host, with his back to the door. I have always thought it heartwarming the way Chinese dinner parties often include the driver in dinner parties. The waitress arrives and begins her duties. If you have put a briefcase or bag on the shiny, polished, clean ceramic floor, they will hurriedly pick it up and place it on the windowsill, or, in some cases, if there are empty seats, they will put your things on the empty chair. I have been informed that all Chinese are taught from childhood never ever to put any bag on the ground, because the ground is dirty. After having Chinese assistants pick my bag up hundreds of times from the ground, I have given up trying to make things convenient for myself, plopping them on the floor. However, I still enjoy sitting on low stone walls, or on curbs, to rest my feet, because I know that there will be a lot of Chinese folks staring at the barbaric foreigner. Because there are rarely ever any benches, and because there are so many Chinese people, when the Chinese want to rest in public, they will squat down on their heels and relax. I used to think this was not restful at all, until one day I decided to try it. I was surprised to find it really takes a load off your feet.

But I digress. The waitress, after settling your bags, hands one menu to the host. I have been aggravated over and over again by the one-menu policy. Since a Chinese meal is a communal one, only one person orders. This means the host usually handles the task, although sometimes there is some good-natured back-and-forth as to who is most qualified to order. The host has a duty to maintain harmony and to keep everyone happy, so he will dutifully inquire as to what everyone wants, or which food each guest does not like, can the guest eat spicy foods, etc. I have learned the hard way that one should vary one's preferences. I got the reputation in one job of liking mutton, and I was served mutton at every meal thereafter, and there wasn't much I could do to remedy the situation. The drinks are handled in special fashion. The host will ask the guest of honor what he wants to drink, without asking the rest of the guests. Once, I was taken out to eat by a high-school class I was teaching. I found out later that they loved to drink beer, and they were really looking forward to this meal, because it was a chance to escape the no-alcohol regulations of their high school. They asked me what I wanted to drink, and I said "mango juice." To my surprise, all the students also ordered mango juice. I thought the mango juice must be especially good at this restaurant, till I discovered later that what the guest of honor orders, everybody else orders. It was a matter of respect. China would fall apart without respect. Everybody is always showing each other respect, even in one's choice of drinks. From that experience I have learned to order what I think the others will probably be happy with.

The waitress pours the drinks, and the guests chat, awaiting the arrival of the dishes. The dishes are not all served at once, Western-style, but arrive one by one. As soon as the first one or two arrive, the Lazy Susan spins, and each guest uses his chopsticks to pick up a tiny bit of food out of the dish when it stops in front of his place. This process will continue for a couple of hours, as new dishes arrive. When I say hours, I literally mean hours. If one thinks of the length of a high school or college graduation ceremony, and multiplies that by ten, one will appreciate the perceived length of a Chinese meal. And since often most of the conversation will be in Chinese that you will not understand, you will appreciate the problem facing the foreigner. If you enter into one of these meals with any sort of jet lag, you are in for a world of trouble, especially if the hours at the table are willed away by gambling and drinking competitions.

Before I address the ritualized drinking that must occur, I need to address the problem of eating. The usually simple process of eating is not so simple in China. Although the fancier restaurants accustomed to serving foreigners will often provide the guests with forks, spoons and knives, one cannot count on that. And in addition, forks and knives just weren't made for certain Chinese food. Six-foot long noodles curled up in soup weren't meant to be eaten with a fork. This might raise a question in the mind of an inquiring foreigner – how in the world are six-foot long noodles curled up in soup to be eaten with chopsticks? Actually, the problem is easily solved, if one remembers that chopsticks must be aided with one's teeth. If the guest sticks the noodles into his mouth, and discovers to his discomfiture that no matter how high he raises his chopsticks, the noodles just keep on coming, he should not panic; rather, he should bow his head towards the noodles, stick them into his mouth, and bite the noodles off. This is perfectly polite, and very utilitarian. Chopsticks, it should be remembered, are not only for squeezing. They can be dipped into a drink or soup to stir the contents. I have seen it written somewhere that chopsticks are not to be directly stabbed into food in order to secure it like a fork, but I do it all the time, especially when the fancy chopsticks are polished and slippery, and I can't squeeze the food properly. There are only two things I don't do with chopsticks, and that is to point them at people when I talk, or stick them straight up in a bowl of rice. The latter maneuver is considered extremely offensive. It appears that two chopsticks sticking straight up in the air remind Chinese of three joss (incense) sticks held up straight in the air in front of a Buddhist or Daoist temple, as devotees pray. Therefore, two chopsticks stuck straight up in a bowl of rice have the appearance that the diner is praying for the evil person sitting in front of him. Here is one last word concerning chopsticks. Yes, it is true, dear foreigner, that the chopsticks that enter one's neighbor's mouth also enters the communal food, after which your chopsticks get the contaminated food, and put that food into your mouth. I have heard stuffy foreigners, Spotless McDermott types, complain about this practice. I respond in this way: first, the Chinese have been doing it for thousands of years, and they have multiplied to the point where they are driving themselves to distraction with population. The practice cannot be deadly. Second, my wife and I have been doing it for about sixteen years, and we're both still alive and kicking. It is true that I have seen an article in a Chinese publication advocating more use of common serving chopsticks for public health reasons. So, perhaps somebody knows something I don't know. But if one is going to do business in China, certain sacrifices have to be made, and this should be a small one, as the foreign businessman contemplates hundreds of millions of potential Chinese customers.

Handling chopsticks is not the only difficulty facing the foreign diner. The lack of a dinner plate, coupled with the foreigner's inability to dexterously handle his chopsticks, increases much the probability that Chinese food will find its destination on the table, or worse, on one's suit, rather than in one's mouth. Before the foreigner leaves home, I would advise him to practice eating with chopsticks out of a teacup and saucer. Another difficulty presents itself when chicken is served. The Chinese love to chop chicken up with huge meat cleavers, with which every kitchen is equipped. They don't chop the chicken according to neat Western rules of logic. The breasts are not separated from the legs and back, etc., rather, the chicken is just hacked like an ax-murderer would do to his victim. The result is a lot of small pieces of chicken surrounding small pieces of bone. The only way to eat these chicken pieces is to put them in your mouth, rotate them around till you nub off the meat, and spit the bone into an available saucer or plate, or on the table, if no saucer or plate is available. There is no need to worry about what Amy Vanderbilt might think about this–her jurisdiction does not run in China.

It is necessary to remember that there is no real segregation of function with regards to Chinese dinnerware. Teacup saucers can be used for plates. Soup bowls are picked up to be drunk from like a cup. Empty glasses can be used to deposit waste. One does what needs to be done with the tools at hand.

There are a few other rules of Chinese etiquette that run counter to Western training. One does not ask for things to be passed to you. The discerning Chinese host, or one of his dinner guests, will see that you need something, and they will rotate the Lazy Susan in your direction. If it turns out (as often happens) that much of the food on the table is unpalatable to your Western tastes, and no one at the table recognizes that you have your eye on a roast beef dish on the other side of the table, you can only wait, hope, and pray. If the Lazy Susan rotates the roast beef to one of your neighbors, and it is close enough for you to reach for it, Chinese etiquette permits this, but you better be skillful enough to hoist the juicy morsel over several neighbors onto your plate, without dripping anything on the way. Another Chinese rule of dining etiquette which has tripped me up is the idea that if one's plate, or a serving plate, is cleaned, then the diner must be hungry, and has not been fed properly. This idea that one's plate must be cleaned in memory of all the starving children in Africa never seems to have occurred to the Chinese. I remember being filled to the brim after a formal Chinese meal, after having eaten for about two hours, and then spying one last piece of roast beef on a platter, which was in the midst of all the other used and empty serving plates. No sooner had I grabbed the roast beef with my chopsticks, than the host flagged the waitress to order another plate. I protested that the meal was over, we didn't have time, I was merely finishing off the delicious roast beef, and I didn't mean to indicate that I was still hungry. My Chinese assistants, who were more culturally savvy than I, explained quickly to the hosts that Americans don't like to waste things, which was an accurate description of a cultural trait of Americans of which I was unaware. Chinese people really love food. I have been present at so many meals in which the dishes are discussed. What are they? How are they different than the dishes in another locality? What is the proper name to call them? How are they cooked? Chinese food is not standard at all, which is one reason Chinese cuisine is among the best in the world. In every city I have moved to, I have had to re-learn the local dishes in order to be able to order food at a restaurant. Every city not only has different dishes with different names, but also has a "specialty," of which they are very proud.

As much as Chinese people love their food, I think they might love their drinking more. They talk about it a lot as they are doing it, the same way Westerners do, as they judge different people's capacities to drink different quantities. The drinking at a Chinese meal is highly ritualized. The host will often figure out the precise amount he and his companions can drink without getting drunk, and then ask the waitresses to bring that precise amount to the room, plus whatever amount needs to be offered to the foreigner to get him sloshed, and off his game. The practice of drinking with foreign businessmen is well known. The idea in the mind of a Chinese businessman is that if one's foreign counterpart trusts you enough to get head-down, stone-drunk with you in a restaurant, the foreign businessman can be sure to trust you further down the line when the Chinese businessmen tries to change the terms of the contract the foreigner has signed, because the Chinese businessman doesn't give a flying frip about the contract, but rather the relationship of the parties who have signed it. This Chinese habit is so well known, that I know of one instance in which the CEO of a major American multinational corporation brought a designated drinker with him to Shanghai. Every time his Chinese counterparts shouted Gan Bei! ("dry glass", ie. "Bottoms Up!"), the designated drinker would stand and guzzle his glass, while the CEO discreetly watched. The CEO didn't drink a drop. The Chinese hosts were too drunk to notice, and negotiations, from the American point of view, proceeded swimmingly.

There are four basic categories of Chinese alcoholic beverages: beer, wine, bai jiu, and mao tai. One famous beer, employed by Western middle-aged professionals temporarily escaping reality in a Jimmy Buffet restaurant, is Qingdao (Tsingdao) beer. Qingdao (Green Island) is a well-known city on China's northeastern coast. Through the vicissitudes of international politics, Germany once ended up temporarily owning Qingdao, and a German beer company set up shop there, and began manufacturing Qingdao beer. Tsingdao is the romanization produced by the pre-pinyin romanization system called the "Wade-Giles" system. Writers have used this system, a very bad one in my humble opinion, before the mid-twentieth century in order to make the pronunciation of Chinese characters intelligible to the Western ear. However, since the Westerner, when reading the Wade-Giles romanization, generally has no idea in the world how to pronounce the "English" that he is reading, the result has been that Chinese culture, geography, personality, literature, history, food, everything, is made even more mysterious than it already is. Having seen Tsingdao beer in the USA long before I saw it in China, I didn't know how to pronounce it till I came to China.

Bai jiu ("white alcohol") is a favorite drink of Chinese diners. It looks exactly like vodka, but it is not as strong, usually containing 40 percent to 60 percent alcohol. It is much stronger than wine, however, and is drunk from small shot glasses. Time magazine recently listed it as one of the world's top ten "ridiculously strongest drinks," going on to say that it was a tough thing for foreigners to swallow. (Time 2010) Bai jiu should not be confused with mao tai. Mao tai is a famous Chinese liquor that is sold in cans that have the size, shape, and appearance of cigarette lighter fluid, which is appropriate, because the individual foolish enough to drink this stuff is doing much more damage to himself than someone drinking lighter fluid could ever do. This white liquor is served in very small, thimble-size cups. I am sure this is for reasons of safety, because to ingest a normal swallow of this stuff would be fatal. I was at a minority folk festival in Shanghai, reclining in a tent, watching some costumed girls doing folk dances, when the gentleman host handed me the little thimble-cup. I don't drink anything stronger than wine, so I refused, but he insisted, so I figured I could take one drop out of that little cup without noticeable effect, in order to keep my host happy. I often replay the image that sprang up in my consciousness after touching my tongue to the surface of the mao tai. The nuclear fireball I saw had the same shape and feel of the explosions one sees in films of the nuclear tests in the New Mexico desert. And the worst part of it was, the explosion wouldn't stop. I have never seen mao tai served at a Chinese business banquet. Chinese businessmen have no interest in killing anyone.

There are certain elegant rituals that are performed in order to get the foreigner properly smashed. Sometimes, one Chinese will stand up, pour fulsome words on his foreign counterpart, hold out his glass for a toast, and then the foreigner, after clinking glasses with the dozen or so other glasses present, will drink. If the toast is accompanied with gan bei!, this means the foreigner should drain his glass. If the foreigner is foolish enough to think there is no problem here, because he thinks he can handle one glass of bai jiu, this foreigner will be rudely surprised to discover that his glass will never find itself dry during the course of the meal. It will continually be replenished, like Elijah's cruse of oil. The hawk-eyed Chinese waitresses hover around the table, searching for empty glasses, which they fill unsolicited by the foreigner. Thus replenished, the foreigner is now a helpless target. Another Chinese host will gan bei him, and the hapless foreign businessman will be forced to drain another glass. And on it will go, until the foreigner is helplessly drunk. However, the Chinese are highly polished and refined as they do their work. They will hold the glass with two hands (a sign of respect), and they will hold it out at a very low altitude, below the foreigner's glass, also as a sign of respect. Foreigners will always feel respected as they sink into unconsciousness.

It is necessary that foreigners develop defensive tactics to deal with Chinese drinking rituals. The simplest tactic is to refuse the very first drink by thanking the offeror, and announcing that you don't drink. This, of course, is probably a lie, but somehow I've noticed that there a lot of lies committed in China in the name of social propriety, and if one's conscience permits, that is your first line of defense. However, if one desires to drink a little wine or beer, there are other methods I have adopted. One is to only sip the glass instead of draining the glass as you are supposed to, and hope no one notices. But nine times out of ten someone will notice your breach of Chinese etiquette, and will helpfully inform you of your infraction, and insist that you drain the glass. I used a very sneaky tactic once in Xiamen, when an official, in his cups, kept insisting over and over again that everyone at the table gan bei. He was drinking beer, and so I poured apple juice in a cup and started gan bei'ing with him. The official was suspicious, and asked me what kind of beer was I drinking. I told him it was a new American brand, Apple Beer. It threw him off his game enough to cause him to quit insisting that I chugalug. In the north of China, folks are much more aggressive about insisting that guests drink to excess. In Yinchuan, they couple a dice game with the drinking. Each table in each restaurant is equipped with a dice set in an enclosed plastic container. The host will take the container, and, starting with the guest-of-honor on his left, take turns shaking the dice. The game of choice was chui niu ("Blow the Bull," an idiom meaning "to brag"). Whoever loses the roll of the dice, must drink up. One particular host in Yongning, a city just south of Yinchuan, was a stickler for the rules. He won every time he blew the bull with me, and I constantly had to drink. Once, I accused him of cheating because he always won, but he insisted that he had not done so. Finally he noticed I was just sipping my ever-full glass of wine, and not draining it. He asked me did all Americans refrain from drinking a lot of wine? I said this one did. Whereupon he started to insist that I drink my whole glass. I calmly asked him a question. "Didn't you tell me this afternoon you were a Muslim?" He replied that yes, he had. "And isn't it true that Muslims don't drink wine?" Everyone laughed. He saw where I was heading, and laughingly responded that when he retired in a few years, he was going to take his hajj to Mecca, where he would received "redemption" for all the wine he had drunk during his lifetime. I am skeptical that there is enough redemption in Mecca to handle his drinking sins. At any rate, my maneuver slowed him down, and he quit insisting that I drink.

All this discussion of Chinese drinking may perhaps give the impression that Chinese meals are not healthy. Nothing could be farther from the truth. Because all Chinese food is chopped into bits so that chopsticks can handle it, the stomach does not have to overwork in order to do its job. In addition, a Chinese meal is long and drawn out, and so only small quantities are consumed at any one time, easing digestion. The Chinese do have a hankering for monosodium glutinate, which most Americans feel is dangerous to one's health. The Chinese do not feel this way. I remember one meal in which MSG was provided in saltshakers on the table. Once, concerned for my health, I asked a waitress to hold the MSG. The food was tasteless, and in fact, horrible. I have reconciled myself to MSG. My American doctor told me that if I had no side effects, it wouldn't hurt me, because that's what I had a liver for. Of course, the doctor, like most doctors, probably was clueless as to what he was talking about, but I have taken his words to be truth, in order to deal with a hamburger- and pizza-deprived diet. Say what one will about Chinese food, one has to admit that Chinese people, generally

119

speaking, are not fat. I wish one could say the same about Americans.

Chinese people are often astounded at the size of fat Americans. I once picked up a Hong Kong friend in the airport near West Columbia, S.C., took him to a restaurant, and noticed that he was staring at the table next to us. I looked over, and couldn't figure out what he was staring at. Seated at the table was a 300-pound woman with a tall, frizzy hairdo, nothing unusual. All of a sudden, my Hong Kong friend exclaimed, "My God! So FAT!!!!!" Another time I was seated at a table in a Chinese restaurant in Sumter, South Carolina with a former student from Shanghai Foreign Language University (SISU). I noticed an extraordinarily large woman, 400 pounds or so, sit down behind the student. I asked the student to turn around and take a look behind her. As soon as the student caught site of the mountain of fat seated behind her, her chopsticks went straight up in the air, she double-clutched lengthwise up and down her entire frame, and gasped for air. That embarrassed me enough, but even worse, my former student continued to stare at the overweight patron. I had another student from Shanghai Foreign Languages University whose mother was sent from Shanghai by her employer on a trip to Disney World, in Florida. Her father stayed behind in Shanghai. Upon the mother's return, she showed the family movies of the crowds at Disney World. The father asked, with a perfectly innocent straight face, why his wife had insisted in only taking movies of fat people!

One last word concerning Chinese table etiquette is offered here. The Chinese are very modest and retiring about eating, especially the women. Sometimes, I feel like they are trying to sneak the food off the plate very quickly so that no one can see them do it, so as not to call attention to themselves. Then, they bow their head close to the plate, and stick the food quickly in their mouths, again, appearing like they are trying to secretly put the food away. And, it is customary for a Chinese diner to bow his head to his bowl, pick the bowl up, and simultaneously slurp the liquid while shoveling the solid part of the soup into his mouth. Actually, many Chinese are consciously altering their etiquette to match that of the west. I have already heard that southern Chinese in Shantou will not insist their foreign guests drink hard with them (this is definitely not true in the north). I have told Chinese high school students how in mid 1990's China, dinner patrons routinely spit bones on the tablecloth and floor, and burped loudly to show appreciation for the food. The students looked at me like I was brainless. How could anyone act so barbaric! Well, they did, because I saw it, and quite enjoyed it, because it took the pressure off when you bit down on one of those ubiquitous, damnable chicken bones. All you had to do was spit, and you were up and running again.

No discussion of Chinese food can be complete without a mention of the cuisine in the south of China, in Guangdong province. There is a famous saying known all over China that goes like this: "If it flies and isn't an airplane, if it's in the water and it's not a boat, and if it has four legs and is not a table, someone from Guangdong will eat it." This, of course, includes dogs and cats, and we all know the American stereotype that leads to all sorts of jokes about the Chinese eating dogs and cats. The people in Guangzhou are the ones chiefly responsible for this stereotype. However, I taught a student in 1995 who was from one of the far western provinces of Xinjiang, or Gansu, I forget which one, who told me that she had crippling arthritis in her legs, until her herbal doctor prescribed some herb which I have forgotten, and dog meat. My student was walking normally, without pain. A professor at Shanghai Foreign Language University (SISU) told me that he regularly bought dog meat and cooked it for himself. I figured that if people in the west and in Shanghai were eating dogs, it was no stretch to accept the common wisdom about what Ghuangdong folks ate. My beliefs were confirmed when I read an article in the China Daily newspaper about an arrest that had been made in Guangzhou. It seems that a man had decided to take advantage of Guandong's desire for hot, fresh monkey brains. The article related that Guangdong diners liked to have the monkey brought to the table, and have his head cracked with a hammer. The skull then was placed on the table as a bowl, so that the brains could be enjoyed hot and steamy and fresh. Since monkeys are relatively rare, this culinary delight was extremely expensive. As we know, everything in China is copied: software, watches, movies, cell phones, running shoes, you name it. Well, monkey brains were apparently no exception. The dastardly counterfeiter took coconuts, split them, and hollowed out the fruit. He then took tofu, which apparently has the same consistency of monkey brains, and dyed the tofu brown with various sauces, and sold his counterfeit delicacy to the unsuspecting public. The stereotype formed in me due to these experiences with Guangdong cuisine was reinforced when my wife and I ate at our first Guangdong-style restaurant, somewhere in the north of China. My wife, who is deathly afraid of snakes, especially large ones, was shocked to see a waiter carry out a snake measuring about six feet in length and two inches in diameter, in order to let one of the restaurant's patrons examine its quality. I live in the country, and I am quite used to seeing snakes, but I didn't especially like seeing that snake in the presence of human company scanning that restaurant from left to right with his evil eye. It game me an extraordinarily bad impression of Guangdong cuisine.

It transpires that I have since spent some time in Guangdong province, and have become more acquainted with some local attitudes towards their peculiar cuisine. Apparently, some folks are a little miffed about the stereotype depicting Guangdong citizens as rapacious consumers of exotic wildlife. I was sitting on a university committee examining student applicants who desired to go to the west to study in an exchange program with my university and a Western institution. One of my fellow examiners was a woman from Guangdong province. She informed one of the student applicants that he would be going to a land where there were stereotypes about the Chinese, and that he would meet people there who would thinking erroneous things about the Chinese. For example, they may think that the Chinese eat dogs and cats. How would he handle this misimpression? The student said that he would politely explain that Chinese people don't eat dogs and cats. After the student had left the room, I asked my Guangdong colleague why she has said that, as everybody knows that Chinese people in Guangdong eat dogs and cats. She told me straight up that no, they didn't. Puzzled, I put this in the back of my mind. I have had the unfortunate experience of over-generalizing many times when trying to understand this mysterious and exotic country, and I thought that perhaps I had done so again. However, after further investigation, I can assure you, beyond a shadow of a doubt and to a reasonable certitude, that the people in Guangzhou will eat anything alive. After enjoying a two-hour lesson on Guangzhou (capital city of Guangdong) cuisine from a Guangdong resident, a foreigner came into the classroom at the end. Seeking to impress him, I asked the Chinese teacher the truth about what is eaten in Guangdong. After each organism was mentioned, the teacher cheerily replied, "Of course!" Here's the list of things I asked her about: cats, dogs, snakes, moth cocoons, scorpions, monkey brains (one of the 108 delicacies prepared for Chinese emperors), shark fins, bear's paw, donkeys, worms, eels, sea slugs, cow scalps, fried pig intestines, pig stomachs, tigers, and elephants. The latter two were illegal, but the southern coastline of Guangdong province is full of rocky inlets, making it very easy for smugglers to illegally ship into the province meat of a rather exotic variety. The fried pig intestines look like little chocolate doughnuts, the holes of which were formerly the passageway for the pig's waste products. My informant also explained to me that Guangdong gastronomic experts delight in eating the poison of poisonous snakes and blowfish. The secret, I was told, lay in how you eat the poison. If you swallow whole the sac in which the poison is contained, you enjoy a culinary treat. If, on the other hand, you bite into the sac before you swallow, you die.

My Chinese teacher also related to me a delightful story about a certain yellow beverage that Chinese traditionally drink on Dragon Boat Festival day, in the springtime. The English translation of this festival drink is "realgar wine," but actually it is a yellow liquor. These spirits cannot be bought at a store; they have to be made at home. A strong white alcoholic liquor is put into a jar, after which are added dead snakes and lizards. My teacher was relating this to our class in English, and although her English was excellent, she stumbled when she came upon the next ingredient that should be added. She said, "You take the... the... I don't know how to say this, it belongs to a bull." I extrapolated that she was trying to dig up the word "penis," and I wanted to help her, but I wasn't about to say the word "penis" to a Chinese woman in mixed company, so I used the Chinese word yinjing instead. I have discovered that you can say anything at all in a second language without shocking yourself. A German linguist once told me that this is because when you learn a second language, you don't have your mother cuffing your ears every time you utter an expletive, and so the impact of a strong word in a second language is not felt. She excitedly responded in English, "Yes! PENIS!" I figured since she was so forthcoming about that, that I would ask her the next logical question, which was: "Do you put the bull's testicles in the drink, too?" She gagged, "No! That's horrible! That's crazy!" So, I guess there are some limits to what a Guandgong resident will eat. Bull penises yes; bull testicles, no.

The story of the bull testicles brings to mind another Chinese food story. An elderly Shanghai gentlemen was casually eating a fish head during a meal he shared with us. I watched him, and finally could not help asking him how the fish head tasted. He said it was the best part of the fish. My teenage son heard him, and thereupon determined to eat the head of the next fish he was served. About a week later, our ayi served us up a fish one day for lunch, and my son started munching the fish head. He got all of it down, except for the bones, of course, and the eyes. He wasn't going to eat the bones, but the eyes he was determined to eat. He hesitated a little, and warily placed the first eyeball in his mouth. When he bit down on it, it surprisingly crunched like a glass marble. I had assumed the eyeball would be squishy and wet. He swallowed the second eyeball as well, and pronounced his feat accomplished. When I related the eating of the eyeballs to the old gentleman who had been my son's exemplar, he screwed up his face and spat out, "That's terrible!! Nobody eats fish eyes!"

THE CHINESE IDEA OF TIME AND SCHEDULING

This section is misnamed, because the Chinese don't have any idea of time and scheduling. None whatsoever. I have concluded, after long and sad experience, that this is the toughest cross-cultural hurdle for the Westerner to clear, if he is going to work in China. All foreigners must learn patience in China, and those who succeed at their foreign assignments indeed must practice an inordinate amount of patience. As someone who has spent many years in China, I thought I had just about overcome every infuriating thing that tended to make me blow my top, like forgetting to take my passport to the post office, or to the bank. But I must confess, I will never, ever get used to the lack of scheduling in the Middle Kingdom. Once, while I was in South Carolina, my niece, freshly arrived in Beijing, was preparing to start her teaching assignment. She Skyped me one day, and breathlessly told me that her Chinese employer, after having told her to prepare for one class, had told her the night before school started to teach a different class, in a different school. She was pretty ticked off. I told her to take a deep breath, and to repeat this phrase like a mantra: "TIC." "TIC" is short for "This is China, and there's not one ding-dong durn thing you can do about it, so suck it up, put it behind you, and deal with the raging anger inside of you that is threatening to explode you into a million cursing pieces." I felt pretty cocky at the time, feeling I could handle this sort of thing. However, at a later time, twice my wife and I were half-way through a one-and-a-half hour trip to our high school teaching assignment in Yongning, a small city south of Yinchuan in Ningxia Hui Autonomous region, when we received a telephone call from our office: the coordinator at the high school had canceled our classes; we did not need to come. A simple phone call would have saved us class preparation, a half-hour taxi ride, and half-hour long bus ride to our destination. One time, I answered my cell phone on the bus, and I heard my assistant's breathless voice: "Get off the bus! Get off the bus!" I shouted for Linda to follow me out the door, as we happened to have been stopped at a bus stop. Linda jumped off the bus not knowing what was going on. Once safely off the bus, my assistant informed me that our classes had been canceled. At this same high school, we would often have planning sessions five to ten minutes before class in the stairway, deciding who was going to teach what, when, and where. It is hard to recall this without growing an ulcer. On one occasion, five employees from my training school took a bus ride from Yinchuan to Helan, a small town one-half hour away. We waited in the principal's office while he smiled and served us tea. He knew doggone well that our class had been canceled at the last minute because of a government inspection, and that no one had bothered to call us. He let one of his teachers come in to tell us the bad news. One of our school's employees asked the teacher why she hadn't bothered to call us before five of our employees wasted about three hours of their time. The lady had the nerve to blame us for not calling, to see whether the class was still on or not.

College holidays and exams are not scheduled before the semester starts. I saw a university of about 20,000 students receive its employees back from summer holidays, schedule all the students' schedule in two days, and start classes on the third day. The reason the scheduling was so easy to do was that holidays and exam dates are completely ignored. If a holiday happened to land on one of your scheduled class days, that was just too bad. And if university officials sent you an email *the day before* your class, and told you that the next day class was scheduled because the freshmen were arriving and needed to be welcomed, also too bad. (Note that I have italicized the day before.) The professor then has to consult with his class and his own schedule to see if a convenient time can be found to make up the class. Once, after having scheduled my final exam, I was told at the last minute that it would have to be moved for reasons which are either unknown to me or which I have repressed. I was told to give the exam at such a time that my students had no time to adjust their schedule in order to study for it. I apologized to the students, saying it was out of my control. Then, I privately asked one of the better students how in the world he could stand this. He said none of the students liked it, but there was nothing they could do about it, so they just accepted it. I usually hate student rebellions. In the 1960s and 1970s, I despised all things hippy, but I found myself fondly recalling slogans like "Up Against the Wall," and wondering how they would look in yellow Chinese characters on a red sign in front of a burning administration building.

A young Chinese working woman in her thirties told me that her friend one day called her thirty minutes before the friend wanted her to meet her for lunch. She replied that she had just gotten out of the shower, and besides, didn't her friend know that it took forty-five minutes to get to the restaurant from her house? Undeterred, the next week the friend called her again asking her the same thing, giving her exactly the same impossible notice. I know a foreigner working as a dean in a Chinese university who received a call past midnight telling him that a meeting had been scheduled for eight o'clock the next morning. A Chinese businesswoman told me that, when she was in high school, the students would arrive in the morning, be told that a cleaning day had been planned for that day, and then turn around and go home. I tell you, weeping, that this sort of thing goes on all the time, and the Chinese are completely oblivious to how crazy this makes foreigners.

The Chinese deal with the dislocations and inconveniences caused by later-than-last-minute scheduling by either ignoring the newly scheduled event, or by canceling the already-scheduled event. And I must say, they make the system work, and they never seem to be upset by it. However, I am convinced that if it is true that planning is the most important aspect of management, then the People's Republic of China could add billions of RMB to their annual GDP if they would just learn how to plan and schedule.

One aspect of Chinese planning that is somewhat unusual concerns scheduling for holidays. I'll take National Day, for example. National Day is October 1, the glorious day in 1949 when the People's Republic of China was founded. It's the Chinese equivalent of July 4 in America, except that it's a little more serious. One would think that it would be possible to make plans for October 1 a year in advance, but not so in China. The government recently made National Day a three-day holiday instead of a one-day holiday. If these three days are juxtaposed next to a weekend, the Chinese have five consecutive days off, making travel easier. But which three days? Monday, Tuesday, and Wednesday, or Wednesday, Thursday, and Friday? The central government in Beijing must make that decision. One would think such a simple decision could be made a year in advance, but no, the word comes down from Beijing perhaps a month in advance. By the time the information has traversed the numerous intermediary bureaucracies and comes to your university, and by the time your university gets the message to you, it might be a mere week in advance before one can start planning one's trip. (But that's OK, because I never, ever have taken, nor do I plan to take a trip on National Day. There are more people on the trains than there are molecules in the sun.) For the sake of discussion, let's say that the government has decided that the three days off for National Day are Monday, Tuesday, and Wednesday. That means the Chinese have Saturday, Sunday, Monday, Tuesday, and Wednesday off. Then, someone had the idea, if we take Thursday and Friday off, and make up the time by coming to work the next Saturday and Sunday, then we'll have a seven-day holiday. Everyone comforts himself with this idea, even though the next week the Chinese have to work seven days in a row. I know several foreigners who resist the encroachment on the weekend high holy days by refusing to come to class, if they are students, or refusing to hold class on those days, if they are teachers. Let's take the case of the university professor. His classes on Thursday and Friday have been rescheduled for the next Saturday and Sunday. But now, if the professor refuses to teach on the weekend (in my humble opinion, justifiably so), he must then reschedule his already rescheduled classes to some other niche in the schedule for next week, or maybe later on in the semester. This process of working on Saturday and Sunday in order to have a longer holiday actually makes some sense, if it were planned for and announced in advance. But consider one New Year's holiday I once experienced. January 1 fell on a Monday. The government made us work on the previous Saturday and Sunday so that we would have a three-day holiday on Monday, Tuesday, and Wednesday. I couldn't help but wonder why those in authority didn't let us have our normal rest on Saturday and Sunday, add those two days to Monday, January 1, and we would have our three-day holiday. The difference would be that our three-day holiday would be Saturday, Sunday, and Monday instead of Monday, Tuesday, and Wednesday. But the government wanted our holiday to be on Monday, Tuesday, and Wednesday. When my wife asked one of the professors the reason for this inexplicable situation, she was informed that Chinese always like to start their vacation days off with the actual holiday. Perhaps if I live in China a few more centuries I will be able to understand the logic in this in order to explain it to you. I realize I probably have failed to make clear what is involved, and so I offer an excerpt from an email home in which I explained the process.

Today is Thursday, and tomorrow would normally be Friday, except that tomorrow this Friday is Sunday, because the Chinese will work this Sunday so they can take this Friday off. Since the schools are off this Friday so they can work Sunday, my Sunday classes will be given tomorrow. I hope you understood that. Because if you did, you will have a better idea about my schedule than I do. Chinese scheduling is a wonder to behold. It's done in elevators, at the tops of stairs, at drinking parties, and always at the last moment, and never for a stretch longer than five minutes.

THE WORKER AND THE BOSS

The Chinese national flag sports a hammer as a symbol dedicated to the teeming masses of laborers toiling within the country, and so I have always thought it strange that labor unions are illegal in China. Even more ironic to me is the relationship often seen between Chinese capital and labor. I have seen many a work situation, had I been in it, in which I would have told an employer to go take a fast, flying jump, and I would be seeking other employment. But the Chinese workers I have seen are very meek, and very concerned not to irritate the boss. I have two theories as to why this is so. One theory is the Confucian culture that informs all Chinese relationships. Confucius was all about authority and one's obligation to submit thereto. I love to ask Chinese single students to imagine if they were in love with someone with of whom their parents disapproved. Would they marry their lover, anyway? I have yet to find anyone to say they would disobey their parents. (Is China a great country, or what?) I suspect that traditional attitudes of respect and authority have not yet been eroded by the freewheeling libertarianism of the west, thus helping explain the Chinese worker's lack of desire to tell the boss to take his job and shove it. My second theory with which I explain worker passivity in the face of managerial offense is the deep-rooted fear of poverty, which is just below the surface of many middle-aged Chinese. They have seen revolution, tyranny, oppression, and poverty during the Cultural Revolution, which Westerners only read about or see in the movies. Workers who are irritated by their boss, or who are unjustly treated by him, I believe are genuinely frightened that they will lose their job and not be able to find another one.

I have seen a college student, upon taking her first job, work for a month or so without getting paid, without even knowing what salary she was working for. When payday finally came, she expectantly went to the meeting with the boss, who lined up the employees, and paid them. I asked her, did she get what she had expected? She said, no. I asked her why didn't she go back and talk to the boss. She wouldn't think of it. At a later time, her company was short of money. Come payday, the boss held a meeting with all the employees, told them that the boss had decided not to pay them that day, and that no one should say anything about it, because the boss was the boss. Not one word of protest was uttered. I later relayed these stories to several high school students, and asked them, was this a normal situation? All of them said yes. I asked the students how then did the parents make it when they didn't get paid? The students responded that their parents would borrow money from family and friends to tide them over. Presumably, the company made up the arrears at a later time. These experiences I have just relayed all occurred at a small private company. But I also know that the situation is often much the same at large multinational corporations. Several of my students in Shanghai have landed employment at well-known international companies. I have asked: what are you doing on your vacation? And, they have responded that they were working on their vacation. I asked whether their employment contract stipulated a certain number of vacation days, and they responded yes, but they never take all those days, because the boss "needs" the worker. I have often said that life is cheap in China. But life is not nearly as cheap as a contract.

CHAPTER REFERENCES

Silva, Alexandra (November 16, 2010). Top 10 Ridiculously Strong Drinks. Time.com.
http://www.time.com/time/specials/packages/article/0,288 04,2031497_2031504_2031466,00.html. Retrieved February 21, 2012.

Before I went to China, I used to think American baseball players were superstitious. But no ballplayer who pops his bubblegum x number of times while scratching his crotch just before leaping over the third base line without touching it as he pounds his glove y number of times can hold a candle to the Chinese. One could write volumes on this subject; however, I will limit myself to three major categories of Chinese superstition.

The Chinese superstition that impresses itself very quickly upon the foreigner is the Chinese obsession with numbers. It is not by accident that the Beijing Olympics began on August 8, 2008, at eight seconds past 8:30pm. All but the greenest foreigners will not give this a second thought. The Chinese pronounce "eight" as ba. Ba rhymes with fa, which is part of fa cai, which means to get wealth. Therefore, 8 is the Chinese prime lucky number. The Chinese pay exorbitant premiums to get cell phone numbers ending in 8. One can see license plates on fancy cars ending in 888. One can see 888 on billboards everywhere, and can hear TV commercials end with phone numbers, the last three digits of which are ba ba ba. And it seems like everyone wants to get married on the eighth day of August, the eighth month. The second number that the newbie foreigner realizes is very important to the Chinese, is the number 4. Si is how one says 4 in Chinese, but it is also (with the exception of the tone) the same way one says die in Chinese. So it is perfectly logical to avoid the number 4 like death itself. When the foreigner buys a cell number, the ones with a lot of 4's in them are always plentifully available.

Another category of Chinese superstition falls around the important task of properly raising babies. Many Chinese will probably see the restrictive taboos placed on the Chinese mother for the first month after birth as scientific, and not superstitious. There are many practices that are looked upon as scientific in China, but which to the Westerner appear superstitious, if not downright occult. I recall one of my Chinese college students who claimed that he was an amateur in the Chinese art of qigong. I expressed some reservations as politely as I could. The student then told me to hold my bare arm up, which I did. He then held the palm of his hand about four inches away from my hand, and became quiet. About 30 seconds later the surface of my skin had become too hot for comfort. Case closed. After spending years in China, I am fast becoming confused by the blurry line between science and superstition. I am constantly asking Chinese about acupuncture and moxibustion and herbal medicine practices, and qi gong, and gong fu, and when they finish telling me what to the Western ear sounds perfectly preposterous, the great majority of them will say, "Of course I believe it!" So perhaps these superstitions about babies that I am about to relate, which were taken from a first-hand account written in the late nineteenth century, are not true. But how can one be sure?

Chinese babies born near the same time should be at least four months old before they visit each other, else they will become sick, and perhaps die. One who has attended a wedding in the previous month should never enter the room of a woman who has just given birth, because this will bring bad luck to the newlyweds. If an infant under four months is laid on a table, he will be afraid of thunder forever. If a parent praises his child's good health, bad luck is sure to follow. Some of the most interesting Chinese superstitions about babies, at least in the nineteenth century, are the ones that illustrate the monumental prejudice against the fairer sex that has deeply permeated traditional Chinese culture. A nurse at that time would not believe that a Westerner would welcome the birth of a baby girl with as much joy as he would welcome the birth of a son. Once, a nurse in Fuzhou, in Fujian province, was asked why a little girl in her presence was crying, and she replied in broken English, "I savy, he too muchy solly he belong girl." Later, the same nurse was asked why a little boy was crying. The nurse replied, "Robin was crying at thinking the he might have been a girl!!" (Mansfield, 1887)

There are many other Chinese superstitions in modern China today, too numerous to mention. A Chinese teacher told me she loved to collect them, and she noted that there are many regional variations. But the Chinese superstition upon which I would like to focus is feng shui, not only because it is becoming popular in the West, but because it has caused me some grief during my employment at Shantou University, in Guangdong Province.

First of all, I should point out that feng shui is not entirely superstitious, certainly not in the eyes of the Chinese, and not even in the eyes of The Skeptic Encyclopedia of Pseudoscience, which states that some principles of feng shui are "quite rational," and that "folk remedies and superstitions… [have been] incorporated into feng shui's eclectic mix." [Michael Shermer. ABC-CLIO. pp. 111-112.] I don't pretend to know which part is rational, and which part is superstitious. I still haven't figured out the distinction with regard to Chinese medicine. I will just tell you briefly what feng shui is.

The characters pronounced feng shui are the characters for "wind" and "water." Wind and water are representative of nature, through which sheng qi, or "life spirit," or "life breath" runs. Central to the concept of feng shui is the idea of placing structures, such as houses and graves, in the optimal position in nature to catch sheng qi, or as it is often more simply described, qi. The principal clue in nature as to where the qi might be found is the layout of hills and the ridges of mountains. These mountains are called "dragons," because they twist, turn, and writhe, and ascend and descend, just like dragons do. Feng shui masters are the people who understand these patterns. Neither the common people, nor you or I for that matter, can figure them out. I have heard of one feng shui master who doubled as a real estate agent. For a high fee, he told my informant where the best place was to be found to lay her relatives in the grave. Fortunately for the feng shui master, the best place happened to lie on some expensive real estate, which quite conveniently was owned by a client of the feng shui master turned real estate agent.

The best shapes of mountain ridges and hills should conform to one of five types: wood, fire, earth, metal, and water, elements which figure large in ancient Chinese philosophy, and each of which has a distinctive shape when represented as a line drawing. Once the proper hills are chosen to site one's grave, care should be given that the site stands out against the prevailing character of the landscape. For example, on a rocky hill, you choose an earthy site; on an earthy hill, you choose a rocky site. If the area is confined, one finds an open place for the grave; if the area is open, one chooses a confined place for the grave. If there are many hills, the site should emphasize water; where there is much water, hills should be emphasized. [March 1968)

What are the benefits of finding an optimal location for one's structure? The benefits are the usual Chinese boons of wealth, success, and lots of wealthy, successful progeny. And this is why feng shui is no laughing matter, no mere superstition. It is deadly serious to the one-third of mainland China's population who are said to believe in the practice. (Debate on Feng Shui, http://www.yuce49.com/showjs.asp?js_id=45) But Westerners, until recently at least, have on the contrary turned a jaundiced eye towards the practice. Westerners who made their influential presence known in China in the early twentieth-century were interested in essentially three things: trade, Christianity, and science. Feng shui was perceived to be opposed to all three. The feng shui masters opposed the building of railroads and telegraph lines because the Westerners willy-nilly chopped through where the qi was running instead of harmoniously running their railroads and telegraph lines in pleasant accord with nature and the universe. The slighting of feng shui by Western businessmen is said to have been a large precipitating factor in the famous anti-Western Boxer Rebellion (1899-1901) http://en.wikipedia.org/wiki/Feng_shui#cite_ref-74, downloaded 12/28/11) The Christian missionaries opposed feng shui for obvious reasons – it was considered occult. Also opposed where those who believed in the rational principles of science, as all Westerners did back then, whether they were businessmen, bureaucrats, or missionaries. They opposed feng shui because it was seen as superstitious folly, unsupported by scientific principle. This opposition gave feng shui a bad name to Westerners. Here are some illustrative slams, all taken from March (1968): feng shui is "a ridiculous caricature of science," and a "farrago of absurdities" (de Groot 1897); it is a "perverse application of physical and meteorological knowledge" (Sarton 1927); ""if any one wishes to see to what a howling wilderness of erratic dogmatism the human mind can arrive, when speculation usurps the place of science, and theories are reverenced equally with facts, let him endeavour to fathom even the elementary principles of that abyss of insane vagaries, the science of Feng-Shui." (Dukes, 1885, p145)

I suspect that given the current intellectual fashion, such statements would be considered culturally imperialistic and dogmatic, unfit for our postmodern age. They remind me of a young French woman, a fellow student in a Chinese class, who was discussing with an American the proper way to drink tea. She gave the American some theory about how or when the tea was to be drunk, and the American responded: is that Chinese medicine? And the French woman responded, "No! This is real medicine." Any philosophical relativist or postmodernist living in China for any length of time, having been assaulted again and again by incomprehensible theories presented as fact, will fast become a dogmatic absolutist about certain things, in order to retain his sense of bearings, nay, even his sanity. And a fortiori, normal people who aren't postmodernists will really take a dislike to certain theories that do not make any sense. I must confess, this has become my attitude towards feng shui. I live and work on the campus of Shantou University, near the southern Chinese coast, in Guangdong Province. The campus is equipped with a large reservoir that serves as a lake, and is nestled among very pretty, steep, jagged limestone hills which are covered with trees and other vegetation. But unfortunately, the whole area used to be a gravesite, and even today there are graves all up in the hills surrounding the campus. This means that there are many complicated feng shui principles that the architects who designed Shantou University could not ignore. As a result, the roads, walkways, driveways, corridors, and anything else linear are juxtaposed in such a way that there is not a single right angle on campus. When I go to my office, it is necessary to take along a compass, and enough food and water for two weeks, because that is approximately how much time it takes to find one's way out of the building once it has been entered. After I had been at the University for almost five months, I still couldn't figure out the layout of my office building. Every time I entered, I tried to find a landmark outside on the horizon with which to orient myself, but to no avail. I was told that I could find my office by noticing the color of the railings on the circular stairwell, all of which are different in different buildings. That was of scant help, especially after the railings were repainted a different color.

One can see, therefore, that feng shui is a superstition with impact. Even Donald Trump lost business because his Trump Towers were not properly aligned with whatever qi there is in New York City. Mr. Trump hired a feng shui master to fix his problem. There is a huge skyscraper in Hong Kong with a large hole built in the middle of it because of feng shui; I suppose to allow the qi to pass through the building unblocked. (Fengshui, Wikipedia, http://en.wikipedia.org/wiki/Feng_shui#cite_ref-74, 12/28/11) An office building may be left vacant because of bad feng shui. At business banquets, feng shui principles often are used to determine the number of guests, the number of courses, and the placement of the guests. (Simmons and Schindler, 2003)

In addition to feng shui, there is a lot of superstition in Chinese culture, which businessmen have to take note of it and deal with it. For example, Simmons and Schindler (2003) performed a thorough study on the ending digits on marked prices of Chinese consumer goods. Simmons found (surprise, surprise!) that the digit in the rightmost places that occurred the most was 8, which occurred 39.9% of the time. Also, they found that the digit in the rightmost places with the least frequency of occurrence was 4, which occurred 1.4% of the time. Apparently, shopkeepers have to play to the superstitions of their customers, or they will lose business. The Economist (1993, cited in Simmons and Schindler 2003) reported that sales dropped more than 30% during "ghost month," the period from August 28 to September 15 each year, the time when good Chinese people make obeisance to their ancestors to keep them from coming back to the land of the living to haunt their descendants.

It is ironic that the Communist Party, in rare agreement with Westerners, has considered feng shui to be pernicious, and has tried (unsuccessfully) to stamp it out. After the founding of the People's Republic in 1949, feng shui has been officially deemed a "feudalist superstitious practice" and a "social evil." During the Cultural Revolution, feng shui was classified as a custom under the "Four Olds" with the intention of wiping it out. Feng shui masters were beaten by Red Guards and their literary works burned. Even today it is illegal in the People's Republic to register as a feng shui business consultant and the advertising of the practice of feng shui is banned.(Fengshui, Wikipedia, http://en.wikipedia.org/wiki/Feng_shui#cite_ref-74, 12/28/11) Ironically, with regard to this practice, communism allied itself with its enemies from the West, Christianity and capitalism, to vehemently oppose feng shui. It is equally ironic that the west seems to have embraced a form of feng shui. Even the term seems to be known by most educated Westerners I meet. A cynic might be persuaded to believe that the post-Christian West is replacing Christianity with that "farrago of absurdities" and that "abyss of insane vagaries" known as feng shui, plus whatever else is necessary to fill the void.

CHAPTER REFERENCES

de Groot, J. J. M. (1897). The Religious System of China, Vol. 3. Leiden, 938.

Debate on Feng Shui, http://www.yuce49.com/showjs.asp?js_id=45, cited in Feng shui, Wikipedia, http://en.wikipedia.org/wiki/Feng_shui#cite_ref-74, retrieved 12/28/11.

Edwin Joshua Dukes (1885). Everyday Life in China. London, 145.

Mansfield, M.T. (1887). Chinese Superstitions. The Folk-Lore
     Journal 5(2):127-129.

March, Andrew L. (1968). An Appreciation of Chinese Geomancy.
     The Journal of Asian Studies. 27(2):253-267.

Sarton, George. (1927) Introduction to the History of Science, Vol.
     1. Baltimore, 345.

Shermer, Michael. ABC-CLIO. p111-112, cited in in Feng shui,
     Wikipedia, ht
     tp://en.wikipedia.org/wiki/Feng_shui#cite_ref-74, retrieved
     12/28/11.

Simmons Lee C. and Robert M. Schindler (2003). Cultural
     Superstitions and the Price Endings Used in Chinese
     Advertising. Journal of International Marketing 11(2):101-
     111.

CHANGING ATTITUDES TOWARDS SEX

One cannot understand modern Chinese attitudes towards sex without understanding ancient Chinese attitudes about sex. The three intellectual and religious streams that most nourished traditional Chinese culture were Daoism, Confucianism, and Buddhism. Daoism's take on the subject, I think all would agree, was unique. It all had to do with yin and yang. Yin represents the female, the cold, the passive, the negative aspects of nature. I have asked two college students, both women, if they found it sad that traditional Chinese philosophy had such a negative view of women. She replied, "No, no! The definition of yin does not represent a negative view of women." I still find that statement very hard to believe. But I digress. The yang represents the male, the hot, the active, the positive aspects of nature. If one lives in China long enough, one will soon get the idea that everything boils down to the balance and harmony of yin and yang – medicine, philosophy, whatever. It is therefore not surprising to discover that sex is an activity that attempts to reach harmony through the unity of opposing forces. If you will think of the yin and yang circle which can now be seen all over the West, consider the curvy line cutting through the middle of the circle that divides the black (which represents the yin) from the white (which represents the yang). Where the white penetrates the black is a sort of Chinese phallic symbol, representing (among a lot of other things) sexual union. So, to the Daoist, the purpose of sex is to create balance in the man. His sperm is yang. The woman during the act of intercourse contributes yin. The yin is transferred to the man at the point of the woman's orgasm. The aim of sex is for the man retain as much yin and yang as possible. This means he must make as many women have as many orgasms as possible; therefore, extramarital sex was countenanced. And since the man needed to keep as much yang as possible, techniques were developed to keep the man from ejaculating. These techniques were described in a famous Daoist sex handbook entitled The Art of the Bedhchamber. One can only speculate as to how all this negatively affected the man's physical and emotional health. The Daoists, on the other hand, felt that these practices enhanced longevity, perhaps even to the point of immortality. Some have thought that the woman came out pretty good under the Daoist theory of sex, but actually, the woman did not. She was merely a passive tool used in order to pass yin to the man. (So and Cheung, 2005) The major purpose of Daoist sex manuals was mainly to secure long life, or offspring, for the man, not to give pleasure to the wife. (Bodde, 1985)

As poorly as the wife fared under the Daoist theory of sex, she probably fared even worse under the Buddhist and Confucian view. The Buddhists apparently believed that sex was dirty (Bodde, 1985), which is not surprising given the Buddhists' philosophical animus against the human body. It would be hard to imagine that this idea would lead to sexual happiness for the woman. But probably worse than Daoism and Buddhism is the Confucian idea of sexual relations. Confucianism approved of sex for procreation only; there was to be no pleasure. In fact, the two sexes could not even properly verbally express affection for each other because to do so would be immoral. They couldn't even touch each other by handing a household object one to another; one spouse had to place the object on the ground, before the other spouse picked it up. They couldn't sleep on the same mat. They didn't borrow things from each other. They didn't share the same clothes rack, and they certainly didn't bathe together. (Bodde 1985). One of the most famous anthropological studies carried out in China was the one done by Fei Xiaotong, who in the 1930s studied a town near Tai Lake, near Shanghai. The rural villagers in that study, if they were husband and wife, and if they were in their house with others present, would insist that the husband not speak to his wife, nor sit near her, nor even mention her in conversation. (Fei 1939, cited in Bodde, 1985) In another anthropological study carried out in western Yunnan province, rural women were taught not to be attractive to men and to not display their charms. Sex was considered dirty, and women were the primary reason. There were various taboos affecting women who had just given birth or who were menstruating. (Xu 1948, cited in Bodde 1985).

With that depressing background, we now turn to what modern Chinese think about sex. In the discussion that follows, the reader will discern a wrenching conflict between traditional (Confucian, Daoist, and Buddhist) influences on ideas about sex with more modern liberated attitudes imported from the West, fueled especially by the modernization campaign China undertook starting some time in the early 1980s. The Chinese have abandoned much of their feudal past, but they have not evolved into Western libertines.

We will start with an overview of changing attitudes in China, starting with ancient China and moving on to the present-day situation. Traditional attitudes toward sex that I have described above were hardened during the Song Dynasty in the 12th century. Before that period, sex was at least discussed. The oldest existing books on sexuality were published in China around 200 B.C. Some books described sexual techniques and the human response to them, others offered advice on how to prevent sexual dysfunction, others offered advice on how to adjust one's level of sexual activity in order to maintain longevity. But during the Song Dynasty, the government began to closely control the people's sexual lives, and also began to restrict open sexual expression until eventually any communication about sex was taboo. This extremely conservative attitude lasted throughout the centuries all the way up until the Communists founded the People's Republic of China in 1949. In the 1950s, the government published a few books aimed at sex education. (Li, et al. 2004) However, this indicated no great thaw in China's frigid attitude toward sex. Because Maoism was ruthlessly collective, the individual was mercilessly subordinated to the ruling statists, privacy was virtually nonexistent, marriage was regulated, and "any direct sexual activity was hard to arrange and consequently rare." (Farquahar 2002, p. 173, cited in Sisson 2003) However, the Maoist regime also struck hard at feudal sex practices. The Marriage Law of 1950 (as well as a later one in 1980) abolished arranged and polygamous marriages in order to reinforce the socialist vision of marriage as a union of two equal partners. In its reaction to feudalism, however, the Communist government in no way turned to Western license. Strict control over behavior in schools and work units kept premarital and extramarital sex in check. (Parish, et al. 2007).

Conservative ideas about sex persevered all the way up until the period that we may mark as beginning in 1978, when China embarked on its famous Reform and Open Policy. At this point, not only were state controls on the economy loosened, but Communist Party restrictions and social strictures on sex practices began to loosen. In a popular reaction against the politicization of private life, an "opening up" of public sexual culture began in the 1980s (Honig and Hershatter 1988, cited in Farrer 2011), leading to greater approval of sex before marriage as well as an increase in premarital sexual behavior among urban youth in the 1990s (Farrer 2002; Pan and Yang 2004; Li 1998; Parish et al. 2007; People's University 2007, all cited in Farrer et al., 2011). Still, even in this period of reform, Chinese secondary schools prohibited dating as a form of "premature love" (Evans 1997; Yang and Yao 2002, both cited in Farrer, 2011). I recall, in a small town in Western China, angering a high school student when, in order to get her to stop talking while I was teaching, I asked her, was the boy with whom she was talking her boyfriend? Her furious reaction I thought was excessive, but I had accused her of doing something that was verboten. In this period, along with conservative attitudes, there was much evidence of "opening up and reform" in the area of Chinese sexuality. Decontrolled book markets began selling pornography, sexual self-help books, sexual hygiene manuals, and books by Alfred Kinsey. Stores sold condoms and other forms of birth control, sex toys and other aids, even clothing for those inclined to fetishes. Prostitutes began roaming the streets. Sexual images in advertising became pervasive. Movies began to show explicit sex scenes. Rates of infection from sexually transmitted diseases soared. Sex clinics selling sexual medicine opened. Sexologists did research and sex education campaigns became popular. (Farquar 2002, p. 215, cited in Sisson 2003). Youth became interested in finding outlets for their developing libido, and many of them became involved in high-risk sexual activity. (Li, et al. 2004)

Traditionally, Chinese people believed that marriage trumped both love and sex. That marriage was the most important thing. Once a good marriage was attained, love and sex would follow. But modern Chinese youth have bought into the Western romantic ideal of love, where both love and sex are at least somewhat disassociated from marriage, and are prior to marriage, in time and perhaps in importance. (Zhang, et al., 1999) I have heard many Chinese students somberly recite to me the proverb "marriage is the tomb of love." This attitude, of course, should logically lead straight to temporary, although committed, sexual liaisons, in which young people try to get the benefits of marriage without the corresponding ultimate commitment. Perhaps these Chinese young people may look one day to the happy state of the American sexual revolution to see what all this opening and reform might buy them.

Here I must pause to relate my observations on this Chinese sexual revolution. I came to China in 1995, and was blissfully unaware of any sexual revolution at all. A professor told me, at my first university, that the virginity rate for girls was about 95%, which I thought was refreshing. I never saw any pornographic magazines or movies for sale in the street. CCTV, the state owned television network, was rigorously censored. Later, when the Internet established itself in the People's Republic, one could watch movies with the sex scenes cut out of them. There was one time, when I was watching a movie with a neighboring foreign expert in his apartment with my wife and three children, aged 16, 13, and 10. I controlled the zapper, and whenever something objectionable appeared, I would zap the VCR, which would turn off and go to the default CCTV program showing at the time, never worrying about what TV show was playing, because they were all squeaky clean. When the first naughty thing in the movie appeared, I shut down the VCR, after which, to my surprise and horror, my young kids get a free shot of some topless Chinese beauties, courtesy of the puritanical, Communist-controlled CCTV television network. To be fair, I think the bare-breasted women might have been artwork, but I was too busy unsuccessfully trying to zap the TV to really notice. Other than that, and other than being approached by a couple of prostitutes in downtown Shanghai, I felt like I was living in Pleasantville, in the 1950s. I only went to one Chinese movie. My whole family of five went to a movie theater in Shanghai in 1995, escorted by two adult high school teachers who were my students. One student (a woman), sat in a row with my three children, and the other student, a man, sat in the row behind to the left of my wife, who was seated to my left. The closest thing we saw to anything explicit in the movie was a husband leaning over to kiss his wife, which he never did, because the scene was cut. However, my wife's Chinese interpreter, not wanting Linda to miss out on any of the action, leaned over at this point and solemnly informed Linda, "He wants to f*** her." Linda's virgin ears reddened. This was the same young man who at an earlier occasion, wanted to tell us that the campus girls wanted to show off their figures, moved his fingers in a walking motion, and told us instead that the campus girls walked around showing off their "fingers." He also earlier had told my son that American women were "fat and aggressive." This obscenity spoken to my wife in the movie theater was the only cuss word I heard in China   for years, because I couldn't understand Chinese obscenities. Everything seemed so much like Wally and Beaver. However, I have since learned that, like most things one observes in China, appearances easily deceive the foreigner. Years later, my wife and I were walking on a Beijing street and randomly came across a "Husband Wife Health Store." It was a small, one-room establishment, with enclosed glass shelves on the right and on the left. At the back was a desk, behind which sat a Chinese girl, with the usual bangs and ponytail, and big round glasses, all of which combined tend to make a 25-year old woman look like an innocent fifteen year old girl. She wore a nurse's uniform, and a 1960s style nurse's cap, the kind that looks like a stiff piece of white cardboard, which is curled around the front of the hair, the kind that one of Dr. Kildare's nurses might have worn. Curious to discover what kind of establishment this was, Linda and I entered, I on the right, and Linda on the left. I glanced at the glass cabinets on the right, and saw contraceptives, lubricants, etc., and so immediately thought, this place is similar to a pharmacy, except it has a nurse on duty. Meanwhile, Linda was looking at the glass shelves on the left, on which were exhibited garish, pink, purple, orange, and yellow sex toys, equipped with pornographic pictures and labels. The nurse sweetly asked Linda if she needed any assistance. After observing the strange juxtaposition of the clinical with the pornographic, and trying vainly to imagine such a shop in the U.S.A., I felt there was something very anti-traditional, yet strangely naïve about modern Chinese views on sex, and this impression has only been reinforced after examining the relevant research into the issue.

MODERN CHINESE VIEWS ON SEX

To illustrate the shift from traditional Chinese views on sex towards modernity, I will take a brief look at modern Chinese views on masturbation, premarital sex, extramarital sex, and homosexuality. It will become readily apparent that, while Confucian China has been changed very much by an onslaught of Western influence, nevertheless, Chinese thinking is, in many aspects, quite different from the thought of the West.

Masturbation

The Chinese view of male masturbation is deeply conditioned by ancient Daoist teachings. As I mentioned earlier, Daoism held that it was essential that the man preserve his yang, and that sperm represented yang; therefore ejaculation during sex was to be postponed and avoided, if at all possible. So then, a fortiori, masturbation was seen as counterproductive to Daoist goals, causing a man to lose precious sperm, which meant that the masturbating man would lose precious yang, without the compensating advantage of a resulting child. These ancient Daoist beliefs have filtered down to modern Chinese. There is a traditional Chinese saying that states that ten grains of wheat produces one drop of blood, and ten drops of blood produce one drop of semen, which emphasizes the value of semen, and that it should not be lost through masturbation. One prominent study reported that almost half the students in the research sample believed this to be at least partly true. (Zhang 1993, cited in Zhang et al. 1999). The traditional Daoist attitude perhaps explains research done on the subject. The percentages of males and females who report masturbating are generally lower than in the West. Examples of research findings of reported incidence of masturbation are 13% male (middle schools students) and 5% women (Liu 1992); 33% urban married males and 12% urban married females (Liu 1992), 9% of rural married men and 11% of rural married women (Liu 1992, cited in Zhang, et al. 1999); 40% men and 13% women (Pan 1995, cited in Zhang, et al. 1999); 53% male and 17% female (Cui & Liang 2001, cited in Higgins & Sun), 18% boys and 12% girls (Liu 1997, cited in Higgins and Sun 2007); 40% men and 13% women (Pan 1995, cited in Zhang, et al., 1999); 59% men and 17% women (Zhang 1993, cited in Zhang, et al. 1999). However, the percentages are apparently catching up with the West. In 2007, China's lifetime masturbation rate was reported to be about half that of the West; however, if one looks at only men and women in their 20s, the percentages are comparable. (Laumann et alo. 1994; Spira et al. 1994; Kontula and Haavio-Mannila 1995; cited in Parish, et al. 2006)   Another interesting phenomenon that indicates that Daoist ideas die hard is the prevalence of questions concerning masturbation on call-in help shows and other events designed to disseminate the sexual knowledge of experts.

Premarital Sex

Of course, premarital sex in traditional China was frowned upon, but things are changing fast in modern China. The research is all over the place with regards to statistics, but in general it may be said with a fair degree of certainty that the practice of premarital sex is becoming more popular. One should distinguish two things when examining statistics, namely approval of premarital sex and engaging in premarital sex, the latter group invariably being smaller than the former. Here are some statistics gleaned from various research articles: 50% of Beijing urbanites approved of premarital sex in 1986, and 70% approved in 1990. In 1990, 80% of a sample of young women was found to have had sex before marriage, and in 1992 the percentage was 95%. One group of college students contained 40% who approved of premarital sex as long as the partners had "fallen in love," whereas 35% approved if both sides want it.   (Pan 1995, cited in Zhang, et al. 1999) These numbers are quite high compared to results obtained by investigating a sample of college students in 1989, which found that 13% of male and 6% of female students had had premarital sex. Another sample of students from 50 universities and colleges in Shanghai reported that 19% of male students and 17% of female students had engaged in premarital sex. (Zhang 1993, cited in Zhang, et al. 1999)

The fact that the incidence of premarital sex is rising is fairly well established. The reasons given for this rise are varied, and include earlier puberty, which has occurred because of increasingly better nutrition in modern China. Coupled with earlier puberty is later marriage, dictated by the government in order to slow population growth down, both of which increase the time that young people are deprived of the connubial comforts afforded by marriage. This in turn increases the temptations to engage in premarital sex. Other reasons suggested include state policies that promote the free choice of partners and which discourage arranged marriages (Yan 2003, cited in Farrer, et al. 2011), and market reforms which lead to greater individual choice (Farrer 2002, cited in Farrer 2011). It seems that, just like anywhere else in the world, increased social and political freedom is not always accompanied with an increase in wisdom to know how to deal with that freedom.

All statistics concerning premarital sex in China should be tempered by recognition of a widespread belief that premarital sex is not approved of, unless the couple is engaged to be married or intends to be married. (Zheng, et al., 2001) This belief, which distinguishes the Chinese from other nationalities, such as the Japanese, is elucidated in a research article in which various attitudes of 111 Shanghai college students were explored in-depth. This research revealed various conservative beliefs that coexisted with the approval of, or engagement in, premarital sex. For example, women are no longer "perfect" if the sexual relationship ends in separation. The premarital sex can result in permanent damage. Sex is a sacrifice a woman makes to a man, and the first sex is a valuable gift that should be preserved for a beloved partner. First time premarital sex should always be in a committed or steady relationship. Commitment was defined by various promises, such as a promise to work hard, buy a house, take the other partner traveling, or promises to love the other partner "forever," or "for a lifetime." (But note: these promises did not extend to promises to marry. Having premarital sex, while not casual, was still not serious enough for these Chinese students to consider the parties engaged to be married.) Sex was not seen as casual, but as a way of enhancing the relationship. Sex was not to be with anyone, but with someone who was loved. It was dangerous and irresponsible for high school students to engage in sex. Abortion is the only reasonable choice for a premarital pregnancy; nevertheless, abortion was a moral shame even greater than the loss of chastity. Most Chinese students defined casual sex as "immoral." Some of the students believed sex was meant for marriage, and therefore would engage in premarital sex only after a formal engagement. (Farrer 2011) It should be pointed out that this is not really premarital sex in the normal sense, because in China sometimes an engagement is tantamount to a wedding. (Yan 2003, cited in Farrer 2011). ." In 1993, it was reported that almost all (89.2%) of premarital sex in China was restricted to the future spouse. (Pan 1993, cited in Higgins and Sun 2007, also see Parish et al. 2007) From these observations, one may deduce that Chinese students are not as "liberated" as their Western counterparts, who sometimes seem to think that sex is the moral equivalent of shaking hands. I will leave this subject with a heartwarming quote from Farrer (2011). This is what a young 22-year old girl wrote upon breaking up with her five-month college boyfriend, who had tried to take liberties with her: "…he thought he could just casually go all the way. He said everyone in the school is doing it. They are always talking about it. I think they are really disgusting."

What about the parents of young people? What do they think of their role as they worry about the effect of China's sexual revolution on their children? One research study conducted focus group interviews with parents of twenty- to thirty-year olds in eight different cities, in China. This study unearthed the following attitudes. First, parents recognized that they were unable to communicate with their unmarried children about sex and contraception, and they were unambiguous about their desire for the government to provide such information and education to their children. The parents were conservative about when to begin such education, often suggesting 18 would be a good age to start. The parents were sharply divided over whether to provide abortion and contraceptive services to unmarried young people. (Cui et al., 2001)

As premarital sex has increased, there has not been a corresponding increase in the knowledge of contraceptives. Low contraceptive use in the sexually active unmarried population has led to an increase in unwanted pregnancy and abortion. (Gao, et al. 1999; Jiang 1997; Qi and Wang 1999; all cited in Zheng, et al., 2001) For example, one qualitative study that explored contraceptive use among young, unmarried, sexually active migrant women workers found that these women who had moved from the countryside to the city lacked basic knowledge of contraception or reproduction. Only a very small portion of these women used contraception, and the resulting pregnancies led to abortions or hasty marriages as the only options to deal with the pregnancy. (Zheng, et al., 2001) A study of 455 Hong Kong college students revealed that 24% of the students were sexually active during the year that the study took place. Of those 455 students, only 38.2% of them reported regular condom use. Only 64% of the students would use condoms regularly if they were to have future casual sexual encounters. (Wong and Tang, 2001) This does not surprise me. I recall hearing a single American woman, a teacher of English, relate the story of two male Chinese students who were bent on discussing condom use during an English corner (English discussion group) being conducted by the teacher, where the participants were both men and women and unknown to each other, and who had come to discuss topics in general, not contraceptive use. These two men were looking to get what Westerners would consider basic knowledge any way they could, just like one woman student who showed her non-sexually active roommate a condom, and asked her how to use it, because her boyfriend had assigned her the task of figuring it out.

Extramarital Sex

Chinese people apparently are becoming more tolerant of extramarital sex, but only in special circumstances. Philanderers still arouse strong disapproval, but when one of the partners has become sexually impotent, or when one of the partners has been forced into a loveless marriage, the Chinese will often have an attitude of compassion and understanding. The strongly negative word "adultery" has been replaced with more neutral expressions like "extramarital sex" or "extramarital love." Here are some relevant statistics culled from research papers. Fifty-six percent of college students, 10% of married urbanites, and 53% of sexual offenders approve of extramarital sex. (Liu 1992, cited in Zhang 1999) It is comforting to see that the billions of RMB spent on the education of Chinese youth has brought them to a level of enlightenment which equals that of sex offenders. In 1988, 2% of Beijing residents admitted to having extramarital sex, and this number had increased to 8% by 1994. (Pan 1995, cited in Zhang, et al. 1999) In a 1990 investigation of 20,000 Chinese people in different regions all over

148

China, the overall rate of extramarital sex among both rural and urban Chinese was found to be 6%. (Liu 1992, cited in Zhang, et al. 1999) The more liberal attitudes towards extramarital sex have been cited as a factor that may have "profound implications" in modern China, more specifically, implications with regard to the rising divorce rate. (Zhang et al., 1999)

Homosexuality

Traditionally, the Chinese have not suppressed or persecuted homosexuals. However, homosexuals have traditionally camped out far in the back of the closet. Most homosexuals, even in modern China, are unwilling to reveal their sexual preferences publicly. Often those few homosexuals who choose to reveal their sexual orientation publicly do so because they have committed some sort of offense, or because they have gone to a clinic to be treated for their homosexuality. This reinforces the common public perception that homosexuality is an illness, crime, or aberration. Something else that reinforces these notions is the ancient Chinese philosophy of the yin and yang, which perpetually strove to find harmony and balance. (Zhang et al., 1999) I suppose that two lesbians would be possessed of too much yin, and two male homosexuals would be possessed of too much yang, with no chance of achieving harmony and balance.

Although homosexuality has been tolerated in China since ancient times, after the founding of the People's Republic in 1949, homosexuality was listed in the Chinese Classification of Mental Disorder as a sexual disorder, and it could be prosecuted under "hooliganism." However, the criminal law was changed in 1997, and now the Chinese legal code is silent on the subject – there are no laws that expressly prevent or permit same-sex relations in China. Later in 2001, the Chinese Psychiatric Association removed

homosexuality from the Chinese Classification of Mental Disorder. (Higgins and Sun 2007).

Although there has been liberalization among legal and mental health professionals, popular attitudes still are quite anti-homosexual. Here are some statistics gathered from research articles. A sample of college students was queried in 1992, and it was discovered that 12% of the men and 6% of the women regarded homosexuality as "normal behavior for some people." Seventy-nine percent of the students overall felt that the practice was "aberrant behavior," 4% of the men and 6% of the women felt that the behavior was "immoral," and 3% of the students overall felt that homosexual practice was "sinful." These statistics dealt with reported attitudes towards homosexuality. In the same 1992 study, it was reported that the actual occurrence of homosexuality was 8% in college students, 1% in urban married people, and 2% in rural married people (Liu 1992, cited in Zhang, et al. 1999), although Cui and Liang (2001) found a lower figure than that. One study reported that the average number of partners for a homosexual man was around 17 per year, and that about 55% of gays were not serially monogamous, but had sexual relations concurrently with two or more partners. (Pan 1995, cited in Zhang 1999) Another study reported that almost 80% of Chinese students considered homosexuality to be abnormal and half of them also believed it to be immoral. The majority of the students in that study would recommend that a friend who was attracted to members of the same sex to go see a doctor. (Cui and Liang 2001, cited in Higgins & Sun 2007) Still yet another research study discovered that most of the students queried disapproved of the statement "homosexuality should be allowed." In addition, research published in 2005 found that 37% of students said that homosexuality should be illegal and 35% would stop being friends with someone they discovered was a homosexual. (Huang et al., 2005, cited in Higgins and Sun 2007)

CHAPTER REFERENCES

Bodde, Derk (1985). Sex in Chinese Civilization. Proceedings of the American Philosophical Society 129(2):161-172.

Cui, Nian; Li, Minxiang; Gao, Ersheng (2001). Views of Chinese Parents on the Provision of Contraception to Unmarried Youth. Reproductive Health Matters 9(17):137-145.

Cui, Y. T. and Liang, L. F. (2001) The Countermeasures And Multi-Dimensionality Analyses Of Mental Disorders Among College Students In The Socialist Market Economy. Proceedings of the Third Pan-Asia Pacific Conference on Mental Health. Beijing: China Association for Mental Health, pp. 26-40.

Evans, H. (1997). Women and sexuality in China: Female sexuality and gender since 1949. New York: Continuum.

Farrer, J. (2002). Opening up: Youth sex culture and market reform in Shanghai. Chicago: University of Chicago Press.

Farrer, James; Suo, Gefei; Tsuchiya, Haruka; & Sun, Zhongxin (2011). Re-Embedding Sexual Meanings: A Qualitative Comparison of the Premarital Sexual Scripts of Chinese and Japanese Young Adults. Sexuality and Culture. Published online November 22, 2011. DOI 10.1007/s12119-011-9123-0.

Fei Hsiao-Tong (Fei Xiaotong) (1939).   Peasant Life in China, a Field Study of Country Life in the Yangtze Valley. London: Routledge & Kegan Paul, and New York: E. P. Dutton.

Gao, E.; Tu, X.; Lou, C. (1999). Reproductive Health Status Of Unmarried Young Adults In China.   Population Science of China 6:47-54.

Higgins, Louise T. & Sun, Chunhui. Social Background and Sexual Attitudes among Chinese Students. Culture, Health, & Sexuality 9(1):31-42.

Honig, E., & Hershatter, G. (1988). Personal voices: Chinese women in the 1980's. Stanford, CA: Stanford University Press.

Hsu (Xu), Francis L. K. (1948). Under the Ancestors' Shadow, Chinese Culture and Personality. New York: Columbia University Press.

Huang, J., Bova, C., Fennie, K. P., Rogers, A. and Williams, A. B. (2005).   Knowledge, Attitudes, Behaviours, And Perceptions Of Risk Related To HIV/AIDS Among Chinese University Students In Hunan, China. AIDS Patient Care and STDs 19:769-777.

Jiang, S. (1997). A Survey Of Sexual Values And Behavior Among Unmarried Urban Young People In The 1990s. Chinese Journal of Population Science 3:265-68. (in English)

Kontula, Osmo and Elina Haavio-Mannila (1995). Sexual Pleasures: Enhancement of Sex Life in Finland, 1971–1992. Aldershot: Dartmouth.

Laumann, Edward O., John H. Gagnon, Robert T. Michael, and Stuart Michaels (1994). The Social Organization of Sexuality: Sexual Practices in the United States. Chicago: University of Chicago Press.

Li, Y. (1998). Sexuality and Love of Chinese Women. Beijing: China Today Press (in Chinese).

Li, Ying; Cottrell, Randall R.; Wagner, Donald I.; Ban, Maosheng (2004). Needs and Preferences regarding Sex Education among Chinese College Students: A Preliminary Study. International Family Planning Perspectives 30(3):128-133.

Liu, C.T. (1998). Health Care Systems in Transition II. Taiwan Part I – A General Overview of the Health Care System in Taiwan. Journal of Public Health Medicine 20:5-10.

Liu, T. B., Zhang, H. and Zang, D. X. (1997) Sex Differences Of Masturbation Behaviour And Its Influence On Mental Health Of Adolescents. Chinese Mental Health Journal 11: 148-150. (In Chinese).

Pan, S. (1993) A Sex Revolution In Current China. Journal of Psychology and Human Sexuality 6: 1-14.

Pan, S.M. (1995) The Contemporary Situation of Sexuality in China. Beijing: Guangmin Daily Publishing House.

Pan, S., & Yang, X. (2004). Xingaishinian: Chuanguodaxuesheng Xingxingweide Zhuizong Diaocha. (Love And Sex Ten Years: An In-Depth Nationwide Study Of The Sexual Lives Of University Students). Beijing: Academy of Social Sciences.

Parish, William L. (2007) Sexual Behavior in China: Trends and Comparisons. Population and Development Review 33(4):729-756.

Qi, Y.; & Tang, W. (1999). Reproductive Health Knowledge And Education Needs Among Unmarried Adolescents. Population Science of China 6:59-62.

Sisson, Kathy (2003) Review of Judith Farquhar (2002), From Mao to Viagra: What a Long, Strange Trip It's Been Appetites: Food and Sex in Post-Socialist China. The Journal of Sex Research 40(2):225-227.

So, Ho-wai and Cheung, Fanny M. (2005). Review of Chinese Sex Attitudes & Applicability of Sex Therapy for Chinese Couples with Sexual Dysfunction. The Journal of Sex Research 42(2):93-101.

Spira, Alfred, Nathalie Bajos, Groupe ACSF, and Ministère de la recherche et de l'espace (1994). Sexual Behaviour and AIDS. Aldershot: Avebury.

Wong, Chi-yan & Tang, Catherine So-kum (2001). Understanding Heterosexual Chinese College Students' Intention to Adopt Safer Sex Behaviors. The Journal of Sex Research 38(2):118-126.

Yan, Y. (2003). Private life under socialism—Love, intimacy, and family change in a Chinese village 1949–1999. California: Stanford University Press.

Yang, X., & Yao, P. (2002) Qingchun Yu Xing 1989–1999: Zhongguo Chengshi Qingnian De Xingyishi He Xingxingwei   (Youth And Sex 1989-1999: A Survey Of Sexual Attitudes And Behavior Of Chinese Urban Youth). Shanghai: Shanghai People's Press.

Zhang, K.; Li, D.;Li, H.; & Beck, E. J. (1999). Changing Sexual Attitudes and Behaviour in China: Implications for the Spread of HIV and Other Sexually Transmitted Diseases. Aids Care 11(5):581-589.

Zhang, S.B. (1993) An Investigation On College Students about AIDS Knowledge. AIDS Bulletin 4:78-71

Zheng, Zhenzhen; Zhou, Yun; Zheng, Lixin; Yang, Yuan; Zhao, Dongxia; Lou, Chaohua; Zhao, Shuangling. (2001). Sexual Behaviour and Contraceptive Use among Unmarried, Young Women Migrant Workers in Five Cities in China. Reproductive Health Matters 9(17):118-127.

A Chinese friend told me once that Chinese people were "tricky." I have years of watching Chinese students hide things from their parents, and hearing about the ubiquitous business practice of keeping two sets of accounts, one to know what what really going on and one set of false numbers to give to the government to keep taxes low. And, after personally observing world-class cheating operations at work in universities, it was very easy for me to believe the common opinion that market reforms, in addition to years of Communist Party bashing of Confucianism, had collapsed traditional Chinese morality, leaving behind a gaping hole which modern Chinese do not know how to fill. I do believe that this sentiment is quite accurate, but there's more to it than that. What Westerners often perceive as unethical is merely traditional Chinese culture in operation. We have already seen that Westerners often dismiss *guanxi* as corruption, even though *guanxi* is accepted and practiced by Chinese as an ethical compliance with moral personal obligations. In addition, saving someone's face often involves lying to him, as also the maintenance of social harmony requires skillfully applied falsehoods. Despite appearances to the contrary, the Chinese do have ethics; however, sometimes their ethics run afoul of Western notions. Confucianism considers authoritarianism and paternalism good, the west values democracy in the workplace. (Ip, 2009) A manager who asked a woman employee to go to beauty school to make it easier on the customers' eyes would naturally be viewed as "unethical" in the West, although perhaps not so in China. It is safe to say that the problem of ethics in modern China is twofold. One aspect of the problem is merely a cross-cultural problem – what Westerners perceive in Chinese practice to be unethical is not actually unethical, it is just different. The other aspect of the problem is that the Chinese actually are operating in a moral vacuum, created by the denigration of Confucian morality by the Communists on the one hand, and on the other hand, by the passionate embrace of shallow Western materialism, devoid of any of the Judeo-Christian morality which gave rise in the first place to the culture of disciplined ordered freedom which produced the wealth of the West.

The Chinese themselves often note the latter point, specifically that the Chinese don't have a moral polestar for guidance. I remember how, in 1995, a middle-aged Chinese professor in Shanghai, after first assuring me that she loved America, and that she had spent time teaching there, told me that it was shocking to her how sexually immoral Americans were. I suspect a decade and one-half later, she has the same attitude towards the younger generation in her own country, who worship Lady Gaga, who swoon over Louis Vitton handbag ads, and one of whom, being short of funds, recently sold one of his kidneys in order to be able to purchase an iPhone. Older Chinese will often bemoan the lack of caring for one another that used to exist in the "harmonious society" of the past. The famous 2011 incident in Foshan, in Guangdong province, in which a baby girl was run over and left to die in the street by unconcerned passersby, provoked a national debate about Chinese ethics, even as it aroused comment in the West. I knew a woman in Beijing whose father was trying to enter a glass door on a windy day, when the door collapsed, and a shard wounded her father in the stomach. Nobody called an ambulance, nobody tried to help him, and he bled to death on the street.

I know that events like the Foshan incident foster a stereotype of the Chinese that life is cheap to them, and that they lack certain basic moral principles. But it is easy to wrongly stereotype a culture that is so opaque to the Western eye. There was an event previous to the Foshan incident, in which someone tried to help an injured Chinese woman in distress, and the woman sued the rescuer for not doing the job properly. This incident was well publicized, and so it could easily be argued that the bystanders were behaving rationally, not unethically, as they contemplated being unjustly sued. Almost all of the states in America have dealt with this problem by passing so-called "Good Samaritan laws," which shield rescuers from liability. One could argue that the Foshan incident was a result of a deficient, undeveloped legal system, rather than deficient Chinese morals.

Discounting for as many mitigating factors as there may be, such as inchoate laws, and Chinese cultural values that make certain actions appear unethical when they are really not, I think one can quite safely say that there is a moral vacuum in Chinese society today. I recall the anguish of a Chinese parent reported in the press, when a young man, competitively racing a sports car through the downtown streets of a crowded Chinese city, killed her son. The boy was the son of a wealthy Chinese businessman, who bribed the judge, who thereupon allowed the boy to walk free. Stories like this are everywhere afloat, all being told to reinforce the idea in the modern Chinese mind that modern Chinese are cast adrift on a sea of moral confusion and ambiguity. I once knew a young Chinese couple, new parents, who attended faithfully, almost religiously, a Chinese house church for almost one year, but who would not convert to Christianity. They said they were looking for moral values to teach their child.

Before we take a look at Chinese business ethics, and specific ethical problems in China such as corruption, product safety, academic cheating, and intellectual property rights, let's look at how Chinese parents teach their children to tell the truth, and how they also teach them to lie. An understanding of this will give the foreigner some insight when he realizes he's been lied to, but can't figure out why he's not offended by it. And I promise you, there's a lot of lying going on in China, if my first-hand observations are at all accurate. I recall listening to a Chinese woman, who I knew to be more morally rigid, straight, and upright than ninety-nine percent of the world's population, without a hint of shame tell me how she used her sister's American university ID card in order to gain access to a printer in a secure room in the university. All Chinese look alike to Americans, she said, so the security guard thought that her sister's picture was hers. I know another Chinese professor with whom I would trust the family silver, who, when his professor wife flubbed an appointment, informed his wife's bosses that her computer had crashed, and she had missed the email informing her of the appointment. When I asked him did it bother him that he had lied to the university, he said, no, not at all, this sort of thing was necessary in China.

Chinese parents, very diligently, seek to inculcate values into their small children. They use many techniques, one of which follows the ancient Chinese practice of imitating the old. Chinese children are persistently instructed to follow the example of iconic role models: the incorruptible official, the loyal servant, and the chaste widow. Chinese parents have recently supplemented these stock exemplars by using peers, famous media characters, characters in famous novels, and teachers as role models. (Wang, et al. 2011) The chaste widow is a pattern that Western children are never urged to emulate, but I have seen this ethical ideal pop up in conversation. I was talking to a Chinese student who was discussing her widowed landlord. The student began heaping praise on the landlord because she had never remarried. I asked her, what was the big deal about that? The student replied that the widow was being faithful to her dead husband! It seems that the ideal traditional Chinese wife will not abandon her dead husband any more than the dutiful Chinese family will abandon their ancestors.

One cultural icon for whom there is almost universal appeal as a role model is Lei Feng. Lei Feng is on everyone's lips, much like Santa Claus at Christmas time. According to the official story line, Lei Feng was a People's Liberation Army soldier who was killed in 1962, when an army truck which he was helping to back up hit a telephone pole, which then toppled and killed him. Ignominious in life, Lei Feng became famous in death when, in 1963 Lin Biao, a famous Chinese marshal in the People's Liberation Army who for years was designated to be Mao Zedong's successor, presented to the public what was purported to be Lei Feng's diary. This diary apparently was a forgery concocted to rehabilitate Mao Ze Dong's image, which had suffered greatly due to the calamities of the Great Leap Forward. (Tanner, 2009, p. 522) The diary was a hagiography of Chairman Mao, chock full of breathless reflections on the Party leader and the Party itself. The skeptic would assume, with a great deal of confidence, that the diary was a forgery. But never mind, due to the world-class nature of Chinese Communist propaganda, the Diary became ubiquitous. If the Internet had existed back then, Lei Feng would be said to have gone viral. Now, when Chinese mothers want to shame their children, they will say "Lei Feng would be ashamed of you." I would dare to say that the Lei Feng phenomenon is one attempt by the Communist Party to replace the outdated moral code of Confucius, which the Party had spent years diligently attempting to trash. The following quote from the official People's Daily will give you a feel for who Lei Feng is:

When Lei Feng died in the line of duty, he was only 22, but his short life gives concentrated expression to the noble ideals of a new people, nurtured with the communist spirit, and also to the noble moral integrity and values of the Chinese people in the new period. These are firm faith in communist ideals, political warmheartedness for the Party and the socialist cause, the revolutionary will to work arduously for self-improvement, the moral quality and self-cultivation of showing fraternal unity and taking pleasure in assisting others, the heroic spirit of being ready to take up cudgels for a just cause without caring for one's safety, the attitude of seeking advancement and studying hard, and the genuine spirit of matching words with deeds and enthusiastically carrying out one's duties. (Editorial, People's Daily 5 March 1993)

Lei Feng sounds a lot like Wally Cleaver. I love to aggravate Chinese students by telling them that I don't believe that Lei Feng was real, or, since I can't prove that, I will say that I'm not sure he was real, and I believe him to be a product of untrue Communist Party propaganda. My students are almost unanimously incredulous that I, a mere foreigner, could not believe in the almighty Lei Feng. I ask who believes in Lei Feng. They all raise their hands. I choose one student with a raised hand and ask: "How do you know Lei Feng exists?" There is dead silence. Chinese students are not taught to think, they are taught to copy, imitiate, memorize, and to emulate past masters, but analysis is not one of their strong points, as any foreign Chinese teacher of English will tell you. I keep asking the entire class, "Someone help your classmate out. How do you know Lei Feng exists?" Finally, one student might say, "I heard someone on CCTV talk about him." CCTV is the state-owned Chinese television network. I persist: "And who controls what goes on CCTV? The same Party that published Lei Feng's diary, correct? So, since you have no independent sources of information, how do you know the Party did not just make up Lei Feng?" The silence is longer now. The students have the same sort of disbelieving look on their faces that I had when I was told that Santa Claus didn't exist. Another student says, "My grandmother told me about Lei Feng." "Really," I respond, "And when did your grandmother ever see Lei Feng?"   And, on it goes. I suspect that when the Chinese masses discover that they have been fed a line about Mr. Feng, China will suffer an existential crisis.

At any rate, whether it be Communist morality or Confucian code, Chinese mothers will endeavor diligently to inculcate values into their children. Interestingly, one prominent value they will try to teach their children well is to tell the truth, except when you are supposed to lie. This requires some casuistry, which, while perfectly understandable to Chinese children, is somewhat over my head. The rules for good lying go something like this. A lie told in order to cultivate interpersonal relations is considered a good lie. If one violates truth and sincerity to maintain harmony, one has done a good thing. Telling the absolute truth is viewed as simplistic and naïve, and is often laughed at. (Blum 2007, cited in Wang, et al. 1011) Apparently, there are exceptions to this rule, if a foreigner with a beer gut is being discussed. Countless times I have been told that my stomach is fat. Once, a perfect stranger engaged herself in an analytical discussion with my Chinese boss in order to satisfy herself whose gut was the largest. At another time, a Chinese student walked into class during a break, saw me sitting in the chair at the front of the room, and made a large circular motion in front of her stomach to indicate to me that, were my stomach located where her stomach was, it would protrude into the atmosphere about two or three yards. I knew what she meant; and so, revengefully, I asked her, "Are you pregnant?" I have yet to discover why fat, especially American fat, is so fascinating to Chinese people, and why they can discuss it in such a carefree manner in the presence of foreigners. One regular masseuse I went to would regularly comment on how much my stomach had enlarged or shrunk from massage to massage. I know one foreign teacher who, while undergoing a weight check during a medical exam, complained that all the doctors gathered around the scale and oohed and ahhed over the large numbers the scale was reporting. It frightened me to contemplate this, because the American teacher was not fat by any stretch of the imagination, at least by American standards. The pangzi (fatso) seems to have a special place in the Chinese mind. I heard a lecture once given by an American who had been doing marketing in China for over fifteen years. A student asked him, was there anything, which, as a marketer, he would not do for ethical reasons? The marketer replied that he would not do what Chinese advertisers do, which is to poke fun at fat people. An incredulous student immediately raised her hand, and asked, why not?

But I digress. In the normal circumstance, the Chinese will favor lying over truth- telling in a situation where there is a conflict between honesty and social harmony, as well as in certain other situations. Here are some classic examples of when it is praiseworthy to lie. Lying should be done to give false praise to someone ("Your son is handsome!"). One should lie in order to provide an excuse ("I did not come to see you because I had to take care of my sick mother." Lying is called for in order to defuse tension ("I didn't really mean it… I actually think you are a fair person."). Lying should be done in order to show false modesty. I can not tell you how many times I have tried to praise the good food of Chinese women, only to hear them inform me that there is not enough salt in the food, or some other imagined deficiency. It is praiseworthy to lie to one's child in order to get the child to do an unwanted task. For example, one may tell a child that if he drinks his soup, his fever will be gone in one minute, or that if he doesn't brush his teeth right now, his teeth will fall out, next week. Here are some examples reported in a research article: "My son won't do anything if it's up to him… When he doesn't want to do things like brushing his teeth or eat balanced meals, I try to persuade him by lying... it often works... I don't see anything wrong to lie for the best interest of the children." Here's another example: "my mother doesn't like my sister's husband. If we tell him the truth, we would create a chaotic family environment. Instead, we tell him that my mother likes him... In this way he feels good... and this has changed the relationship between my mother and my brother-in-law; they are now getting along well." (Wang, et al. 2011) I recall an example in my own experience of being serially lied to and feeling good about it after it was over. My wife and I were attending Chinese language school in Beijing. I wanted to take a one-on-one tutorial with one of the teachers there, but I was too late to sign up. I know that if this had happened in the U.S.A., the administrator would have told me, "I'm so sorry, the deadline for enrollment has passed, maybe you can sign up next semester," and that would have been the end of it. But this is what happened to me, instead. I asked the teacher in charge if I could enroll in a one-on-one class. The response was: "I think that class would be too easy for you." Knowing my pitifully weak Mandarin, I was surprised to hear that. I thought she really meant it. She was actually lying to me, because she was too embarrassed to have to tell me that there were no more slots available for me. I continue: "No, I don't think it will be too easy, because So-and-So, whose level of Mandarin is much higher than mine, is taking a one-on-one class, and it's not too easy for her." The teacher responds: "One-on-one classes would be tiring for you." I knew that wasn't true, because I had been enduring three hours per morning plus homework in the afternoon, so I told her that I was a "strong American," and therefore I wasn't worried about being too tired. She then said I wouldn't like the class, because it would be too boring. I quickly responded, "Of course it won't be too boring! I love to talk to this school's Chinese teachers." Persisting, she told me that the class would be too expensive. I told her it would be worth it, and I would be willing to pay. Finally, she gave up trying to give the dumb American the hint, and she straightforwardly told me the one-on-one classes were fully enrolled, and there was no room for me. At last, the truth had emerged. A Chinese person would have realized at the beginning that the teacher was lying to either save me from the embarrassment of waiting too late to enroll, or to save her from the embarrassment of not being able to serve her customer, would have taken the hint, and then retired gracefully.

BUSINESS ETHICS IN MODERN CHINA

In the chapter in which I discussed *guanxi*, I mentioned how the demarcation between *guanxi* and corruption can be easily blurred. I will discuss that idea more thoroughly here, and then discuss Chinese business ethics in general.

It is a subtle thing, the difference between *guanxi* and corruption. The Chinese assume *guanxi* as a part of their existence, and yet they (the ones who aren't doing it, at least) decry corruption, so one is inclined to think that the two are distinct, even if they seem to be closely conjoined in the minds of Westerners. I propose to examine the relationship between *guanxi* and corruption to see if it might be possible to discern meaningful distinctions.

It is useful to distinguish between two opposing forces in Chinese culture. The first is "particularism," which describes how *guanxi* operates between a particular pair of actors, regardless of organizational and societal rules and structures. We have seen how pervasive particularism is in China. It operates so strongly that often parties to a contract will refuse to introduce commercial law in contract discussions, because the other party will feel mistrusted. (Chan, et al. 2002, Hoivik 2007) However, there is a countervailing force in Chinese history and culture, and that is the impetus for procedural justice, which emphasizes neutrality, impersonality, objectivity, rationality, and rules over relationships, all of which, of course, are diametrically opposed to the practice of *guanxi*. One immediately thinks of all the Western corporations who enter China, with their codes of business ethics, and their standard operating ethical procedures. However, besides Western influences operating on modern Chinese culture, there is also a quite strong and quite famous cultural imperative that has cultivated strongly in China the notion of procedural justice. The imperial exams were designed to be neutral arbiters between all those seeking advancement in the imperial bureaucracy. The ancient Chinese were among the first to introduce merit-based government service, and in fact own one of the earliest and longest-lasting bureaucracies in the world. Even Confucius, who almost worshipped personal relations, wanted government officials to be promoted on the basis of individual integrity and merit, and in fact did not approve of the inheritance of offices based on blood relations. (Wang 1999, Lunyu 1991, both cited in Chen et al. 2004) In addition to modern Western corporations and the imperial examinations system, another force in

Chinese culture giving impetus to rational, objective, procedural justice was the Communist Party's long battle with *guanxi* and other forms of personal and family loyalty, for which they attempted to substitute ideological identification with, and loyalty to, the Communist Party. (Chen et al. 2004)

There are two problems facing the Westerner doing business in China. The first is acquiring parts, supplies, permissions, etc. and the other things necessary to do business. The second is to avoid getting caught up in unethical or illegal behavior in an attempt to get the things necessary to do business. If *guanxi* that is promised is actually bribery, there is a high risk of becoming involved in illegal or unethical behavior. (Su et al, 2003) In other words, *guanxi* may be necessary, but corruption should be avoided. Some findings gleaned from research might perhaps provide some orientation. It has been reported that when employees see that promotional decisions were done based on *guanxi*, management is perceived by employees as less trustworthy than before. In addition, perceptions of untrustworthiness in this scenario rise in proportion to the degree that merit is omitted in the hiring decision. Thus, if the hiree is an old schoolmate of the person doing the hiring, this is perceived less negatively than if the hiree is a relative, because the schoolmate will be seen to have more education, and thus more skill, and consequently merit is more of a factor in the decision. Blatant personal favors based on *guanxi* will be seen as unjust, but if two applicants are seen as equally qualified, *guanxi* may be used as a tiebreaker without causing disapproval by those looking on. (Chen et al.2004) Favors done publicly, and in an organizational setting, are more likely to be seen as corruption, rather than an acceptable practice of *guanxi*. Also, favors that assist a person in his personal capacity, rather than as a representative of his organization, are also frowned upon. (Chen et al. 2004) And one last important thing to remember: just because a Chinese person practices *guanxi*, he should not be viewed as unethical. Research has shown that there is no connection between higher ethics and lack of *guanxi* practice. A Chinese businessman who heavily practices *guanxi* is not necessarily unethical, nor is an unethical Chinese businessman more likely than not to be heavily involved in the practice of *guanxi*. (Su et al. 2003)

Research into business ethics in mainland China is in an embryonic state. There have been few studies about business ethics in the People's Republic, although there have been an increasing number of research articles published about business ethics in Taiwan, Hong

Kong, and Singapore. These articles typically explore cultural differences in viewing ethical problems in business, and business ethics problems relating to specific functional areas, such as marketing. Except for the Chinese concept of *guanxi*, the research is all from a Western point of view, in that the methodologies and research instruments all assume Western concepts. (Hoivik 2007) Because of this, it is somewhat difficult to know the precise state of business ethics in mainland China. There are indications, however, that things are not so rosy. For example, it has been argued that during the transition from a command to market economy, the accounting profession is experiencing a "moral vacuum," and that CPAs don't understand very clearly the difference between ethical and unethical behavior, and that there is increasing concern about the lack of independence for auditors and concern about their lack of professional standards. (Chong and Vinten 1995, Tang 1999, p27; cited in Gul et al. 2003). In addition, it is said that China lacks a proper theory of the ethical culture and ethical foundation of the corporation. As Chinese enterprises were rapidly thrust from a world of state-owned enterprises, which lacked any ideology or culture with regard to operating in a free market, into a globally-competitive world which required different ethical bearings, many Chinese enterprises were at sea, when it came to discerning and practicing ethical behavior. This was especially true because state-owned enterprises had previously operated on an assumption that private enterprise was evil, and now they were suddenly asked to believe that private enterprise was a good thing. This ideological shift was so profound that one private enterprise actually delayed production until it had educated its employees that capital indeed was not evil, but was something that should be respected. Thinking on business ethics produced in the West did not fill this ethical vacuum into which state-owned enterprises were thrust at the dawn of the era of market reform. In the 1990s, some publishers in China began to market business books from the United States, but these business books were from the 1970s and earlier, and said nothing about business ethics. (Lu 2009) Somehow, the Chinese idea of capitalism did not correspond with those theories of capitalism that say the capitalist system promotes, and requires, ethical behavior much more than socialism, as George Gilder has so eloquently suggested. (Gilder, 1993) Rather, the Chinese relied on Chinese proverbs such as "the marketplace is a battlefield," and depended on lectures from Chinese professors of management who compared corporations to an organized group of robbers. It seems that a strong strain of thinking amongst Chinese businessmen is that whatever is necessary to be done, should be done in order to make a profit. Of course, not all Chinese firms act like robber barons. Well-known Chinese companies such as Lenovo, Haier, Fuda, and Ming Yuan strive to behave ethically. It is said that in China a few "uncivilized" companies coexist with the civilized ones. (Lu 2009)

One researcher has divided into two periods the development of whatever business ethics there are in China at present. The first period is said to run between the beginnings of Deng Xiao Ping's market reforms, starting in 1978, to the end of 2001 when China entered the World Trade Organization. During this period of great economic transition from statism to the free market, there existed three sources from which a new business ethic might have been derived: traditional Confucian ethics, Marxism, and business ethical ideas imported from the West. The attempt to meld a coherent business ethic from this mishmash of contradictions was done entirely at the academic level. Research papers were written, books were published, courses on business ethics were established in MBA programs, conferences and seminars were held. The second period for the development of business ethics is said to stretch between early 2002, just after China entered the WTO, up to today. There were several forces pushing for further development of Chinese business ethics. For example, the WTO had rules that needed to be complied with. Another push came from China's widespread lack of credibility on ethics issues, which led some to advocate the application of Confucian ethics. The third impetus came from the rising Chinese middle class, who became quite conscious of their rights and interests, and who, armed with the Internet, created public opinions favoring ethical business practices. The final force favoring the development of business ethics during the current period was provided by the Chinese national government, which began to promote chengxin (honesty and integrity) for corporations as well as government. As an example of this, and I am being serious as I relate this to you, the national government required the three national accountancy schools to adopt as their official school slogan this inspiring motto: "Don't Cook the Books." Companies began to adopt corporate social responsibility as a goal. In the second period, the current period, practitioners as well as academics are becoming interested in the idea of business ethics. (Lu 2009)

Specific Ethical Issues in Chinese Business

We will now turn to specific ethical problems, many of which have created for Westerners anti-Chinese cannon fodder, as some of these issues have risen to the level of international scandal. We will look at product safety issues, academic cheating, employee evaluation systems, and intellectual property rights.

Product Safety

At times, it seems the whole world is awash with news of defective Chinese products exported to other unsuspecting countries, whose consumers become more and more afraid to use Chinese products. The United States Food and Drug Administration has warned American consumers to "throw away Chinese toothpaste." (Lu 2009) This comforting admonition came at a time when I was living in China and using Chinese toothpaste every day. By the time the warning had filtered through the popular press, and through my friends and family's emails sent to warn us, it had become quite apparent that, if we continued to use Chinese toothpaste, we would be ingesting antifreeze that would curdle our organs and send us on our way to eternity by means of an excruciatingly agonizing death. Two Chinese companies poisoned some American dogs by adding melamine to pet food. Many Americans are constantly griping about Chinese currency manipulation, the buildup of the Chinese military, violations of human rights, and other sundry matters, but killing pet dogs? What could possibly be worse? Not only have Chinese companies killed American dogs, one Chinese company also indirectly caused the suicide death of a Hong Kong businessman who had been swindled by a mainland Chinese company. The company sold the businessman fake unleaded paint, which actually contained lead, which the Hong Kong businessman used to paint toys his company sold for export. He had to suspend his export operations completely, and lost 30 million US dollars in one year. As a result, he decided to end it all. We now must ask ourselves, is the situation really as bad as all this? Have Americans over-generalized and concluded that all Chinese products are defective, if not dangerous? There is plenty of evidence indicating that Americans need not be overly concerned each time they consume a Chinese product. Assuming his statistics are correct, the Chinese Minister of Commerce in 2009 stated that China's exports have steadily grown at an annual rate of 17% for 29 years. Presumably, if Chinese exports were injuring or killing people, people all over the world would not keep buying them. Again, if China's official statistics can be believed, 99% of all of Chinese food products exported to the United States, the European Union, and Japan, passed acceptable quality standards. (Lu 2009) My favorite statistic is a personal one. I have been living off and on in China since 1995, and I have gotten sick only three times, twice in hole-in-the-wall restaurants that would not be allowed to operate in the United States, and once in a nice four-star hotel restaurant. I must confess that all three times I thought I was going to die, and in fact wished I would die, so perhaps the food contamination is deeper, at least qualitatively, if not quantitatively, in China than in the U.S.A. The last food poisoning occurred in a Shanghai restaurant, outside of which I squatted and curled up on the sidewalk outside in a pouring rain, while all the restaurant patrons standing around me scarfed up all the available taxis. Fortunately, my Chinese dinner hosts called the police for my wife and me, and the policeman dropped us off at our hotel. However, despite these several untoward experiences, I have become accustomed to eating Chinese food and using Chinese products without worry. However, when I am in China, I keep my ears open for the latest poisoning rumors, of which there are many. I generally wait to see if someone else sickens before I partake. I trust, but I also verify.

Considering once again the famous toothpaste scare, the following facts should put things in perspective. Glycerin is what the world uses in toothpaste now, and some small Chinese companies used glycol instead as an ingredient, in order to save a little bit of cost because glycol is cheaper. Even though glycol does sound an awful lot like antifreeze, it cannot be all that terribly dangerous, since the European Union and the United States both certified glycol as safe ten years before the Chinese toothpaste scandal occurred, and in fact, glycol was used for many years around the world as a substitute for glycerin. Some Chinese, observing the hysterial reaction in the United States, became suspicious that the real reason for the outcry was protectionism, and the fear of economic competition from China. (Lu 2009) Perhaps so, but I suspect that the real reason is that Americans have become a nation of Spotless McDermotts, afraid that our pantywaist immune systems can't take care of a germ or two. I love watching newly arrived Americans eating in down home Chinese restaurants. While I am enjoying the wonderful Chinese food, the American is suspiciously eyeing the torn carpets, the dog or cat curled up on the floor, the smelly toilets, and the general overall tumbledown shabbiness of the place. If I am feeling particularly naughty, I remind them that the reason the lettuce is cooked along with all other vegetables is that they are grown with "night soil" used as fertilizer. "Night soil" is an elegant euphemism for human feces, just like "Palmetto Bug" substitutes for "roach" in South Carolina. I can't prove it, but I am convinced that the reason stomach upsets in China are often so devastating is because of the human organic methods of fertilization. I love to tell foreigners this, as I invite them to eat from the plate of gong bao ji ding.

Academic Honesty

I will now turn to look at academic cheating in China, of which there is plenty. Chinese college students are world-class cheaters. I will relate to you several incidents that have occurred at three of the four colleges that have employed me as a professor. My first experience with Chinese academic cheating occurred in 1995. I was told by an experienced foreign professor at my university to put a strict time limit on an English exam, which I did. When the time for the exam elapsed, I told the class to please turn their paper over on their desk, as the time had expired. No one paid me a whit of attention. Frustrated, I walked into the class, intending to take up the papers one by one. I reached for the nearest student exam paper, tried to pick it off the desk, and immediately became engaged in a tug-of-war with its owner. I finally won that battle, and proceeded to the next paper, and the process repeated itself. I finally started yelling in a most undignified manner for the students to hand in their papers, but to no avail. I suspect the students hoodooed me out of about ten extra minutes on that exam. That same year, I was giving another class a midterm exam in Business Law. A student raised her hand, and I went to her desk, standing to the left of her. She asked me what the answer to a particular question was. I told her I couldn't tell her. So, without hesitation and without exhibiting even one modicum of shame, she turned to her neighbor to the right and asked her what the answer was, with me standing six inches away from her. Another university at which I taught required all the students to pass a standardized English exam. This exam was an annual one, and it was a big deal. No classes were in session during the session, hundreds of students took the exam, and the university had proctors all over the campus administering the exam and watching for cheating. Outside the exam rooms, on a public billboard on the street, was an advertisement by a company that volunteered to help students pass the exam. For a small fee, the student would be provided a set of earphones and a radio receiver. Outside the classroom, someone who worked for the company, and who had a copy of the test being administered, would transmit the answers to the student customer using a radio. The sign was in large letters, on a university-administered billboard, in plain sight of everyone, and yet the university did nothing. None of the foreign professors at the university trusted the administration, or the proctors, when it came to stopping academic cheats. If a professor left an exam off at a print shop, the owner would secretly make a copy, and sell the exam to the students. The students would take the exam, memorize answers, leave the classroom, and use their cell phones to text answers back to the students still taking the exam. Before I taught in China, I always considered exam day a relaxing day in which I could take time off from lecturing. But in China, I prepared for exam day like I was going to war. All cell phones were placed at the front of the room in my sight. All papers were cleared from the top of desks, and under the desks. I patrolled the aisles. If I saw eyes wandering, I stared at the guilty student till I broke his gaze down, and he started to sweat. I say he was guilty, because everyone, whether their eyes were wandering or not, were presumed guilty until proven innocent.   Often, three different versions of the exam were necessary so neighbors could not profitably copy. The American college that was administering the exam, very nervous about maintaining academic integrity, required I insert into my syllabi a long boilerplate section about the horrible things the college was going to do any student caught cheating, which I solemnly read to each class at the beginning of the semester. When I interviewed with the college for the job, one of the first questions I was asked was, "How do you intend to stop cheating?" Even with all this, I still gave one exam in which the answers were suspiciously alike, and was forced to interview about half the class, during which I discovered that students with evidence of cheating would not betray their classmates, even if their life depended on it. They wanted to maintain the traditional Chinese group harmony, I suppose. I told them, fine, if you don't tell me, the grades won't change, and the cheaters get higher scores than you do. The Chinese officials in the university, no doubt concerned that the American college in partnership with them would be unhappy with all the cheating going on, created a huge bright red canvas sign, about eight feet high and twelve feet long, with huge bright gold characters, and put it in the lobby of one of the classroom buildings. The sign said something like "Cheaters are scumbags." It didn't do one bit of good, but I'm sure it made everyone feel good. At another university, I caught a student's eyes wandering, and moved her to a desk in the front of the class, next to me. A few minutes later, I discovered that she was examining a cheat sheet, right under my nose. Steaming, I jerked the paper from her desk, and announced to her and to the class, that she had just earned a zero. She just sweetly smiled, looked at the class and laughed, packed her belongings, smiled at me, and left. There was not a trace of anger, sadness, or shame. She was playing a game, she had lost, but she would be back to play another day. That was my experience at three Chinese universities, in three different cities. From those experiences, I extrapolated that all Chinese universities would be the same. However, at the fourth Chinese university in which I taught, the cheating was minimal, so much so that my department didn't even have an academic honesty policy. It was a wonderful experience giving exams in that university. However, I am not naïve enough to believe that this university is in any way typical.

Evaluation Systems

Chinese group-oriented culture intrudes itself into the operation of foreign companies doing business in China in unforeseen ways. I am sure that Western managers would not anticipate problems like the following, when trying to operate an employee evaluation system. Evaluations, of course, have a notorious history, being difficult to implement and to operate fairly and in way that ensures employee trust is gained. But when cultural differences are added to the problem, the unforeseen becomes routine. Here is an example that is said to be "typical." In one company, Chinese managers were not willing to discriminate between a good performer and a poor performer. They promoted group results instead of personal results, which perhaps might have been all right, but then the Chinese managers rotated the "excellent" evaluations and the "partially meets the criteria" evaluations amongst the group members, so that everyone ended up being just average. The untoward result was that low performers were rewarded for poor performance, and high performers went unremarked, and the purpose of the evaluation system was thwarted. I wonder how much good it would do to recognize superior performance, especially among older Chinese. The Chinese have an old proverb that says "the nail that sticks up will be hammered down." (Hoivik 2007) The Chinese generally don't like to stand out in a crowd. I recall a friend of mine, an extraordinarily extroverted guy, being present in my living room in America, during my daughter's birthday. I mentioned that my Chinese student, who was also present, would soon have a birthday.

My friend began loudly serenading her, singing Happy Birthday to her. To the surprise of all, the student's response was anger, not appreciation. She said the "honor" should be directed toward my daughter, not to her.

One Chinese manager claimed that "Western companies view employees as individuals and company resources, while we think of employees as collective resources for developing our company and a harmonious society." (Hoivik, 2007) Imagine, if you will, a manager at Enron announcing to his employees: "We hired you to develop Enron and to promote a harmonious American society." I'm sure that would get them out of bed in the morning! Another cultural difference that could foul up the smooth operation of evaluation systems is that evaluation systems are designed to highlight problems, so that managers can know where to intervene and fix problems. But the Chinese are very nonconfrontational. They instinctively strive to smooth things over in order to maintain harmony. To point out a problem in a work unit might cause someone to lose face.

Intellectual Property Rights

China has such a reputation for harboring pirates who steal intellectual property rights, that it is easy to forget that, yes, actually, China does have laws that protect intellectual property theft. But as we shall see, the reality on the ground is that there are all sorts of faking going on. I remember an incident at the Ya Shou, the market in Beijing that foreigners love to go to and get snookered by wily Chinese peddlers, who sit in their stalls, smile, and use their limited English to gouge the star-struck tourist as he enjoys his cultural experience. I went to the Ya Shou market in 2005 to buy some sandals. A Chinese friend told me that you are getting ripped off if you pay more than 30% of the asking price. I found a small, crowded stall selling footwear, sat down on a stool, and let the young twenty-something salesgirl begin her spiel. I looked at the shoes on the walls, and discovered a pair of Adidas running shoes that were quite cheap, so cheap, in fact, that my suspicions were aroused. I asked her, were those Adidas shoes real or fake? She immediately responded that those shoes were fake Adidas shoes, the real ones were on another shelf. I looked to where she pointed, and saw what looked like an identically branded set of shoes, but with a much higher price tag. I have discovered that this is a very typical phenomenon. The fakery is not hidden. The fake brand still has a certain cachet, and is worth something, even if less than the genuine brand. Very expensive fake Rolex watches are for sale all over the place in Hong Kong. After I walked away three different times to another stall, to see if they would match the inflated price the salesgirl offered me, and after her asking price was 70% lower than when I first entered her stall, I agreed to buy a pair of sandals. The salesgirl was tight-lipped and angry, with fire in her eyes. I suspect she had never faced off with such a foreign tightwad before. She wrapped my sandals, handed them to me, looked me in the eye, and pronounced solemnly: "I don't like you." I looked at her with a smile, and triumphantly replied, "Ah, but I sure like you!" I wish I had had the cojones to kiss her on the cheek.

The issue of intellectual property rights in China is somewhat complex. I'll analyze it by first giving some historical background, which might help explain China's difficulty in enforcing intellectual property rights. Then we'll examine some present-day causes that might explain China's relative disrepect for intellectual property rights, after which we will examine some modern-day factors that may lessen piracy, and some that may increase it.

Western nations have long attempted to gain Chinese acquiescence in a legal regime that would enforce intellectual property rights. After decades of hot negotiation, the issue is still a bone of contention between China and the West. Successive Chinese governments have regularly adopted legal models constructed in the West, and yet Chinese citizens continue to ignore these laws. (Lehman 2006) I can testify, from first hand experience, that, in universities all over China, even over the professors' objections, which are completely ignored, universities assist students in copying entire textbooks. Every year, United States industries are estimated to have lost billions of dollars due to piracy and counterfeiting. In 2001, the State Council of the People's Republic of China estimated that the country was awash with counterfeits valued between $19-24 billion, and that counterfeiting accounted for eight percent of China's GDP. Multi-national companies in China indicate that fifteen to twenty percent of their brands in China are counterfeit, causing annual losses in the millions of dollars. Made in China goods are now exported to markets in all parts of the world, and, in fact, according to some accounts, China now accounts for eighty percent of all counterfeits in the world. Counterfeiting and commercial piracy have become a vibrant component of the economies of many local municipalities, and there are now millions of Chinese involved in the counterfeiting business. And yet, in the last several decades, China has actually undertaken a considerable amount of intellectual property reform, including introducing its first modern copyright, patent, and trademark laws. At present, China is a member of many multilateral intellectual property agreements, including the Berne Convention, the Geneva Convention, the Paris Convention, the Patent Cooperation Treaty, and the International Union for the Protection of New Varieties of Plants. One would think this would do the trick, but not only have the government's efforts failed, they have actually led to apathy, reluctance, and resistance on the part of local authorities and their citizens. (Yu 2007) Later, we will see why this is so.

One reason that intellectual property piracy still exists in China is that the judges and courts in China that can enforce those property rights are located in the major cities and coastal areas. In those areas, in the early 1990s, specialized courts staffed with judges with intellectual property expertise have had good success. However, the counterfeiters have moved inland and to the smaller cities, where they continue to pirate with abandon. This has created a situation fraught with the possibility of misunderstanding between China and the United States. American firms look at China as a whole, and see their intellectual property being robbed. The Chinese look at Americans and think that Americans give them no credit for making real progress in some areas of the country, and, instead, unleash upon them a constant barrage of criticism. This tends to make the Chinese feel that, no matter how much progress they make, it will not satisfy the Americans, so why bother? This attitude, of course, undercuts the objectives of the Americans, who would like to see more vigorous enforcement of intellectual property rights, not less. (Yu 2007)

Just like in so many areas of conflict between the West and China, there are things in China's history and culture, things hidden from the Westerner's eye, that inform the attitudes of modern Chinese toward the protection of intellectual property rights. That the Chinese take a different attitude appears quickly to the foreigner living in China. I remember the story of an Ivy League professor, teaching at my university, who discovered that a student had plagiarized an entire paper. He gave the student a zero, which failed the student for the course. The dispute ended up in the administration of the university, which instructed the professor to restore the student's grade, because (as I heard the story) the student

173

had done nothing wrong. The professor refused, and shortly thereafter shipped back to the States. I suspect the university looked at the situation through the eyes of an examinee at an imperial exam, who spent days sitting in his cubicle, preparing and eating his food, while copying down from memory, word for word, ancient texts. If you look at it that way, copying from someone else's paper, and copying from one's own memory, is not all that different, at least not different enough to warrant failing the student.

There are two prominent strains in Chinese history we can isolate that tend to explain Chinese denigration of intellectual property rights. The first is that the Chinese have historically used scholars in the administration of justice, and not lawyers. It takes lawyers to staff the legal apparatus that is necessary to deal with the infringement of intellectual property rights, and lawyers, perhaps as the result of the historical Chinese bias against them, are still in short supply in modern China. To illustrate this need for lawyers in modern China, I will relate to you the story of how the university that first hired me in China hired me because I was able to teach contract law, having been a lawyer in the past (but, please don't tell anybody). The department in which I taught was, in the year or so before I arrived, an English department, stocked with students who had entered the university with not one thought of pursuing a legal career. But the university, seeing the huge demand for lawyers that had arisen because of the swelling tide of international trade, switched the academic department in which I was teaching from an English department to a law department. Of course, this was done without asking any student their personal desires in the matter. That's what's so nice about top-down, authoritarian Communist-controlled universities – they can make decisions for the social good (a "harmonious society") without having to worry about such bourgeois notions as individual rights. The students, who woke up one morning and suddenly found that they were now preparing to be lawyers, were not allowed to transfer, because Chinese students, once they choose a university, do not have the right to transfer. When I see the things American college students complain and protest about, it almost makes me want to laugh. Do they not have access to enough beer or condoms on campus? I wish they would consider this. A certain group of students at a very prestigious Chinese university where I was teaching had graduated, and were waiting on campus for the graduation ceremonies. To celebrate, they had imbibed a little too much beer, and had become rowdy. They were told by the administration to stop. This injunction was ignored, and the inebriated celebrations continued. The administration thereupon informed them that their degrees were cancelled, to please depart the campus, which they did, probably going out to the fields to plant rice.

But, once again, I digress. My previous point was that modern China is short of the lawyers needed to staff the legal apparatus necessary to control intellectual property theft, and that shortage may have arisen from a traditional lack of appreciation for lawyers in Chinese history. But the communist chapter in Chinese history probably also contains reasons which might explain modern China's lack of enthusiasm in protecting intellectual property rights. Intellectual property rights are rights held by intellectuals in private property, and the communists hated both intellectuals and private property.

Let's first take a look at Chinese history, compare it with Western history, and see how the West has favored lawyers but the East has favored scholars. The history of modern Europe is much concerned with the process by which the modern centralized state gradually usurped the power of feudal nobility. To replace the legal and administrative functions of the feudal nobility, the kings turned to graduates of European universities that had kept alive Roman law. Roman law itself tended to foster centralization, because Roman emperors had to deal with a far-flung empire administered from the center at Rome. China, under the Ming Dynasty (1368-1644 AD), went through the same centralization process, as did the West, as the power of local lords was curtailed. However, the situation in China was different. First of all, the law, as a means of administration and social control, had been discredited during the harsh rule of China's first emperor Qin Shi Huangdi (221 – 210 BC). Han Feizi and the Legalists imposed extraordinary draconian measures on the populace, and famously burnt the Confucian books that had stored up the ethics and rituals of the idealized Zhou Dynasty (1122-255 BC). Ever since Qin Shi Huangdi, Chinese intellectuals have distrusted law, law codes, and lawyers. They have turned to scholars instead, who have transmitted a body of Confucian ritual and etiquette through the centuries down to modern China. This scholarly tradition was merged into the administrative apparatus of the Chinese empire, and perpetuated by the famous imperial examination system. This body of Confucian ethical conduct had nothing in it concerning intellectually property rights. However, in the West, European civil law, a descendant of Roman law, developed the concept of intellectual property rights in the seventeeth and eighteenth centuries. (Lehman 2006)

Therefore, there are deep cultural reasons that militate against an open-armed Chinese embrace of the legal protection of intellectual property rights. The Confucian scholarly tradition I just mentioned also was wary of artistic production, seeing it as both immoral and low class, (Lehman 2006) which would tend to make a government sluggish in protecting that sort of intellectual property. I think the story of the great classic novel Jin Ping Mei is perhaps illustrative of why Confucian scholars might tend to think of literature as immoral. This excellent novel is peppered with passages of such exquisite obscenity that the English translation I used translated those passages into Latin, instead of English. I thoroughly enjoyed presenting the Latin to a Catholic priest, who began to translate in my presence, until we both felt nauseated enough to stop.

So, how may we summarize how the history and culture of China has affected the present day Chinese attitude towards intellectual property rights? First, in Chinese thought, there was no such thing as intellectual property. Second, in Chinese legal codes there is nothing concerning intellectual property rights, and besides, legal codes were not all that important in Chinese history, because ethics was more important than law. Third, in traditional Chinese thought it was considered trashy and immoral to make money on art. This cultural drag does not mean that no Chinese respects intellectual property rights, and it does not mean that in the future the protection of intellectual property rights will be neglected in China. But it probably does mean that the way forward will not be successfully negotiated with the use of the law. Rather, there will have to be a change of the Chinese heart with regard to the matter, which may take some time. (Lehman 2006). I suspect that the change of heart will be effected by means of the Chinese pocketbook, because sooner or later, all the piracy is likely going to come back to bite the Chinese in the wallet, as I will suggest shortly.

Some have suggested that Chinese theft of intellectual property will decrease when the Chinese consumer tires of buying shoddy pirated goods. This theory states that when Chinese consumers don't have a lot of money, they will be content to get a warm and fuzzy feeling being associated with a popular brand, even though they know it's fake. However, when they have more money, they will not be content with the fake brand, but will insist on the real thing. The lessening of demand, say those who buy into this theory, will put the counterfeiters out of business. (Yu 2007) That might sound well and good, but I'll believe it when I see it. It seems to me there will always be demographic slices of the consumer market that will be poor enough to want fake brands.

It seems to me that a more likely scenario is that, as the Chinese economy continues to develop, and as it continues to produce its own intellectual property, the Chinese themselves will start demanding protection from those who pirate their intellectual goods. For example, China has incentive to provide intellectual property protection to its fast-developing biotechnology, software, semiconductor, and movie industry. (Yu 2007) This might mean the Chinese will continue to install the legal apparatus necessary to protect Chinese intellectual property rights all across the country, and perhaps those courts will then also protect the intellectual property rights of foreigners who want to invest in the country. In addition, such legal protection might encourage more foreigners to invest, who might otherwise be deterred, knowing that a certain percentage of their profits would inevitably be robbed from them.

However, there are others who pessimistically forecast an upward growth in Chinese piracy. They see that development, contrary to the argument in the previous paragraph, will produce an increased desire for products that people cannot afford, and therefore the demand for product fakery will increase. In addition, as there is more and more foreign investment in the country, there will be more and more products to which Chinese consumers are exposed, thereby increasing the number of products that are candidates for piracy, claim these pessimists. Other pessimists point to the fact that China's obligations to the World Trade Organization have forced the government to ease its restrictions on export privileges and rights, thus allowing counterfeiters within China to produce aggressively for other countries that are hungry for low-priced counterfeit goods, such as Southeast Asia and Eastern Europe. In addition, these pessimists might point to the economic reality that the enforcement of intellectual property rights in China has a cost. Every enforcement action has the potential to throw people out of work. If Guangdong Province, for example, decided to shut down counterfeiters in the Chaoshan area in the south of the province, all the workers who specialize in making fake electronics, cigarettes, pharmaceutical, or CDs would be jobless. Also, strict enforcement directly hurts the Chinese economy, in some areas. China uses a great deal of pharmaceuticals, chemicals, fertilizers, seeds, and foodstuffs, many of which are imported. If domestic counterfeiters of those goods were inhibited by strict enforcement of the foreign companies intellectual property rights, it would directly impact large sectors of the Chinese economy. Another factor which inhibits the Chinese when they are asked to control intellectual property piracy is the nature of the communist system, which insists on thought and information control. It would be hard for a Chinese communist court to give copyright protection to a book or movie that explicitly or impliedly criticized things the government doesn't want criticized. (Yu 2007) And lastly, there are many practical difficulties facing a firm who wants protection of its intellectual property. There are difficulties in monitoring large territories, in collecting evidence of wrongdoing, in collecting judgments. There is widespread corruption and abuse by government officials. Local protectionism repels enforcement of foreign companies intellectual property rights. Government decentralization is harmful, because even if the central government in Beijing wants to enforce intellectual property rights, local governments may not. (Yu 2000, pp 230-231, cited in Yu 2007).

Who can say what the future holds? I think, as someone once famously said, that in conflicts between optimists and pessimists concerning what the future might hold, the pessimists are almost always right.

CHAPTER REFERENCES

Blum, S. D. (2007). Lies that bind: Chinese truth, other truths. Rowman & Littlefield Publishers, Inc. New York.

Chan, Ricky Y. K.; Cheng, Louis T. W.; and Szeto, Ricky W.F. (2002). The Dynamics of *Guanxi* and Ethics for Chinese Executives. Journal of Business Ethics 41(4):327-336.

Chen, Chao C.; Chen, Ya-Ru; Xin, Katherine (2004). *Guanxi* Practices and Trust in Management: A Procedural Justice Perspective. Organization Science 15(2):200-209.

Chong, H.G. and Vinten, G. (1995). "The Auditing System in China and the U.K.: A Critical Comparison," in J. Blake and S.Gao (eds.), Perspectives on Accounting and Finance in China. Routledge, London, pp319-345.

Gilder, George (1993). Wealth and Poverty, San Francisco: ICS Press.

Gul, Ferdinand A.; Ng, Andy Y.; Tong, Marian Yew Jen Wu (2003). Chinese Auditors' Ethical Behavior in an Audit Conflict Situation. Journal of Business Ethics 42(4):379-392.

Hoivik, Heidi von Weltzien. (2007) East Meets West: Tacit Messages about Business Ethics in Stories Told by Chinese Managers. Journal of Business Ethics

Ip, Po Keung (2009). Is Confucianism Good for Business Ethics in China? Journal of Business Ethics 88:463-476.

Lehman, John Alan. (2006) Intellectual Property Rights and Chinese Tradition Section: Philosophical Foundations. Journal of Business Ethics 69(1):1-9.

Lu, Xiaohe (2009). A Chinese Perspective: Business Ethics in China Now and in the Future. Journal of Business Ethics 86:451-461.

Lunyu (1991). New Interpretations of Lunyu. Sa Ming Book Company, Tapei.

People's Daily (5 March 1993). Editorial.

Su, Chenting; Sirgy, Joseph M.; and Littlefield, James E. (2003). Is *Guanxi* Orientation Bad, Ethically Speaking? A Study of Chinese Enterprises. Journal of Business Ethics 44(4):303-312.

Tang, Y.W. (1999). Issues in the Development of the Accounting Profession in China. China Accounting and Finance Review. 1:21-36.

Tanner, Harold Miles (2009). China: A History. Indianapolis, Indiana: Hackett Publishing Company.

Wang, Xiao-lei; Bernas, Ronan; & Eberhard, Philippe (2011). When a Lie Is Not a Lie: Understanding Chinese Working-Class Mothers' Moral Teaching and Moral Conduct. Blackwell Publishing.

Wang,Y . S. (1999). Chinese Traditional Political Philosophies. Chinese Language Teaching Publisher, Beijing.

Yu, Peter K. (2007) Complex Guoqing and Intellectual Property Reforms in China. Abridged and adapted from Yu, P.K (2007), "Intellectual Property, Economic Development, and the China Puzzle," in D. J. Gervais (ed.) Intellectual Property, Trade and Development: Strategies to Optimize Development in a TRIPS Plus Era, Oxford University Press, Oxford, pp 173-220.

I hadn't lived in China for very long before I came to an ironclad conclusion: in China, the family is God. It became apparent that rarely did a young Chinese make a decision that was not subject to veto by his or her parents. What college to go to, what major to enroll in, what boy or girl to date, all were subject to parental approval. I began to ask a stock question to single people with a boyfriend or girlfriend: would you marry your current significant other if your parents didn't approve? I have yet to find someone who answered that they would buck their parents' wishes. It seemed to me that, everywhere I turned, the Chinese were trying to please their parents: buying them refrigerators, taking them on trips, bringing them to live with them in their homes. At the time, I did not understand the Confucian concept of familism, which has endured throughout the centuries, and which has not yet been erased by the corroding influences of Western romantic ideals. Writes one scholar: "…family… plays a fundamental role in Chinese theories on cosmology, religion, and many other subjects. In other words, Chinese culture as a whole is imprinted with reflections on family… " (Zhang Zailin 2009) There is a great deal of current Chinese family life that can be understood with just a glancing acquaintance with Chinese philosophy and history, so before I give you my observations on Chinese family life, I will give you a quick summary of the Confucian idea of the family.

The key to understanding the Confucian concept of the family is to think vertically, across the generations. Inter-generational ties conquer conjugal bonds. A man is more concerned about his parents and his children (especially his son), then about his spouse. In Confucian philosophy, there were five famous relationships. If one lists these relationships in descending order of importance, the rankings are as follows: (1) ruler – subject, (2) father-son, (3) elder brother – younger brother, (4) husband – wife, (5) friend – friend. One sees that a husband's duty to his wife is quite overshadowed by his duty to his son. China's patrilineal kinship system emphasized vertical family ties traced through men, in an unbroken line of descent connecting a man with both his ancestors and descendants. Marriage took place to maintain the line of descendants, not to benefit the husband or wife.[Pimentel, 2000)

Confucian philosophical concepts had implications in practice. First, the parents arranged marriages, in order to ensure that healthy reproduction would occur. Estranged or unhealthy spouses would not make babies, and the parents, with the help of professional or amateur matchmakers, did their best to arrange a proper match. Second, girls, when married off, left the father's household, and were completely absorbed into the domestic and economic life of the new husband's family. Thus daughters provided no old-age security to a father or mother. Daughters developed a second-class status, and were subject to neglect in their family home, and domination and abuse in their new husband's home. Third, sons would often take their new wives into the sons' parents' home, and the two generations (three, after the marriage produced children) would live together under the same household. This created closeness between father and son, because the son was living in his childhood home. The wife, on the other hand, was divorced from her birth family, she was often living geographically apart from her family of birth, she had not had time to become loved by her husband, and she more often than not had to contend with her po po, her mother-in-law, who was living in the same house with her, and who had been living in that house a lot longer than the new wife. The po po had herself been stripped of her security, when she had left her birth family's home, and she had spent much of her life securing the affection of her son to protect her against her own mother-in-law living in her home. Thus, the new wife was faced with a po po jealous of her son's affections, which had been nourished carefully over the years. When a conflict arose, and they often did, the poor husband was caught in the cross-fire between his wife and his mother. [Pimentel, 2000]

Despite many attempts in the modern age to swim against the tide of Confucianism, illustrations of every one of the concepts listed above can be seen in modern Chinese society. Favoritism for a son, parents living with sons, wives' conflicts with po po's, the lack of romance between the sexes, parents' control over marriages, even matchmakers... I have either seen it directly, or heard of it, since my arrival in China. I saw it before I understood the Confucian reason for it, and so, on the occasions I encountered it, I would be jarred. I knew that I was dealing with people who were wired entirely differently than me, but I didn't know why. Before I relate some of these experiences, I do need to point out that, as China becomes more westernized, the younger generation is moving more towards the Western idea of companionate marriage. Young people have come a long way from feudalism. In the pages that follow I will recount some of the historical movements away from traditional

Confucian marriage concepts, but even as I do, the reader should be aware that Confucianism dies hard. The Communists tried mightily to eradicate Confucian "feudalism," and although they accomplished much, they have in no way completely succeeded. Years ago, when Americans would ask me what it was like living in a communist country, I would respond that I didn't live in a communist country, I lived in a Confucian one. The research I cite below will indicate how, in the domain of marriage and family, China is somewhere in the middle between feudal and western.

The traditional Chinese marriage and family system bore hardest upon youth and women, and starting in the early 1920s, these two groups of Chinese began demanding more freedom from family control, starting with the urban intellectual elite. The Communist Party encouraged even more change, through two actions that had far-ranging effects. The first was the promulgation of the Marriage Laws of 1950 and 1980. The second was moving most women into paid employment. The third action taken by the Party that gravely affected the traditional Chinese family system was the extension of socialism into areas previously the domain of family elders.

The Marriage Laws of 1950 and 1980 had as their purpose the shrinking of the outsized power of the family to make marriage decisions for the young. The state now controls whom, when, and how a person may marry. Concubinage and other forms of polygamy are outlawed, men cannot marry before 22 and women cannot marry before 20, and no third party can interfere with an individual's right to marry. Article 3 of the 1988 Marriage Law states that "Marriage upon arbitrary decision by any third party, mercenary marriage and any other acts of interference in the freedom of marriage are prohibited. The exaction of money or gifts in connection with marriage is prohibited..." The prohibition against "marriage upon arbitrary decision by any third party" directly counters the authority of a parent to arrange a marriage, as was done in pre-revolutionary times. (Engel, 1984)

Moving women into paid employment in the factory labor system was the second method the Party employed to fight traditional Chinese familism, by giving women financial independence from their husband's family. The state mobilized more than 90% of urban women into the paid workforce during the reign of Mao Zedong (1949-1976). Having more money, the social and economic status of

183

women was raised, compared to men. Women were told that working in the workplace was going to lead to their ultimate emancipation. As a result, the traditional female role of "virtuous wife and good mother" (xian qi liang mu) was undermined by the State. However, an unfortunate thing happened on the way to emancipation. First, women's employment outside the home was mainly "externally pushed rather than internally driven." Many of the women working in the factories did not, in fact, want to be working there. Second, most of the jobs were labor-intensive, low-wage jobs. Third, domestic chores continued to bind workingwomen. The husband didn't help, and to make matters worse, this was at at time when laborsaving devices in the kitchen were not to be found. Thus, the Communist Party destroyed a woman's freedom to choose between marrying and raising a family, or working. (Zuo & Bian, 2001)

The third action taken by the Communist Party that tended to erode the traditional power of the Chinese patriarch was a side effect of socialism itself. Since the Party strove to control the means of production, such decisions as job assignments and schooling decisions, traditionally in the hands of parents, fell instead within the purview of the state. Formerly, family elders made those decisions, and in doing so, bound the young to them and made them dependent on them. After the advent of communism, young people became less dependent on their family members and more dependent on the state. (Riley, 1994)

As time has gone on, the Communist Party has continued its push against Confucian marriage traditions. Current Chinese divorce law acknowledges that affection between spouses is a necessary part of marriage, and the lack of such affection is a ground for divorce. (Pimentel, 2000) However, the Party has not at all eradicated deep-rooted gender distinctions that were characteristic of feudal times. The education and skills that women learned in the workplace during the times of Chairman Mao allowed women to compete with men in the workplace, thus tending to eliminate a woman's dependence upon her husband and her husband's family. This was a push against familism. However, during the time of the post-Mao market reforms, state-imposed requirements for full-employment for women were weakened, and women, instead of trying to use their skills and education to make themselves equal to men in the marketplace, began to restore their "feminine" identity in the domestic sphere. Two national surveys in the 1990s revealed that more women then men believed that men's role was primarily outside the home and that women's role was primarily inside the home. Women predominately believed that a woman should sacrifice her own career to support that of her husband's. Unmarried young women, including college students, now seek men with more education, ability, and income for their husbands. All of these attitudes push back against the Communist Party's ideal of anti-feudal marriage "equality." (Zuo & Bian, 2001)

So, for modern China, what is the result of the intersection and clash of Confucian marriage and family ideals against the countervailing forces of both communist ideology and Western marriage concepts that emphasize conjugal love? The result is neither traditional nor Western, but a hybrid. Men and women in China have free choice in their marriage decisions just as they do in the West, but parents are nevertheless highly involved, holding in effect a veto power over a child's choice. Sometimes, the contrary occurs, and the parents present a choice to the child for the child's veto. Parents have much more power over a child's choice in China than in the West. Another example of the in-between state of current Chinese family mores can be seen in one researcher's survey and focus group results which confirmed that, for her research sample, interaction between spouses apart from the family during free time together is not an important part of marriage quality for the Chinese, whereas the contrary is true for Western couples. Another example from this research: China does not have the "dating culture" of the West. The above-mentioned researcher discovered that 77% of her women respondents and 66% of her men respondents dated no one or only their spouse, prior to marriage. One final example of Chinese-Western differences: Chinese are decidedly less romantic in their idea of love than Westerners. Chinese couples tend to think of love more as "companionship," "respect," "mutual understanding," and "support," and do not tend to think of love in terms of "passion," with "sparks flying." However, an example of where Chinese marriage and family ideals tend to converge with Western ideas, if this research is accurate, is in the desire of a more egalitarian marriage where decisions are shared equally. And finally, illustrating Chinese convergence to Western norms, most of this researcher's focus group participants said that husband and wife's relations are relatively more important than parental relations, when there was a conflict between parents and spouse. (Pimental, 2000)

My own observations from living in China mirror Pimental's in all but one aspect: I have yet to meet anyone that thinks husband and wife relations are more important than parent-child relations. There is a famous hypothetical question that Chinese are all the time asking each other. It goes like this: "If you and your wife and your mother were in a boat, and neither your wife nor mother could swim, and the boat sank, and you could only save one of them, which one would you save?" I have asked many Chinese that question, and I have yet to find one to say they would save their wife. I have asked, why would you let your wife drown? After all, your mother's old, she's had a full life, your wife perhaps can have more children, your wife is young and still has a lot of life to live. These arguments are to no avail. One Chinese answered me and said, "But my mother gave me life!" The real reason, of course, is thousands of years of Confucian filial piety, which may or may not be understood by the Chinese contemplating the answer to the question. I do think that the very fact that the Chinese are always asking this famous question of each other at least shows that they are aware of a certain conflict of loyalties, that perhaps they should have at least a twinge of conscience as their wife sinks beneath the waves. One time, I had a boss in China, whose wife and son lived in the United States. While we were both in China, I asked my boss whether he was excited to be going home to the States for a visit. He replied, "Yes! I want to see my son!" I knew his wife; she was my former student. I also knew that this man and his wife had been happily married for two decades, and that there was no hint of marital discord. So, I asked my boss, "What about your wife? Would you like to see her?" My boss steadfastly replied: "I want to see my son!" After trying one more time, and getting the same answer, I gave up.

I observed the run-up to one marriage which confirms the idea that Chinese marriages today, while not arranged without the participation of the child as they were in feudal times, are nonetheless, not as freely entered into as they are in the West. The bride-to-be was a college senior. Her parents had introduced her to her boyfriend two years or so, before. She talked about handsome boys, and perhaps she would meet some boy one day that she would marry, but actually, she was for all practical purposes, engaged, and her options had been foreclosed. Her grandparents had raised her, her parents having taken a home next to the grandparents. So, every decision she made had to win the approval of the grandparents, with the father and mother's approval being secondary. Her fiancé was in England, studying for a Master's Degree. Her plan was to get a marriage license, and a visa, and then go to England in the autumn, after her graduation from college, and also study for a Master's Degree. Her situation was complex: coordinating visa, marriage license, and university requirements with the family's desire to have a traditional wedding feast at a restaurant was a challenge. I asked her often during the summer before she left for England: when are you getting married? And she invariably replied, "I don't know, I am waiting to see what my grandparents say." She was like a lonely sea-traveler floating on the waves of the ocean, with no power to do anything, in no position to make any decisions, with no option to do anything but to wait to see what the tide and weather might bring. She chafed under the situation, but only just a very little. Her story brings to mind a young man I met in Beijing. He showed me a picture of his girlfriend, and I told him she was pretty. He replied, yes, she was pretty, but he didn't love her. Surprised, I asked him, "Why, then, are you marrying her?" And, he said he was marrying her because his father told him he had to marry someone by the time he was thirty, and he was almost thirty. As someone who is sixty years old, I have often bemoaned, as older people are wont to do, the deficiencies of youth. So, I have surprised myself by siding with Chinese youth against their elders on more than one occasion. I feel like Chinese family elders and schoolteachers put entirely too much academic pressure on their children and their students (as a college professor, I cannot begin to tell you how much it pains me to confess this). And sometimes I feel as though Chinese parents put too much pressure on their kids in the matter of marriage, especially when they hound them all the way up to the "unmarriageable" age of 30, and after they are married, how they ask their children almost daily when they are planning to have a baby. However, I must say, that however overbearing towards children the Chinese system might look to my American eyes, the system at least produces a form of communication and cooperation across the generations, something which, it seems to me, is sadly lacking in the West.

I find it very easy to see in modern China that the old Confucian family ideals die hard, especially the idea that the (married) son live with his parents, rather than the (married) daughter live with her parents. I am friends with a family in Beijing, a couple with two very young children. The husband's two parents live with them in the same apartment. The wife's mother, a widow, lives alone in a different city several hours away traveling by bus. To my Western mind, it would make more sense for the wife's widowed mother to live with the wife and her husband. She's alone, she could use the companionship, she takes up less room than the husband's two parents. The husband's two parents could provide each other companionship, living together in another household. I am sure there could be other factors of which I am unaware, but I suspect there is a traditional Confucian pull on this family that has led to their living arrangements.

Professor Pimentel's conclusion that love is quite less romantic in China is indisputable, in my considered opinion. One young Chinese wife told me that her husband had never told her "I love you." However, I saw a card from him to his wife that said, "I love you" in English. I told her that it seemed her husband was becoming more romantic. She said, no, saying "I love you" in English didn't count, because it didn't have the same impact as wo ai ni ("I love you") in Chinese. I guess it's like cussing – the words in the second language don't have nearly the same impact as they do in the native language. I remember women college students in Shanghai, telling me they called their boyfriends ge ge ("Older brother"). I remember theorizing that, perhaps the reason Valentine's Day, with the usual boxes of chocolates, roses, and Valentine's Day cards, is so wildly popular in China, is because there is a romance deficit among young love-starved Chinese women. I also heard a theory that Chinese women loved Western men compared to Chinese men, because they were ever so much more romantic than Chinese men. Chinese women, not being used to being treated chivalrously, were said to especially respond to romantic attentions granted to them. I used to believe this theory, but now I no longer do, for two reasons. First, the usual Western single man in China is far from your Clark Gable type. Second, I believe that Chinese women are attracted to Western men not for their romantic allure, but rather for their money and their power to bestow upon their Chinese lover a green card. Please, forgive me for reinforcing a timeworn stereotype, but one should remember, there is a reason the stereotype exists.

I propose now to look deeper into the modern Chinese family. I will examine Chinese marriages first, and then I will take a look at Chinese family life through the eyes of Chinese parents. In discussing Chinese marriages, I will defer to traditional Chinese thinking, and focus on the production of an heir to the family name, and leave off discussion of the conjugal relationship to the end. Therefore, I will begin with how the Chinese find a spouse, proceed to the sex life of modern Chinese married couples, go then to contraceptive use for the planning of the birth of the heir, then to the birth of the baby and the immediate postpartum period, and finally, I'll conclude with the relationship of the husband and the wife.

MODERN CHINESE MARRIAGES

Finding a Spouse

Young Chinese men and women do not find their spouses the way Westerners do. Neither do they find them the way their grandparents and more distant ancestors did. Completely arranged marriages are now rare in urban areas. However, many marriages can be characterized as "negotiated," which means that the choice is strongly influenced by parental input. That input may be in the form of a prospective partner being set forth to the child as a suggestion, subject to veto by the child, or the input may be approval or disapproval of a child's choice. (Pimental, 2000) However, although Chinese marriages are normally not formed through arrangement, neither are they created through Western casual-dating methods. Pimental's research indicated that 77% of women and 66% of men dated no one (or dated only their future spouse) before they were married. (Pimental, 2000) Dating is often different from the dating encountered in Western countries. Sometimes, young couples do not date until after they are engaged. (Beijing Review, 1981b in Engel, 1984) Dating is considered much more seriously in China than in the West. The acceptance of a movie date may be interpreted tacitly as an agreement to marry. The single foreigner would be well advised to understand this. A single man visiting a single girl's parents is considered a very serious thing. I recall a student of mine who had another young and single American instructor for her teacher. The American teacher was not a China newbie, he had been here for years, and spoke Mandarin. He informed me that our mutual student had recently asked him to visit her parents during a vacation. The poor guy looked pale in the face and green around the gills. The thought of going to those parents' house scared him to death. It could have been innocent; it could be that the traditional Chinese honor for the teacher (which really has to be seen to be appreciated) perhaps was the main motive for the invitation. But my colleague was very wise to decline the invitation. To read research that states that there is not a dating culture in China is somewhat surprising, because I had seen plenty of dating on the college campuses where I had taught in China. But I had not realized that the students were practicing a form of serial "monogamy". They wouldn't date around, and then settle on a boyfriend or girlfriend. They would settle on a boyfriend or girlfriend, and then date only that person, until such time as they broke up, or became married. I asked an undergraduate college co-ed, was it true that Chinese people didn't like to casually date? She responded that, yes, it was true. The reason? If a college student was seen alone by a member of the opposite sex, they would be subject to a good deal of ribbing from their fellow students. Therefore, Chinese college students would gather up a group of the opposite sex, when they went out.

Not only does their culture press against dating, but also the Chinese who want to date are inhibited by practical constraints that lead to a lack of privacy. The cities are dense and packed, and there are almost no personal automobiles available to a young couple. As a result, the parks are dotted with couples that have carved out their little zones of privacy in the midst of the public. I recall fondly the time in 1995, when my family was exploring a little park near a KFC in Shanghai, near Renmin Guangchang, the big public square in the middle of town. My youngest daughter, about nine at the time, came breathlessly running up to me, and pointed out to me a young man and woman standing in the middle of the park, tightly wound around each other like it was their wedding night, passionately kissing, and completely unaware of the masses of people around them. I thought to myself, at least they censor the TV in China.

So then, if Chinese young people are averse to casual dating, and find it difficult to date when they want to, where does the love of their life come from? College is a good place for college students to find their life partners. However, it is quite interesting to see how many boyfriends and girlfriends break up before they graduate. They know they are just enjoying a temporary romance, that family connections, jobs, graduate education, social status, and all the other unpleasant things in the outside world will break them up eventually, so they just enjoy their two or three years together, while they have them. Another place that Chinese can find their mates is through their parents. The parents might have "inside information" through work and social contacts that they will exploit in order to find a suitable match for their son or daughter. (Pimental, 2000)

The pervasive practice of Chinese *guanxi* (relationship) partially explains the source of marriage material for children. *Guanxi* is an exaggerated system of mutual back scratching that often results in miraculous results, when one is attempting to find something that is in short supply. It is important enough that I have given it a separate chapter in this book. Folks in a *guanxi* network supply each other with jobs in certain work units, or enrollment in certain schools. If a parent wants his child to meet the right sort of potential mates, the parent might well "pull *guanxi*" and get his offspring located where he or she might make a favorable match. (Riley, 1994)

Parents may also assist their children in finding a spouse by the simple act of helping the child to socialize at home. Socializing is often done at home, and parents are thus well placed to encounter their children's friends at gatherings in the home, and to judge them, and make comments on them to their children. In this fashion, parental disapproval beforehand can prevent an unpleasant situation when the prospective mate is brought to the family home for a formal introduction to the parents, and the parents subsequently disapprove. (Riley, 1994) Parents' assistance might extend beyond simple influence. The parents sometimes actually introduce the two young people to each other. In one survey, nearly 45% of the respondents had been introduced to a potential spouse by their parents. (Riley 1989) Parental introductions are considered especially vital for those daughters approaching the deadly age of thirty, beyond which, if a girl remains unmarried, her life becomes worthless, and is, in all practical respects, over. In addition to parents, Chinese young people may rely on help from those around them, such as classmates, friends, and relatives. (Riley, 1994)

One thing is constant: Chinese women do not, and I repeat, do not, want to marry any man who is inferior in age, education, or height. (Higgins 2007) Especially height. I recall a conversation with a young 25-year old single, unattached Chinese woman who was deprecating her fellow Chinese single women who put so much emphasis on the usual important things: money, education, parents' social standing, and more money. She said she was interested in more ethereal things, such as companionship, love, spiritual compatability, nobility, etc. I asked her: "Would you marry a man shorter than you?" Her instant retort: "Of course, not!" She wasn't trying to be funny. She didn't even realize the irony of her statement till I pointed it out to her the next time I saw her.

I should take the time to address the special concerns of any single men reading this. You may have found yourself in the same situation as a man I met on an airplane on his first trip to China. He had become enamored with a Chinese girl he had met on the Internet. She knew no English, and he knew no Chinese. One periodically encounters such couples. They can't talk to each other, so they can't fight. This Internet couple communicated using Google Translator. After the man's plane landed in Shanghai, and he had met her for the first time, the next day he was going to the marriage bureau in order to marry her. This poor gentleman was afflicted with what may be called the "China Doll Syndrome." Uninitiated Western men do not understand that when they are gazing upon a young Chinese beauty, they are looking at the endproduct of Confucian training that has been going on purposely, for millennia. Chinese girls are trained to be feminine by their mamas, and their mamas know exactly what they are doing: the minced steps, sitting on the edge of the seat and listening attentively, not being intrusive and rude, the blushing, the giggling behind the backward hand over the mouth, the bangs, the ponytails, the long eyelashes over the averted Oriental eyes; in other words, all the things that our Western feminist culture has abandoned. The Chinese even have a word for it: nuxinghua ("feminization"). I ask you, what Western man's bank account is safe from this arsenal? These poor victims will soon learn that, behind that wall of Confucian charm lies the rumbling energy of a weaponized Iranian nuclear reactor.

Sex

I recall being in Beijing, talking to an old Chinese man in his eighties who had lived for years in the state of New York, working for IBM. He referred to the old stereotype that Chinese don't have sex too much, and weren't interested in it. He then asked me, where did the 1.3 billion people come from? He had a point.

Sex is a notoriously taboo subject in traditional China. I recall reading an account by a New York Times reporter who recounted an interview with a married Chinese woman who was having a good deal of trouble in her sex life with her husband. When her work unit found out about the interview, she was shamed and censored. Because of its sensitive nature, I have never had a conversation with any Chinese person about married sex. I remember being unexpectedly told by a married Christian woman that Christian churches in China love to have marriage and family seminars, and they all involve whatever the first subject was, and whatever the second subject was, and sex. I was so shocked that a Chinese had mentioned the taboo word to me, I froze, and did not pursue the subject. If I had known I would be writing this book, I would certainly have continued the conversation. Sex in China is rarely a subject of empirical research, and as a result, the relationship between sex and marriage remains mysterious. (Guo and Huang, 2005) I will shortly turn to some serious academic research to try to shed some light on the matter, but I suppose I should mention some second-hand evidence I accidentally obtained when an American professor born in France told me about several Chinese girlfriends he had had. He said they were terrible at sex, and knew nothing about it. Of course, this evidence is biased, being based as it is on hearsay, limited sample size, and the possibility that the professor himself was the one who knew nothing about sex. However, given that the professor was French, and given the way that information (or misinformation) about sex floats around in China, I suspect that the professor's observations were quite accurate. Sex education in China is problematic. Here is a snippet of a conversation between two college girls in 1987: "Zhenzhen, I'm pregnant because Weiwei kissed me." Zhenzhen responds, "Who told you that, silly girl, you don't get pregnant from being kissed by men, it happens when they touch your breasts." (Ma and Rosenberg 1998) Think of what a happy country America would be, should misinformation like that be spread abroad. I recall a young unmarried student in Shanghai, telling me that she would read magazines at home as a child, and find holes cut in certain pages where her parents had censored the material. A Chinese college instructor told me that Chinese sex education instructors taught sex education classes in the high schools (which are often co-ed, incidentally) without ever mentioning the word "sex" during the whole semester of instruction. Many of the instructors were single women who themselves knew nothing about the subject. A young university woman student of mine told me that her roommate asked her how to use a condom. My student asked her roommate, whatever did she need to know how to use a condom for? The roommate responded that her boyfriend felt that they should use one, but he didn't know how to use it, and was thus asking his girlfriend to figure it out. These experiences, and others like them, have made me feel that perhaps Chinese wives (and their husbands) are enjoying their sexual relationship in a less-than-optimal fashion. It is interesting to note that one researcher hypothesized, before doing his research that, given both traditional and previous Communist Party negative attitudes towards sex, and the general Chinese cultural message that sexual pleasure is restricted to men, Chinese wives would probably not be very satisfied with their sex life, which was exactly the suspicion I had. However, Renaud, Byers, and Pan (1997) discovered that Chinese women reported significantly greater sexual satisfaction than did their husbands. Let's turn to some research to see what can be gleaned about this subject, in which we can find learned commentary describing modern Chinese married couples' sexual satisfaction, non-sexual physical expression of affection, who takes the initiative, wives participating in unwanted marital sex, the effect of previous sexual experience on the married couple's sex life, the frequency of married couples' sex, sexual problems of Chinese married couples, and the contrast between husbands and wives' in their attitudes towards sex.

Sexual Satisfaction

I will begin with the counter-intuitive finding by Renaud, Byers and Pan (1997) that, surprisingly, wives were more satisfied with their married sex lives than were husbands. Before premature conclusions are taken from this, it should be pointed out that the authors give reasons for this conclusion that differ from an assumption that Chinese wives are having good sex. These researchers write that their results may reflect different expectations women have from their sexual relationship, expectations different than their husbands'. In other words, they speculate that because women have been socialized not to expect pleasure from sex, when they don't get it, they don't miss it. The authors write that the findings may reflect Chinese culture's message to women that they should not, in fact, respond to their husband's stimulation. In addition, these researchers report other findings that tend to suggest that the sex life of a Chinese wife is less than rosy. For example, husbands reported certain "costs" in having sex with their wives, and one of those costs was the difficulty in getting their wives to participate in a mutually pleasurable sexual experience, in particular, the effort to get his wife to respond sexually. In addition, the research found that women were more "erotophobic" than their husbands, and reported more "sexual concerns." The women in this research were more likely than men to report that their partner provided insufficient affection, lack of kissing during sex, or extramarital sex on the part of the spouse. Later research on this topic by Parish and Luo, et al. (2007) reported that Chinese women were not as satisfied as their husbands with their sex life. Those researchers speculated that the wives' lower level of satisfaction could be due either to the effect of Chinese traditional values on the women, or else due to insufficient knowledge about sex on the part of the husbands.

Sexual satisfaction research suggests five determinants of sexual satisfaction: (1) social-emotional aspects of the the relationship with the sex partner, (2) general physical vitality and health, (3) environmental impediments to sexual satisfaction, (4) knowledge, values, and attitudes about sexual matters; and (5) variety of sexual practices. (Parish, Luo, et al., 2007) I have found nothing in the research that would contradict the commonsense statement that the greater the affection of Chinese spouses for each other, the more satisfied they (both husbands and wives) are with their sex lives, and the more satisfied they are with their sex lives, the greater their affection is for each other. (Parish, Luo, et al., 2007, Renaud, Byers & Pan, 1997)) The same is true for health: the better the health, the better the sex. (Parish, Luo, et al., 2007). Environmental impediments to good sex for Chinese couples were found to be as one would expect. Children, parents living in the home, fear of pregnancy, and small apartments cramped the sexual style of Chinese husbands and wives. (Parish, Luo, et al., 2007). Does an increase in knowledge, values, and attitudes about sexual matters increase sexual satisfaction? Parish, Luo, et al. (2007) found that higher knowledge of sexual technique increased the variety of sexual practices, which in turn indirectly produced higher levels of satisfaction, but at the same time made some respondents feel more inadequate, and thus decreased their level of satisfaction. The direct effect of education about sexual technique (as well as more permissive values concerning sex) was to diminish reported satisfaction, to diminish perceived partner affection, and to diminish (for women) frequency of orgasm. It is apparent that China is in the midst of its own sexual revolution, as more and more Western attitudes and information seep into the country. Unfortunately, many Chinese men are using pornography to educate themselves. (Pan 1993, Parish, Luo et al. 2007). If this is the method used for sex education, it would not be surprising to me that such education would diminish the married partners satisfaction.

The fifth determinant of sexual satisfaction, as suggested by research into the subject, is variety of sexual practices. It is believed, with some reservation, that variety of sexual practice can be used as a surrogate for sexual satisfaction. Parish, Luo, et al. (2007) asked about nine specific sexual practices, and reported the following percentages. The men and women reported separately, thus the different percentages for the two genders in the following table.

Table 1   Relative Frequency of Sexual Practices of
Chinese Couples

Practice	Never		Sometimes		Often		Total	
	Women	Men	Women	Men	Women	Men	Women	Men
Kiss	.20	.00	.55	.52	.25	.34	100%	86%[1]
Caress woman's breast	.13	.05	.49	.45	.38	.50	100%	100%
Caress woman's genitals	.18	.13	.59	.56	.23	.32	100%	101%[2]
Caress man's genitals	.27	.12	.55	.62	.17	.26	99%[2]	100%
Woman on top	.42	.39	.48	.52	.10	.09	100%	100%
"Doggy style"	.53	.47	.43	.49	.04	.04	100%	100%
Oral sex to woman	.76	.75	.23	.24	.01	.01	100%	100%
Oral sex to man	.74	.72	.24	.28	.02	.01	100%	101%[2]
Anal sex[3]	.96	.96	.04	.04			100%	100%

[1]Parish, Luo, et al. give no reason that the percentages do not add to 100%

[2]Presumably rounding error causes the percentage not to equal 100%

[3]Categories for Anal sex are "No/Yes"

Source: Parish, Luo, et. al (2007), Sexual Practices and Sexual Satisfaction: A Population Based Study of Chinese Urban Adults

A few observations can be made about these results. First, men reported statistically higher levels of kissing and caressing (woman's breast, woman's genitals, and man's genitals) than did women. This might suggest that Chinese women feel that their menfolk are not quite doing their duty; or, to put it into more scholarly language, this possible feminine dissatisfaction could be due to "insufficiently transformed male behavior." (Parish, Luo, et. al, 2007) Second, the levels of oral sex seem to be quite low. However, the Chinese might see it differently. I recall a conversation I had with a Chinese college professor, a Fulbright scholar who has lectured at Harvard, a genuine polymath. He told me that only "criminals" participated in oral sex.

Frequency of orgasm is said to be directly related to sexual satisfaction. Parish, Luo, Stolzenberg, et al., 2007 reveal the following reported orgasmic frequency for both Chinese men and women:

Table 2   Relative Frequency of Chinese Couple's Orgasms During the Past Year

Never		Rarely		Sometimes		Often		Always	
Women	Men	Women	Men	Women	Men	Women	Men	Women	Men
.04	.02	.14	.03	.49	.21	.26	.32	.08	.43

Source: Parish, Luo, et. al (2007), Sexual Practices and Sexual Satisfaction: A Population Based Study of Chinese Urban Adults

We see from these statistics that women often or always have orgasm only 34% of the time, whereas men often or always have orgasms 75% of the time. It would seem that the Chinese wife's orgasmic contribution to her marital satisfaction is less than optimal.

Before I conclude this brief look at sexual satisfaction in Chinese marriages, I should point out something that research confirms and which may or may not be intuitively obvious, namely, that more sexual satisfaction leads to more marital satisfaction (Renaud, Byers, & Pan, 2007) Guo and Huang (2005), in reporting on research that confirms Renaud, Byers, & Pan (2007), state that sexual satisfaction is a "profoundly significant predictor of marital satisfaction." Guo and Huang (2005) go on to say that the effects of sexual satisfaction on marital satisfaction were more pronounced for women than men. Every "unit of increase" of sexual satisfaction experienced equally by women and men leads to a greater increase of marital satisfaction for women, than for men. In other words, if one would desire to see an increase in marital happiness, there is more bang for the buck for any method that will increase the wives' sexual satisfaction. Pan (1993, in Gua & Huang, 2005) also points out that fifty percent of

197

Chinese people seeking marital counseling and wanting a divorce gave sexual difficulties as the primary reason. More education and counseling for the spouses, and communication between husbands and wives would help, according to Guo and Huang (2005), especially since Chinese couples tend to avoid discussing sexual problems in marriage.

When all is said and done, I think I may conclude the research on married sex and satisfaction by safely saying that both men and women report a moderate level of satisfaction with their sex lives, and that it is inconclusive which gender is most satisfied. In addition, the moderate satisfaction that is reported may be due to low expectations, which are subject to being overturned by a sexual revolution of rising expectations, which seems to have begun in the Middle Kingdom.

Non-Sexual Affection

I now turn to other interesting aspects of the relationship between Chinese husbands and wives. First I will discuss their expression of love and affection to their spouse in ways other than sex. Studies clearly shows that most other such expressions, such as hand holding, kissing in public, saying affectionate mush like "sweetie pie honey bunch" are not very popular in the People's Republic. In fact, hugging in general, even between family members, has traditionally been considered inappropriate. I remember reading Lin Yutang, a famous Chinese intellectual who wrote around the 1930s, who was educated in the West and whose English was as good as his Chinese, remarking about the usual scene at a Western train station and airport. Lin said that the typical Chinese would consider it disgusting, watching all the hugging and kissing going on as Westerners departed from and greeted each other. I recall also a former student who, having lived in America for several years, returned to visit her parents in China. As she prepared to board the bus for departure, without thinking, she hugged her father, who recoiled in horror, and asked her what in the world she was doing. I remember showing a class an American movie in which Harrison Ford had a tearful reunion with his family at the end. As I was wiping the tears away from my eyes to prevent my students from seeing, I heard them break out in what I considered to be highly inappropriate laughter. I asked them why they were laughing. The response: Harrison Ford was hugging his family! I also recall a college official in a Chinese university who was allowed to visit my college in America. This man reportedly had propositioned just about every female staff member of his Chinese university. While he was staying at my college in the United States, not caring if she were a woman or a lady, he would hug every woman from eighteen to eighty. He apparently had figured out that the American sexual harassment laws didn't cover him. He reported that he loved American culture with regards to hugging, I suppose because he had become liberated from his own anti-hugging Chinese culture. I am not sure if his victims ever realized what was going on. I recall one time having just arrived in Beijing, after having been in America for several months. I had not adjusted my mores to match my location yet, when I unexpectedly ran into several of my old Chinese teachers in their office. I was so glad to see them that I instinctively hugged the closest one, and she recoiled like I had tried to shoot her. Prior to the 1980s, even holding hands in public was considered "deviant behavior" or a "social transgression." (Pan, 1989b, in Renaud, Byars, and Pan, 1997) The communist ethic taught that love should be kept within the heart, rather than shown overtly through hugging, kissing, and cuddling. (Renaud, Byars, and Pan, 1997) I would suspect that this ethos applied to indoors hugging, kissing, and cuddling, as well as outdoor public displays of affection.

Having personally experienced the Chinese way, I was not surprised to read research that states that the frequency of sexual behavior and the frequency of affectionate non-sexual expression is just about the same. This implies that physical affection is mostly done at sex time. This doesn't mean that Chinese couples don't love each other, they just use alternative means to show it. Renaud, Byars and Pan (2007) suggest looks and body language are means often employed. I would suggest rather that gift giving is perhaps the means most often employed. In China, everybody is Santa Claus. I remember reading a famous Chinese novel (Jin Ping Mei), whose English translations was four volumes long. After I finished it, I decided that about fifty percent of the novel was consumed by long descriptions of who was giving gifts to whom, and how many rolls of silk or taels of silver were given, and that I was thoroughly sick of reading about people giving presents to each other. I just heard about a man who had managed to break up the civil harmony of his home by fighting with his wife and not talking to her or his son for one month. One day, he came home with three movie tickets, and without one word of apology or reference to the last month's unpleasantness the wife and son took the tickets and went to the movies with him. So, it would be a mistake to assume that the dearth of hand holding and hugging in China can tell us anything about the state of a Chinese relationship. The Chinese are like the country singer who is not good at "love out loud." However, it was interesting to note that Renaud, Byars, and Pan (2007) reported that, at least in their research sample, more frequent physical affection was related to higher relationship satisfaction and higher sexual satisfaction. They reported that more overt expressions of non-sexual affection were increasing among the young, which suggested that the cultural norm restricting public displays of affection had shifted somewhat. I saw this illustrated at one Chinese university where I was employed. This university was different than most universities where I have worked. Many of the students would hold hands as they walked around campus. I asked one of the students about it, and they said that, actually, many other students would like to hold hands, but the older professors frowned on the practice and scared the students out of doing it. This provides one more example of the superiority of Chinese culture over the West's.

Who Takes the Initiative?

I will now turn to that perennial question: which spouse takes the initiative in sex? I suspect that you will not be surprised to learn that research supports the idea that the Chinese husband is the spouse who makes most of the advances. (Liu, et al., 1997 in So & Cheung) Wives rarely report taking the initiative. This was especially true of rural wives who felt too shy to initiate sex, even when they might want to do so. However, as Chinese sexual mores make the transition from the traditional to the modern, it appears that young women are beginning to reject the traditional idea that their role should be asexual, passive objects at the beck and call of men. (Zhang et al., 1999, p.585, quoted in So and Cheung, 2005) Some surveys have indicated that more young women, even though they are a minority, have become more active in sex than they were in the past (Xu, 1990, quoted in So and Cheung, 2005)

Unwanted Sex

Next, we turn to the question of unwanted marital sex. In a Hong Kong survey, it was determined that over 82% of the married women surveyed believed that wives should have the right to reject their husbands' request for sex, whereas only 67% of the men surveyed said that their wives should have the right to refuse.

(FPAHK, 1997, in So and Cheung, 2005) This unchivalrous attitude probably reflects traditional Chinese thinking that sex is for the man's pleasure, and the woman is just supposed to lie back and take it. However, through contact with foreigners and foreign media resulting from the post-Mao era of openness and reform, those traditional attitudes are probably changing. Research was published in 2007 that analyzed a survey exploring unwanted sexual activity among married women in urban China. The authors stated that it was quite plausible, given traditional attitudes in China towards sex, that there was a good deal of unwanted sex being participated in by Chinese wives. However, because of the advance of liberalized ideas since the post-Mao opening to the West, it was also plausible that Chinese wives were, as a matter of fact, not enduring unwanted spousal sex. The researchers defined unwanted sex as a situation "in which a person freely consents to sexual activity with a partner without experiencing a concomitant desire for the initiated sexual activity." Thus unwanted sex included forced (qiangpo) sex as well as sex in which interest was feigned. The authors reported that during the lifetime of their current marriage, 52% of wives reported that at least one incident of unwanted sex had occurred, with about one-fifth of the respondents reporting that at least one instance of the unwanted sex involved force. When the question was asked about unwanted sex occurring one year before the survey, as opposed to the lifetime of the marriage, 27% of the women reported unwanted intercourse, 22% unwanted sex acts, and 72% said they had sex at some point merely to please the husband. The women reported that unwilling intercourse occurred several (48%) or many (43%) times during her marriage, and only 9% said the unwilling sex occurred only once. Of those women who had participated in undesired sex, the median span of time for the occurrence of these unwanted events was five years, which was 67% of the duration of her marriage. Therefore, the condition was chronic. The authors also reported that, on many dimensions, the Chinese results are not very different from other societies. (Parish, Luo, Laumann, et al., 2007)

What were the reasons for the undesired sex? A poor relationship with the husband was a risk factor, as would be expected. Hitting the wife, lack of daily intimacy, lack of foreplay, unsurprisingly made more sex with the husband unwanted. A weak economic status compared to the husband or the husband's family, children in the house, the wife's physical and psychological problems were also causes for unwanted sex, which also should be of no surprise. Increased residential housing that allows for the couple's mobility away from the wife's relatives was an interesting risk factor. Being forced to stay in the old neighborhood with the parent, or having the husband's or wife's parents stay in the home, decreased the chances of unwanted sex. Leaving the old neighborhood perhaps caused women to feel isolated from family and friends, and thus lacking in a social network to make her feel secure. The wife will then submit more often to unwanted advances from her husband. Traditional attitudes towards sex also increase the incidence of unwanted sex. If the wife feels compelled by "wifely duty," or if the wife feels that "sex is dirty," she is likely to more often feel that the sexual relations she engages in are undesired. (Parish, Luo, Laumann, et al., 2007)

The argument that a wife's equal financial status with her husband would decrease unwanted sex with him is plausible, but weakened by other considerations. Even though the income, occupational status, and education of modern urban Chinese women often approximates that of their husbands', wives are nevertheless often insecure enough that they will submit to unwanted sexual advances from their spouse. There is the chance that a challenge to the traditional idea of male authority will lead to a backlash from the husband, who might resort to violence, withdrawal of economic support, extramarital affairs, or prostitution, which is growing and becoming more available. (Fox, Benson, et. al, 2002, Rivers et al., 1998, Im-em et al., 2004, Knodel et al., 1999 all quoted in Parishb)

Interestingly, an increased familiarity with a variety of sexual techniques was significantly correlated with an increase in reported unwanted sex on the part of wives. Parish, Luo, Laumann, et al. (2007) speculate that pornography was the culprit. The researchers discovered that among currently married, sexually active urban men of all ages, 40% reported having viewed pornography during the last year before the survey. It was discovered that there was a statistically significant increase in the variety of sexual techniques used with wives when the men reported watching pornography through the year. Thus it could be surmised that the men had learned the new techniques watching pornography, after which they tried them on their wives. The wives perhaps interpreted these new procedures as too abrupt and too rough. These researchers also reported that only 30% of women and 56% of men knew what an orgasm was, and that only 39% of women and 56% of men knew where the clitoris was. I suspect that the difficulty of finding sexual information in China has led to both a dearth of knowledge concerning sexual technique as well as an increase in pornography, as curious Chinese men search for what they can't find. I recall in Beijing seeing near the zoo, in the area where my wife and I lived, women holding small infants and standing on small streets and in alleyways. We were told that the infants were a signal to potential customers that the women were selling pornography. I suppose it was thought that the police would not suspect a woman carrying a small infant. However, I thought it strange that a foreigner could figure out what was going on, but the police couldn't. I think the statistic that 40% of married men used pornography in the year before they were surveyed is interesting in another aspect. Given the Communist Party's vaunted efforts to reign in pornography and prostitution, how has it become so easy to find both in China?

How much harm has been done to women who have suffered undesired sex in their marriage? Parish, Luo, Laumann, et al. (2007) report that of those women in their research sample reporting unwanted spousal sex, 40% reported at least some harm, and 6% reported considerable harm. The authors' suggested cures for this harm are directed at, first, the husband, and then the wife. The husband should be more caring of his wife in daily life; he should take more time in foreplay. The wife should lose traditional attitudes such as the one that makes them feel that "sex is dirty." She should learn of new sexual techniques, but not through the use of pornography, which, because of its ill effects, may "provide for a troubled move towards more liberal sexual practices." Her education in new sexual techniques will be of no benefit to her, and in fact may be counterproductive, unless accompanied by "affective care" from her husband.

Is Married or Unmarried Sex More Satisfying for Chinese Couples?

Parish, Luo, Stolzenberg, et al. (2007) reported a finding that I thought was interesting. In the West research has reported that married couples are more satisfied sexually than sexually active unmarried couples are. (Laumann et al., 1994; Waite & Joyner, 2001) However, the situation is reversed in China. Continuously married, urban Chinese women and men were no more satisfied sexually than anyone else. In fact, continuously married Chinese women were significantly less satisfied sexually than those who were not married. The authors, citing Xu and Ye (1996) plausibly theorize that the reason for this dissatisfaction is that Chinese marriages, at least some

203

of them, are held together by duty rather than romantic love, which would then impact sexual satisfaction. This finding is consistent with Pan (1993a, in Renaud & Byers) who states that as many as half of Chinese couples marry not for love, but just to get married.

Do Chinese Men Prefer Virgins for their Brides?

I remember that, in 1995, China was abuzz with a human-interest story concerning a famous Chinese male athlete who decided to dump his fiancée because the required premarital physical exam revealed that the girl was not a virgin. At least, it appeared that she was not a virgin, because it was possile that the examining doctors made a mistake. At any rate, the country was caught up in an emotional argument about whether the man had done the right thing or not. This athlete was exhibiting a very traditional Chinese sexual concept that holds that female chastity is prized about all else, including male chastity. Two research articles tend to show that the traditional attitude still prevails among Chinese men. One article reported a survey that showed that male respondents (compared to the female respondents) were more tolerant of men having casual sex then they were of women having such sex. (FPAHK, 2000a, in So and Cheung, 2005) Another article reported that more male respondents than female respondents felt that their relationship would be adversely affected by irreparable damage, if their fiancée had prior sexual relationships with someone else. In citing these articles, So and Cheung (2005) conclude that "the traditional attitude emphasizing female chastity still prevails." (So & Cheung, 2005)

Not Having Babies and Having Babies

Now that we have discussed how Chinese couples view and practice sex, we will now turn to examine how they deal with the consequences. We'll start out with contraception, an interesting topic in light of the One Child Policy, which makes contraception necessary to avoid violations of the law. Then, we'll talk about how Chinese mothers have babies, and more particularly, how they handle the postpartum period when they "do the month."

Contraception

I will rely on a study that analyzed a very large sample of 7,336 newly married couples living in Shanghai between 1987 and 1995.

This study analyzed which methods couples adopted, the switching of methods, and discontinuation of methods. Twelve percent of the sample reported that they had had sexual intercourse before marriage. Only one-third of that 12% had protected themselves with some form of contraception. The form of contraception used by that one-third was mostly withdrawal and periodic abstinence. As a result, a majority of that one-third of 12% conceived. Of the ones that conceived, one-fourth resorted to induced abortion or rapid marriage to deal with the contraceptive failure. (Che & Cleland, 2003)

After marriage, about one half of the 7,336 couples used contraceptives to postpone the birth of their first child. Of the half that was using contraceptives, 40% experienced unintended pregnancy. What sort of contraceptive methods led to that rather high failure rate? The methods that were chiefly chosen were condoms, withdrawal, and abstinence. (Che & Cleland, 2003)

After the birth of the first child, almost all the couples (98 percent) resorted to the use of contraceptives. I suspect this was in order to avoid violating the One Child Policy. Of that 98%, one-third experienced pregnancy, failure and discontinuation of contraceptive methods being high. Because of the second pregnancy, there was a high rate of induced abortion. In the entire sample, increasing numbers of couples switched to the IUD, until this became the preferred method of contraception by the third year following the birth of the first child. (Che & Cleland, 2003)

Family planning is difficult in China, having been made problematic through the one child policy, forced abortions, failed contraceptive methods, a dearth of sexual and medical knowledge, and the rise of premarital sex due to the breakdown of traditional Chinese sexual mores.

Giving Birth

Traditionally, midwives delivered Chinese babies. Although one has to read behind the lines when examining Chinese history texts, it can safely be said that most Chinese midwives, throughout thousands of years of Chinese history, were competent, knowledgeable, and compassionate. Their practices were based on the traditional "yin and yang" theory of traditional Chinese medicine, and they kept the Chinese race going into the twentieth century, when Western missionaries, adventurers, and traders brought Western science to China. At that time, China began to worship science and technology the same way Westerners did. As a result, the first Western style midwifery school was set up in Beijing in 1929, instructing the midwives in Western techniques of birthing babies. These modern midwives met resistance from the traditional ones, as one might imagine. But Chairman Mao gave the traditional midwives a boost, as the Cultural Revolution (1966-1976] destroyed the medical system, and the educational system which trained midwives. Mao felt that "barefoot doctoring" and midwives would help the poor rural people, because the old Western-style system was helping privileged elites. The modern Western-based midwives reestablished their schools in 1972 near the end of the Cultural Revolution, and these schools continued to function until 1993. At that time, ironically enough, the same Western influence that had made modern (as opposed to traditional) midwifery possible, worked to destroy the profession. In 1993, the Communist government, enamored with the Western world's love affair with science, power and technology, committed the country to the international scientific approach, which replaced midwives with obstetricians and nurses. The result has been that modern Chinese women are becoming unacquainted with natural, vaginal childbirth. A majority of Chinese women today give birth via caesarean sections, and in some areas, the C-section rate is one hundred percent. (Huang, 2000 in Cheung, 2007) Two researchers found a C-section rate in their research sample of 62.9% and another rate close to that (The national rate has been estimated at 46.2%.) (Lumbiganon et al., 2010 and Zhang 2009) I am sure the idea is order, efficiency, and convenience for the doctor. However, as someone who watched my youngest daughter brought into the world by an American midwife, and who has since seen the medical profession attempt to squeeze midwives into irrelevance, it seems to me that China might do well to appreciate the midwife profession. It would seem that Chinese women have enough burdens already, without having to be carved on in order to have a baby when there is no medical necessity for it.

"Doing the Month"

"Doing the month" (zou yue) is the Chinese term for the peculiar set of rituals and practices designed to take care of the mother when she returns from the hospital. These practices include dietary modification, protective rituals, social seclusion, mandated rest, and the assistance of older female relatives with daily tasks. "Dietary modification" includes eating or not eating whatever the assisting women dictate. Their dictates are constrained by their knowledge of Chinese medicine, which is thousands of years old, and which differs from region to region and woman to woman, and is, in point of fact, weird. The mothers are laid up in the bed like empresses, and can't lift a finger. If they feel like getting up and about, they can forget about it, because they will be straining against thousands of years of Chinese culture. Some of the common practices include: not allowing the mother to wash her hair for an extended period of time, for example, for twelve days, or for perhaps a month, eating six times a day, eating a lot of ginger, not allowing visitors for a certain period of time (for example, twelve days), not squatting, not taking baths for a long time because the pores will open up and allow wind to come in to the body, thus raising the risk of arthritis, not touching unboiled water, washing the mother's hair with ginger. The practices vary, and are becoming less of a ritualized duty to the family, and more of an instrumental thing to increase good health. Younger mothers are not as strict as their mothers were, and if a practice is too much trouble, she will often violate the mother or mother-in-law's requirements. (Holroyd, Lopez, and Chan, 2011)

The postpartum period is a difficult time for all families everywhere, of course. But the difficulties of Chinese mothers are exacerbated by several factors. First, most childbirths now in China are first-child, and only-child childbirths. Doing something for the one and only time in one's life is stressful. In addition, although the desire for a male child is lessening now in modern China (Wu & Lu, 2009), some families expect the first child to be a son, and when the first child is a girl, first-time parents have been found to experience greater anxiety. (Wang & Zhang, 2008 in Lu et al. 2011; Mao et al., 2008) Concern with the proper gender of the baby apparently still remains a concern in modern China, so much so that some Chinese parents attempt to determine the gender of their one baby through the illegal practices of selective abortion and infanticide (Gao, et al., 2009 in Lu et al., 2011) Second, (this is my speculation), family relationships being as complicated as they are in China, the young mother is quite likely to face "po po problems" from her mother in law. Of course, the presence of the mother-in-law (as well as other older female relatives) is designed to assist the new mother. However, it has been suggested that the presence of a female relative during the "doing the month" time may not facilitate the mother's adaption. (Leung et al. 2005) I can well imagine the presence of the po po not only being unhelpful, but making matters worse. At any rate, a small study with a sample size of 96 found that nearly half of the new parents experienced unsuccessful family adaptation during the postpartum period, which may have been aggravated by dissatisfaction with the marriage, lack of childbirth knowledge, and (if the pregnancy was a surprise) dealing with an unplanned pregnancy. (Lu et al., 2006 in Lu, et al., 2011)

The Relationship between Chinese Husbands and Wives

Marital Satisfaction

Researchers have stated that, among other factors, marital satisfaction for Chinese couples is a function of sexual satisfaction, education, and health; the more of the latter three factors the more marital satisfaction there is. (Guo & Huang, 2005) This, of course, should not be surprising. More interesting is the discovery that the more children Chinese couples have, the more marital satisfaction there is. This is surprising for two reasons. One, research into the marital satisfaction of Western couples has shown that the more children there are present in the family, the less marital satisfaction there is (Marini, 1980; Twenge, Cambell, & Foster, 2003 in Guo and Huang) Thus, the situation in China is reversed from the West. The second reason this finding is interesting is that despite the One Child Policy, Chinese parents are more satisfied when they have more children. Other research has discovered that the more egalitarian (and thus non-traditional) a marriage is, the more maritally satisfied the Chinese couple is. Modern Chinese men and women seem to be happier when decision-making is shared. There is a prominent exception to this egalitarianism, however, and that is in the division of household chores, which I will discuss next, separately. (Pimentel, 2000)

Another factor that greatly affects marital happiness and satisfaction is parental approval (Pimentel, 2000), which exerts a very strong hold on Chinese couples. As I mentioned in a previous chapter, I once asked two university students, one a man and one a woman, to give an impromptu speech in their Business English class. The man was to give the five most important criteria that his future wife should meet, and the woman was to do the same for her prospective husband. The woman said her top criterion was that her husband should be a plastic surgeon and make a lot of money, and the second was that her parents should approve. The man said his top criterion was that the girl should be "curvy" (aotu, the Chinese characters being 凹凸, which should give an idea of what was on the young man's mind). The man's second criterion was that his parents approve. This was notable to me. I didn't expect desire for parental approval to supplant the Chinese woman's desire for money, or the universal male appreciation for the female form. But I thought to myself, I doubt that, if I asked the same question to Western college students a thousand times, I would get parental approval to rank number two.

Two peculiar Chinese characteristics that might plausibly affect the satisfaction of Chinese married couples are son preference and arranged marriages. Research appears to be conflicted on whether a girl baby creates dissatisfaction in the marriage, because of the traditional Chinese idea of son preference. Guo and Huang (2005) found no dissatisfaction when a girl was born. However Zeng, Schultz, and Wang (2002 in Guo and Huang) found that son preference was significantly associated with the risk of divorce. As far as arranged marriages go, Xu and Whyte (1990) report that women in free-choice marriages uniformly report better marriage quality than those women in arranged marriages, and the there is only a small tendency for the arranged marriages to "warm up" over time. I must confess that my attitude towards arranged marriages has sunk considerably since living life in China. Having witnessed the disastrous marital situation in America, which ostensibly, at least, is the fruit of a free-choice system, at one time I wondered if maybe the Chinese were on to something about arranged marriages and matchmakers. However, I have heard of too many disastrous marital situations in China that sprang from an arranged marriage to believe what I toyed with, before. However, I do appreciate the degree of involvement of Chinese parents in the children's decisions. It seems to me the hybrid "negotiated marriage" system the Chinese have might perhaps be the best of both worlds.

Who Does the Housework?

It is of course notorious that Western men, no matter how liberated their wives feel or how egalitarian they think their marriages are, do not share household chores equally with their wives. Except for men in Shanghai, a special case with which I will deal with shortly, Chinese men don't seem to be any different than their Western counterparts. I will rely on research by Zuo and Bian (2001) in order to explore this. Do wives think it is fair that they have to do more unpaid work inside the home even as they have to do paid work outside the home? Do masculine and feminine roles exist for husband and wife, and if so, are husbands and wives who do role reversals looked down upon? Has there been a retreat from Communist Party egalitarian dogma towards an acceptance of domestic femininity for wives?

The answer to the first question, (do wives think it is fair that they have to do more of the household chores?), is quite interesting. One would think that wives would chafe under the inequality, but as a matter of fact, they do not, being quite satisfied with the arrangement. Even though more than 90% of married women are in the labor force and almost equally share economic resources with their husbands (Bian, Shu, & Logan, 2000; Wolf, 1984, both cited in Zuo and Bian 2001), the unequal division of household chores has survived even the Communist revolution. (Honig & Hershatter, 1988; Whyte and Parish, 1984) Few couples see the situation as unfair (Feng, Anderson, Wang, & Zheng, 1997, cited in Zuo and Bian 2001), which tracks the situation in the West (Lennon & Rosenfield, 1994; Thompson, 1991, both cited in Zuo and Bian 2001). To see why Chinese wives think their unequal burden is fair, one has to appreciate the gender roles that exist in China, despite the egalitarian pressure from the Communist Party. The traditional gender roles require that the husband be the provider and the wife be the homemaker. The Communists tried (and failed) to obliterate that distinction by moving almost all women into the workplace and proclaiming that both men and women should be family breadwinners. But now that strict Maoism has come and gone, in the post-Mao era, husbands and wives have been moving toward what has been called a "neotraditional, postrevolutionary" ideology, in which the husband is the main (not the only) provider and the wife is the main (not the only) homemaker. The husband is thus expected to fulfill his role as someone who works outside of the home for pay. For this sacrifice, he expects to be relieved of the main burden of household chores. The wife, on the other hand, because of her contributions to family and homemaking, expects to be relieved of the main burden of breadwinning, although she is expected to earn some money to contribute to the family budget. Both parties, on the whole, perceive this arrangement to be fair.

It is ironic to me that marital gender roles in China, a Communist country, are more rigidly defined then they are in the West. Two national surveys taken in the 1990s revealed that more women then men believed that men's role was primarily outside the home and that women's role was inside. A predominant view in this data was that a woman should sacrifice her own career to support that of her husband (Sha, 1995; Tao & Jiang, 1993) Some women were even bent on becoming full time housewives (Zheng, 1997). When asked "How do you feel about doing a larger share of housework, while still working on a paid job?" most wives showed that their heart was primarily with their family when they answered: "This is my family, I am doing it for my family." They felt that family work and paid work outside the home were equally important, and that therefore a good wife should be able to combine her family responsibility with her career work. Some of the wives even felt that, to pursue a career, was to sacrifice her womanhood. The wives felt that their family work was so important that they were entitled as a matter of right to their husband's money. "His money is my money," said one. And if anyone tries to reverse the expected role that he or she is fulfilling (like a house-husband), this is frowned upon. Role reversal in Zuo and Bian (2001) was rare and generally viewed negatively. In the eyes of both husbands and wives, househusbands were men of "failed aspiration," "incapable," "lacking ambition," and "eating soft rice" (chi ruan fan). In the eyes of wives, such a husband was "overengaged" in household chores. He was considered "unmanly," "nonambitious" and "chained to the stove."

Everything I have just written should be completely disregarded, were I to write about gender roles and housework in Shanghai. Shanghai is notoriously famous in China for having the best husbands in the country. They cook. They clean the house. They shop. In fact, they do everything their Shanghai wives tell them to do. If they don't, they won't have the privilege of marrying the Shanghai girl. I had an instructive conversation with the husband of one of my former students at Shanghai Foreign Languages University, a Shanghai girl. I asked the husband: was it really true that Shanghai men cook, clean, shop, and do everything their wives demand? Without flinching, he said "yes." I then asked him why Shanghai men do this. He took me to a family photo album. He showed me a picture of his wife's grandmother. The grandmother was very beautiful. Then, the husband showed me a picture of his wife's mother. The wife's mother was also very beautiful. He then looked at me laughing, and said, "This is why I do it. This is what I have to look forward to in my old age." I laughed, too, because I was very aware of the well-deserved reputation of Shanghai women as being the most beautiful women in China.

211

It is completely off the subject, but I am going to take some time to discuss the question of the beauty of Shanghai women. First, not all admit it. Some say the women in Chengdu or Dalian are prettier. I suspect that those Chinese who think that are subconsciously exercising the universal prejudice of the Chinese against the city of Shanghai. I have been in Chengdu and Dalian and have not been particularly struck by the beauty of the female inhabitants. Dalian was notable for the fashion that the women wore. At midday, I walked down the street and felt like I was at a Hollywood first showing of a movie. However, the women themselves, in my humble opinion, could not match the beauty of a good percentage of Shanghai women, who not only dress very fashionably, but also are fair of face. They are noticeably whiter-skinned, which Chinese value very much, and they dress very fashionably, if not as fashionably as the ladies of Dalian. I asked a professor from Shanghai what could possibly account for this excess of pulchritude, and he responded that there were several theories. One theory said it was because there were special minerals in the local water, which beautified the faces of Shanghai women. Another theory was that there were special minerals in the face creams that were used in the area. Another theory was that, since Shanghai had only been in existence for less than two centuries (a very short time by Chinese standards), there had been an influx of all sorts of racial groups into the area, and the resulting mixture was, for some reason, very beneficial.

Since I am already way off the subject of Chinese husbands and wives, which I will return to shortly, and since I am talking about Shanghai, I am going to discuss the incredible rivalry between the city of Beijing and the city of Shanghai. Beijing is the capital, and thus endowed with political prestige. The standing stereotype is that that Beijingers talk about is politics. I used to love to ask Beijing taxi drivers what they thought about Mao Zedong. I would get a free political dissertation all the way to my destination. Shanghai is larger than Beijing, and is the leading commercial city of China. The standing stereotype concerning Shanghai is that the only thing the people of Shanghai talk about is making money. If these two cities were ever to acquire nuclear weapons, the peace and stability of the Orient would be destroyed. I recall talking to a young Beijing woman who had a cousin living in Shanghai. When she was in high school, the Beijing girl went to visit her cousin, in Shanghai. While they were driving with their families in a car, the two girl cousins became engaged in an animated discussion revolving around the topic of which city was the greatest, Beijing or Shanghai. The two cousins were soon mutually hitting, hissing, slapping, scratching, clawing, and generally behaving in a most unladylike fashion, all in the service of their native city. I was touched by such local patriotism. I have never in my experience ever seen two Americans fight over the superiority of one city over another. It seems to me that such energy should be reserved for discussions of the superiority of the American South over a certain other region of the U.S.A.

Divorce

The divorce rate in China has increased considerably since about the mid 1980s. I know a lawyer who used to work for a government agency that was in charge of handling divorces. His job was to try to counsel the troubled couple and talk them out of the divorce. Such counseling does not seem to be working. I have heard of another couple that obtained a marriage certificate for 10 RMB (about USD $1.50 in 2011), and three days later obtained a divorce certificate for 50 RMB (USD $7.50 in 2011). The government officials did mock them a little bit for their stupidity, but they gave them a divorce for $7.50, and there were no attorneys' fees.

In 1985, the divorce rate, as indicated by the number of people who become divorced in one year per 1000 people, was only 0.9. However, the divorce rate had jumped to 1.96 people becoming divorced annually in 2001. To express these percentages in absolute terms, in 2002, there were 1.2 million marriages that ended by dissolution. Does this increase reflect an increase in dissatisfaction by Chinese husbands and wives towards each other? Not necessarily, for this reason: there has been a powerful traditional belief that even if there are serious difficulties in marriage, divorce is nevertheless highly undesirable both socially and morally. Thus, intact marriages often were social covers for dysfunctional families. The increase in the divorce rate might be due to a changing perception of the desirability of maintaining a family in the absence of spousal love, rather than a decrease in the amount of spousal love. There has apparently been a "drastic shift" in China's long-standing views about marriage and family. Married couples seem to be more concerned about the quality of the marriage looked at from the spouse's viewpoint, rather than looked at from the perspective of the family as a whole. (However, despite the strong uptick in the Chinese divorce rate, it nevertheless should be remembered that the divorce rate in China is still quite low compared to the rate in America. In 2001, the annual number of persons divorced was 1.96 per thousand in China, whereas in America the number was 4.01 per thousand, double the amount. (Guo and Huang, 2005)

CHINESE PARENTS AND CHILDREN

I have already mentioned the historical idea, deeply rooted in Chinese culture, that the vertical parent-child relationship is more important than the horizontal conjugal relationship. Something happened during a student role-play that really drove this point home to me. The student was playing the part of a businesswoman at a conference, making small talk with another businessman (me) whom she did not know. I asked her, "Did you come with your family to the conference?" She replied, "No." I then said, "That's a shame, you must be lonely here after the meetings with no one to talk to." She replied, "No, I have my children, and we go to look at the sights in town." I responded, "I thought you just said you did not come with your family." She replied, "I didn't. My mother and father are not here, they are in their home town." I then asked the class what they understood the English word "family" to mean, and they all agreed it meant their mother and father. This, of course, confuses the Westerner, who is used to conceiving of the family as the immediate family. The Chinese conception, held even by young college students in 2011, is the old traditional Chinese idea of the family being ancestors and descendants, not husband, wife, and children. This old Chinese idea of filial piety is reflected by the high rate of parent and adult child co-residence in China, to which we now turn.

Co-residence and Filial Piety

Researchers have been interested in the connection with Confucian familism and the co-residence of adult children with their parents. Does filial piety account for the extraordinarily high and long-lasting rate of co-residence? Or perhaps are some other factors at work, factors that both increase the rate, and other factors that bring the rate down? Another question intriguing researchers concerns the effects of modernization (the growth of industrial capitalism and the free market) on the old Confucian concept of the family. As long ago as 1949, Marion Levy predicted that modernization would fundamentally transform the Chinese family. The traditional Chinese family was patriarchial in authority, and descent was patrilineal. One of the adult sons would live with his father and mother, while the other sons and daughters would move out of the childhood home. Levy predicted that modernization would change all that. He predicted that daughters would be granted greater autonomy and respect because of their newfound economic empowerment, and thus role distinctions between sons and daughters would lessen, causing the pattern of the son (and his wife, if married) living with the son's father to dissipate. Children's needs as individuals would begin to rise above the desires of parents, as the nuclear family began to take precedence over the intergenerational one. This movement, Levy predicted, would drive down the rate of parent-son co-residence. (Levy, 1949 in Logan, Bian, & Bian, 1998) Levy was wrong. The following statistics will clearly show that he was wrong. After we look at the numbers, we will explore several of the various theories that try to explain the staying power of Chinese son-parent co-residence.

A few explanatory notes will be in order, before we begin this discussion. First, a fundamental distinction must be made between actual residential patterns and preferred residential patterns. The research almost universally reports that both Chinese children and their parents prefer to live apart, but that actually they live apart a lot less than they prefer to. (See Zhang, 2004 for much evidence of this) Another point to keep in mind is that there is a difference between child-centered versus parent-centered co-residence. Child-centered co-residence occurs when parents and children live together to benefit the children, as for example, when parents move in to help the children with childcare, or when children newly-graduated from college return to their family home and live there until they later marry. Parent-centered co-residence occurs when the parents and children live together for the sake of the parents, as for example, when the parents became aged and need someone to take care of them. I will not make an issue of whether the co-residence occurs in the parents' home or the children's home. A technical term that is quite useful in this discussion is patrilocal, which means a married child lives with the husband's father.

Here are some relevant statistics: Seventy-one percent of all elderly persons lived with an adult child in 1984. During the first five years of the reform era (1977-1982), newlywed couples were more likely to live with a parent than in any previous historical period in nearly half a century. (Unger (1993), cited in Logan, et al. (1998)). The well-known Chinese anthropologist Fei Xiaotong conducted a famous survey of a rural village in 1936, and found that 49% of all the households there contained a parent with married children. Professor Fei returned in 1981, and found that the percentage had essentially held steady, declining only slightly to 43%. (Fei 1982 cited in Logan, et al., 1998) A 1993 survey of two large Chinese cities discovered that the proportion of elderly persons living with an adult child was 67%, which was only a slight decline from 71% that was observed in 1984. This 1993 survey illustrated that Chinese Confucian familism was very much still alive. Single children living with their parents were just as likely to be women as men, but upon marriage, co-residence became highly patrilocal, which is to say, a high percentage of children upon marriage were sons who moved themselves and their wives in with the husband's father. (Logan, et al. (1998) cited in Zhang (2004))

Marion Levy's prediction in 1949 that traditional Chinese familism would fall by the wayside under the onslaught of westernization and economic modernization seemed entirely reasonable. More housing, which would ease the housing shortage, should have made it easier for children and parents to live separately. Western ideals of privacy should have made their way into the minds of both parents and children, impelling them to live apart. It is somewhat puzzling that Levy's prediction fell flat. Next, we will take a glance at several theories that have been proposed by researchers in order to explain this surprising persistence of intergenerational cohabitation in the face of modernization.

The first explanation proposed is simply that Confucian family ideals were simply stronger than were predicted, and that modernization, although cutting against the old familism, was not strong enough to overcome it. The argument against this proposition is that co-residence behavior does not reflect the Chinese people's values; rather, co-residence might spring from necessity imposed on parents and children by government action or by market forces. This leads us to the second explanation of co-residence behavior, which is that the Communist state (ironically) reinforced Confucian patrilocality by certain actions it had taken. For example, the government control of the real estate market led to housing shortages, which forced many three-generation families to live together. Another example: the Chinese government has not installed a secure, large-enough social safety net for old people, thus forcing them to live with their children. A further example: state bureaucracies and danwei (work units) gave preference to men when housing allocations were made before the real estate market was decontrolled. Thus, more men than women had access to the short supply of homes, and therefore, more men than women were able to ask their parents to live with them, thus generating more patrilocality. In addition, the state laid great emphasis on seniority when granting reward packages. The relative wealth of their parents, as compared to the children, forced more dependence by adult children on their parents, many of whom would then have their adult children live with them. (Zhang, 2004)

The second argument against the proposition that traditional Confucian ideals endured throughout the Maoist era states that market forces in the modern, post-reform economy forced parents and children to live together, much like state policies did, and that this co-residence did not spring from Confucian cultural values, but rather, from necessity. The collapse of hardline communism meant that state enterprises were compelled to face market competition, and as a result often collapsed, either through competition or mismanagement. When these enterprises collapsed, older people's nest eggs went up in smoke. The same free market revolution that was destroying the "iron rice bowl" of their parents was opening up economic opportunity for children. The new order placed a premium on education, not seniority, and thus resources were shifted from the older generation to the younger. Old people now needed assistance to make it through old age, and they turned to their increasingly wealthy children in order to get it, and one way they did this was by living with them. (Zhang, 2004)

Here is a final note concerning the causation of co-residence. The state's famous One Child Policy may have affected co-residence rates. Families with one child have now become the majority in cities (Li, 2007 in Lin & Yi 2011). This means that a typical husband and wife will have one child to take care of and four parents. Obviously four parents cannot co-reside with the children. If there are more children, there is an increased possibility that there will be a child willing and able to co-reside with the parent. Thus it would seem that, given the One Child Policy, the percentage of co-residing parents would decrease over time. If so, one would then have to ask the question, is it modernization that's decreasing co-residence, or is it the decline of Confucian values, or is it the One Child Policy?

When all is said and done, it is very difficult to know for sure why so many Chinese live with their parents. But we do know for certain that a great many of them do.

Child-Rearing Practices and Tiger Mamas

Recently Amy Chua, a Chinese woman teaching law at Yale University, in her book Battle Hymn of the Tiger Mama (2011), created quite a splash by indicting wholesale the wussy-puss parenting methods of soft Americans, who aimed at self-esteem for their children rather than achievement. This Chinese mother was probably an extreme case of the proverbial Chinese Tiger Mama. But her thinking runs deep in the soul of Chinese mothers, everywhere. And like most things in China, the origins of Chinese parenting philosophy come from Confucius.

Two Chinese concepts describe the Chinese approach to parenting. Jiaoxun ("teaching and training") and guan ("management, discipline, control") are designed to to enforce standard conduct expected by the parents and by the society at large. The motivation is not to dominate the child, but rather to assure that there are harmonious relations between the child and others in the family and outside the family. (Lau & Cheung (1987) cited in Chao (1994)) A staple tenet of Confucianism is the desirability of harmonious relationships between the five hierarchically arranged relationships: emperor-subject, father-son, older brother-younger brother, husband-wife, and friend-friend. Harmony, or at least the aspiration for it, is everywhere in China. The English word "harmony" may be seen on billboard after billboard. The idea for children is not so much that they will be independently-acting moral agents, but rather that they will be smoothly-turning cogs in society's machine, which should purr harmoniously along. Children are lower in the hierarchy, but the parents, because they are higher in the hierarchy, are required to responsibly and justly govern, discipline, and teach, even as the children should display loyalty and respect. (Chao 1994) Confucianism affects greatly the type of society into which Chinese children are being trained to grow up. Chinese society emphasizes group values. To the Chinese, what is important is that which is important for groups (family, society) as a whole, such as harmony, interdependence, and connectedness with others. (Triandis 1989, 1995; Triandis et al. 1988, cited in Bush, et al., 2002) Individualistic values, such as independence, creativity (Ho 1986, cited in Bush, et al., 2002), personal agency, freedom, autonomy, and assertiveness are not valued so much. (Ching 1997; Triandis, McCusker, & Hui 1990; Yang 1981, cited in Bush, et al., 2002) Not surprisingly, research reports that Chinese parents discourage independence and creativity (Ho 1986, cited in Bush, et al. 2002), and that children are socialized to view themselves as serving societal rather than individual goals, and they are expected to conform to socialistic ideology, to become self-sacrificing, and to respect family and group decisions (Ching (1997), cited in Bush, et al., (2002)).

My experience confirms two aspects of this Confucian upbringing. The Chinese are always talking about an individual's sacrifice for society. My Chinese language textbooks constantly give examples and exercises in which the subject of the sentence or essay is sacrificing himself to take a train to western China in order to help teach in small rural schools in order to "build the country." I even had an adult student in 1995 whose given name was Build the Country! (Jianguo). I had another student in 1995 whose name was Soldier Yang. She had pigtails and weighed about 60 pounds. The prototypical Chinese role model is Lei Feng. Lei Feng is (supposedly) a soldier who died for his country. He is a super Chinese Boy Scout. He is pure, heartwarming, hardworking, and always helps little old ladies across the street. He is kind to animals and little children. And of course, he is always building the country. I once complimented the Chinese father of a very accomplished Chinese scholar on all of his son's remarkable individual academic achievements. The father immediately commented on all his son had done for "society."

The other aspect of a Chinese child's Confucian upbringing can be seen in Chinese students, whose inability to reason, think creatively and solve problems is matched only by their ability to memorize and do arithmetic with huge numbers. I have heard foreign teachers all over China comment on this. Thinking outside the box is not conformity and harmony, but rather it is sticking your neck out and subjecting it to possible ridicule from the mass of people who don't think creatively. This, of course, means shame and losing face, which Chinese people hate to death. For years I have been getting Chinese students to raise their hands to vote on an issue, or to express their opinion. Most of them will sit there and stare at me. I have given them training in how to raise their hands – your elbow must be extended straight up in the air so that your fingertips are above your head, so that I can see your hand. I have grabbed elbows and assisted them upwards. It is hopeless.

Given that a Chinese mother is imbued with traditional Confucianism, what are these Tiger Moms' goals, and what are the techniques that they adopt to attain their goals? Two of the most prominent objectives pursued by Chinese mothers when rearing their children are social conformity and academic excellence. These goals are actually not separate, but closely intertwined, because one way to measure the success that parents have in getting their children to conform to social norms is to measure their success in school. (Wu & Tseng (1985), p. 11, cited in Chao (1994)) And believe me, Chinese moms lust for their children's academic success. They would sell their soul for their child to get top marks. I once worked as the American Headmaster for a Chinese English language training school, and I had the privilege to speak to many, many mothers who were shopping for the best school for their child. I remember one wealthy mother whose son was placed in a special class designed for students who were going to go study in America. Sending their child to study in America is like dying and going to heaven for Chinese mothers, so this particular mother was quite sad when I told her that her son was academically hopeless, because he couldn't understand a word I was saying. She responded that the boy was "naughty." I don't think it ever occurred to her that wanting a boy who can speak two or three words of English to go study at a university in America was a little too ambitious, notwithstanding the declining standard of American colleges and universities. I gave the boy an impromptu oral English test in front of his mother. I asked him what his name was, where he lived, how old was he, what was his favorite color. The mother, who knew rudimentary English, answered every question I asked, then looked at her son, and said, "Answer him!" I don't even think she realized she was cheating for him. She refused to take him out of my class for the college-bound. Thereafter, the boy sat in each class for two hours not understanding a word that was being spoken. He was not naughty; he was heroic.

Chinese Tiger Moms devote themselves sacrificially for their children during their children's early years. The mother provides an extremely nurturing environment by being physically available at the child's beck and call and by attending to their young one's every need. (Wu (1985); Young (1972), cited in Chao (1994)). Therefore, Tiger Moms are not just tough for the sake of being tough. They do their work in the context of a "supportive, highly-involved, and physically close mother-child relationship. (Chao 1994)

How might the values of Chinese mothers be described? I will describe certain "ideologies" taken from a table by Chao (1996) in which Chinese mothers outranked their "Euro-American" counterparts. From this list of beliefs, we will be able to easily understand why Chinese mothers have the reputation of being "authoritative." Chinese mothers scored higher than Euro-American mothers on the following beliefs. The beliefs that are flagged with an asterisk mean the difference was statistically different at the $p < 0.5$ level.

- Parents must begin training the child as soon as it is ready*
- Children can improve in almost anything, if they work hard
- Mothers must train their child to work very and and to be disciplined*
- Mothers should teach their child by pointing out good behavior to others*
- The best way a child learns how to behave is to be around adults
- When a child continues to disobey you, he/she deserves a spanking*
- Mothers primarily express love by helping their child succeed, especially in school*
- A mother's sole interest is in taking care of her child
- A children should be in the constant care of their mothers or family*
- Mothers should do everything for her child's education and make many sacrifices

Amy Chua, I am sure, has helped to stereotype Chinese mothers firmly in the minds of Americans as cudgel-bearing harridans bent on destroying the joy of their children's childhood. This stereotype, as I will show, is erroneous. I have discovered that, when trying to understand a culture so exotically different than my own, I have inevitably made false generalizations time and time again, which have taken years to correct. I have also listened to the Chinese struggle to understand America the same way. I like to ask the Chinese to guess the number of Americans who own guns. The actual percentage of Americans who keep guns on their premises is around 40% (Carlson 2005), but the typical Chinese estimate is 100%. They think we all pack heat, we all have living rooms filled with enough guns to stock an arsenal, and that, for recreation, we go out into fields with our machine guns and our wives and kids and shoot old cars to hell. Well, actually, that is pretty much true of where I live in South Carolina, so I have to explain that there are regional differences in America, so please don't over-generalize. I also love to tell Chinese I own guns. It gives them a charge. However, not all Americans own guns, and to say we all do is an almost universally held Chinese stereotype. Likewise, the Tiger Mama stereotype is an over-generalization, partially born out of ignorance of the true nature of Chinese mothers, and partially springing from fundamental cultural differences. There is a lot of scholarly psychology literature that describes Chinese parenting as "restrictive," "controlling," "authoritarian," "rejecting," "hostile." But scholars discovered that when Western children were so described, they performed poorly in school, but when Asian students are so described, they perform quite well in school. It seems that it depends on what "authoritative," etc., is. The psychological tests that are used to discover "authoritarian" attitudes are ethnocentric and misleading, biased towards a Western concept of "authoritarian." Western ideas of "authoritarian" and "strict" include ideas of parental hostility, aggression, mistrust, and dominance. However, to Asians the idea of "strictness" is more often related to parental concern, caring, or involvement. "Parental control" conveys more of an idea of an organizational control of the family to keep it running smoothly rather than the idea of limiting individual freedom. (Chao, 1994) In other words, "authoritarian" is good to the Chinese mind, but bad to the Western mind. An example of how misunderstanding can occur across the two cultures can be seen in the standard dictionary definition of guan (管,) which my dictionary defines as to "run, manage, administer, have charge of, subject to discipline," which has a feeling of cold formality and efficiency about it. However, in actual usage in China, the word guan has a very positive connotation, having meanings such as "to care for" or even to "love." So, parental care, concern, and involvement are synonymous with firm control and guidance of the child. (Tobin et al., (1989), cited in Chao (1994)).

With the above caveat firmly implanted in our minds, let's proceed to examine some techniques used by Chinese mothers in order to raise their children. One technique mentioned in the research literature is jihui jiaoyu ("opportunity education"). Chinese parents often realize that too much didactic preaching in the abstract, instructing children to behave themselves and to follow the rules, is ineffective, and perhaps even counterproductive. Therefore, parents should watch carefully in order to find "teaching moments," if I may use that hackneyed phrase. For example, a parent might see another misbehaving child disciplined by his parents, and then take the opportunity to point out to her own child that, if he does the same thing, the same unhappy results will follow in his life. Another technique that perhaps is more questionable is hei lian bai lian ("black face, white face"), which is the Chinese way of doing a Mutt and Jeff, good cop-bad cop routine. Chinese opinion is apparently divided on this, because some parents in one study said that it was most important for the mother and father to present a united front to the misbehaving child. The "black face" parent will read the child the riot act, and the "white face" parent will try mitigate the wrath of his or her spouse. (Fung 1999) But for Chinese parents, the parenting technique that stands out above all the rest is shaming the child. I will give some examples, and ask you to thank God you never had to run the guantlet of a Chinese upbringing.

First, shame needs to be defined. It is so close to guilt that it is difficult to separate the two concepts without some focused attention. Although both emotions are similar, and both follow on an action that the principal wishes he hadn't done, there are several distinctions. First, guilt is a violation of a moral or ethical principle, whereas shame may or may not be. One may be ashamed of losing a ping-pong game, but one is not guilty of doing so. Second, guilt does not need anyone else in order for it to be experienced; shame, on the other hand, is felt by receiving the disapproval of one's group members, whether family, work unit, society, etc. One can feel guilty without anyone else knowing about one's infraction. It comes from within; it is the voice of a violated conscience. Third, the punishment experienced by those experiencing shame is more particular, consisting of the fear of social expulsion and abandonment. Fourth, guilt can be assuaged by confession and reparation, whereas shame is irreversible. One does not make shameful actions right, one avoids them. (Fung 1999) China is an honor society, and to lose one's honor by being shamed is so serious that shame can actually strike one dead. (Darwin (1872), Nathanson (1992), cited in Fung (1999))

Chinese parents shame their children in a way that Western parents would, well, find shameful. However, their shaming does have limits. A Chinese mother or father will be careful not to shame his or her child so much that the child will withdraw and give up on its task.

Also, a good Chinese parent will not shame a child for doing something that the child has not actually done. This is somewhat off the subject of shaming, but I should mention here that although I have heard of some Chinese parents who apologized for mistakes made, I think as a general rule, it is very hard for Chinese parents to apologize, once a parenting mistake is made. In Shanghai, in 1995, my wife, three children, and I were chatting with a group of students in my apartment. They were asking about my children's childhood, and as we were talking, I made a minor factual mistake, which was pointed out to me by my oldest daughter, and I said "sorry," whereupon all the Chinese students in the room broke out laughing. To this day I often experience unexplained, and sometimes inappropriate laughter, and I constantly have to ask for explanations. So, this time, I asked why everyone was laughing. One of the student's responded, "Parents in China NEVER apologize to their children!" Therefore apparently, children are shamed constantly, and when the inevitable mistake comes, they rarely receive a parental apology!

I suspect you will cringe at the several incidents of shaming that I will describe below. First, however, I should point out the interesting fact that a Chinese child's initial sense of shame is said to be instilled within him by the tender average age of three-and-a-half years. Something poured into a child's nurturing that young will stay with him his entire life. The implications of this are simple. Every foreigner should be very, very careful not to cause embarrassment or shame to a Chinese person. They cannot help but be very sensitive to an embarrassment or shame a foreigner may cause. And the sad political state of China in the nineteenth century, the Opium Wars, the burning of the Summer Palace during the Boxer Rebellion by the foreign powers, the loss of Taiwan, etc., etc., are something they are very, very sensitive about. It is much harder to engage a Chinese person in order to dispassionately discuss an historical or political question, because it seems that shame is right under the surface. It's not a question of law or treaty (it seems to me), but rather a question of "the world made us look bad and shamed us, and robbed us of our honor". I remember a student once told me that I must feel great as an American because America was the strongest military and political power in the world, and that everyone "respected" us. I responded that no, it didn't feel great, it felt dangerous and expensive, it might subject my son to military service and death, and besides, most countries in the world don't respect us. I got the feeling that it wasn't world peace and the comity of nations that was driving this discussion, it was rather honor, and how China could get some more of it.

Before I mention some incidents I uncovered in a research paper, I should like to mention when the Chinese concept of shaming entered my consciousness. I noticed that parents would put their index finger on the nose of a child and say the equivalent of "Do better!" (We put our index finger on someone's chest when we want to be forceful; the Chinese put the finger on the other party's nose. In fact, when they want to refer to themselves, they will place their finger on their nose and say "Me?" instead of putting the finger to the chest like Westerners.) It doesn't matter how well the poor child did, he was always being compared to someone else who did better. If the child made a "B," he was questioned as to why he did not make an "A." Or, he is told that his cousin made an "A," so why can't he make an "A," too? Whenever I would praise a child to his parent, the parent would always say that whatever I was praising was "no good." This perhaps was the famous Chinese modesty in operation, but I was told that the practice originated in the Chinese idea that if you praise the child too much, he will get lax and quit working; but if you keep telling him how lousy he's doing, it will shame him and make him work harder. Chinese students are constantly being compared to each other in order to shame them to greater efforts. Their grades are publicly posted on the walls of schools (including middle schools), and the students are ranked in each subject, and the rankings change periodically. As a professor, I love this, because I can publicly post on the college computer network students' grades (by name, not just by student number), and not have to worry about some privacy-crazed, crybaby student going to the ACLU and costing my university and me tens of thousands of dollars in time and money. Chinese students are taught to put up with some shame, because they have endured so much of it, as children. (Fung 1999) I recall judging a mock case competition, and hearing a Chinese professor smilingly tell one of the teams, in front of all the participants, that if he were giving them a grade, it would be an "F." As I internally cringed, the team members happily smiled back to the professor.

Punishment for a Western child generally ends after the transgression ends. But a Chinese parent will often bring up the past transgression and continue the shaming. How does the parent shame the child? The mother (or father) will use words, such as "I want to bury my head in the ground," or "You made your mother lose face."

The parent will use gestures, such as turning the whole body away from the child, and then saying sarcastically, "How come I have such a child?" A Chinese mother will enlist other children to use as benchmarks in order to carry out her campaign of shame. Other children are "normal" and "well-behaved," her child is not. The mother may suggest to the child that the whole family should go to the playground without taking the child. Public spanking of the child is resorted to often, as is name-calling, derogatory attributions, threats of abandonment, invoking a third party to sit in judgment of the child, angry intonation, loud or slow delivery of chastising words, sighs, making disapproving sounds, staring at the child, frowning, pursing up the lips, and reticence or silence. (Fung 1999) Is it any wonder that Chinese use the phrase "soft American?" After surviving childhood, they don't need military training.

Here is an example of child raising recorded by an anthropologist. A three-year old Chinese child named Didi approached the researchers' unattended camcorder. Approached, mind you, not destroyed. I suspect the Western parent would have stopped the little kid and that would have been the end of it. But listen to what poor little Didi had to endure. The mother threatened to spank him. She announced to everyone that her child was the sort of child who didn't obey rules. The kid was now perfectly obedient. Nevertheless, his mother spanked him, and the child sat down on the floor, crying. Not satisfied, his mother continued to publicly chastise him, saying "We don't want you," and "Let him cry; it doesn't matter," and "Look how ugly your crying will be on tape." But this wasn't enough for poor little Didi. His five-year old sister had to get in on the act. She started to call him "Ugly monster! Ugly monster!" She urged her mother to reprimand him some more, and then turned, and spanked Didi herself! (I have heard of several examples of siblings being authorized to spank their younger counterparts). Didi's torment, excuse me, training, lasted four-and-a-half minutes, all for the terrible crime of approaching a camcorder. (Fung 1999)

It is ironic that a stereotypical figure has arisen in China in recent years, whose essence is diametrically opposed to the fine children produced by Chinese Tiger Mamas. I am speaking of "little emperors." They are only children, products of the One Child Policy. Their parents are survivors of the Cultural Revolution, who suffered untold privation and indignity during that troubled time, and who want to compensate by spoiling their children into extinction. You can see these sad rotund creatures standing in front of MacDonalds, licking feverishly on an ice cream as their mother or father hurries inside to buy them a Big Mac. My feeling is that the "little emperor" phenomenon is a relatively unusual one, being notable especially because it is out of the mainstream. I remember little emperors the way I remember that a young teenage girl in the early 1990s was known by name to tens of millions of people in Ningxia Hui Autonomous Region. She was famous because she was unmarried and pregnant, and back then, that condition was nigh unto inconceivable.

No discussion of child rearing would be complete without a mention of that universal parental bugaboo of potty training. It is not so true anymore in the cities, where Pampers are now readily available, but in the late 1990s, they weren't to be seen. But interestingly, cloth diapers weren't to be seen, either. The little kids would wander the streets with their mother with pants vertically split in the rear. Even in the coldest winter, rotund little children could be seen bundled up like the Michelin tire man, with their cherry-red bottoms exposed to the elements. I have a naturally inquisitive nature, so upon confronting this phenomenon, I asked myself, where do these kids go to the bathroom in public? They must not hold it; otherwise their pants wouldn't be split. I began to closely observe the little tykes, as I encountered them in public. I observed that their mothers would simply position their charges over a spot of grass, a curb, wherever. The effluent was so small as to not upset the delicately balanced ecosystem of a Chinese city. I was beginning to think that the Chinese were on to something, having done the environmentally friendly thing by eschewing Pampers, until I saw a little child parked by his mother upon a counter at a store where I was contemplating a purchase. Suddenly, I saw liquid running down the front of the glass showcase, obscuring my view of the products on sale. I have now become utterly convinced of the necessity of Pampers for openness, development, and a harmonious society.

The former scarcity of Pampers illustrates the overall general lack of paper in China, which was noticeable in the 1990s, but which has became less aggravating in the 2000s. I have become accustomed to hoarding scratch paper, printing on the back of paper, and doing whatever I can to preserve paper. The paper napkins at restaurants are really tiny little Kleenex packets, which my wife hoards religiously. The foreigner who attempts to use a public restroom expecting to find toilet paper there, is very foolish. There was a time when even airports didn't have toilet paper in the restrooms, but that problem has gloriously been remedied. Although times are changing, any foreigner who ventures into the public without his personal stash of toilet paper had doggone better be well-regulated. I knew a young Chinese woman who, having used a public toilet, reached for her private toilet paper only to discover that she didn't have any. Using typical Chinese resourcefulness, she stuck her hand out from under the stall door into the public space, and begged plaintively, "Does anyone have any toilet paper for me?" A Good Samaritan anonymously placed her gift into my friend's open hand. But you probably won't be able to do that, because you don't speak Chinese.

The One Child Policy

The One Child Policy was implemented by the Chinese government in 1979 for the simple reason that the government felt there were too many people in China. Ironically, one reason that there were too many people in China is because Mao Zedong felt that population was a weapon, and he wanted to increase it in order to wield it in world politics. Once, Mao urged Josef Stalin to start a nuclear war with America, because Russia and China together had more population than the U.S.A., and so after the radioactive dust had settled, even though hundreds of millions of Chinese people would be killed, there would still be more Chinese left standing. (Chang and Halliday 2005) Mao felt that more people meant more hands to build the Communist state; however, the government shifted its thinking to consider that more people would mean more mouths to feed. This attitude, plus improvements in medical technology which lowered the mortality rate, resulted in a nation with seven percent of the world's landmass having to feed 23% of the world's population. Since 1949, when the People's Republic of China was founded, till 2005, China has doubled the size of its population from 540 million to 1.3 billion. China has the largest national population on the entire planet. (McLoughlin 2005) The One Child Policy was itself initiated in 1979, but the government had taken steps before that to get a handle on its proliferating population. Contraceptives were officially approved in 1954, and were made widely available in 1962. Family planning was voluntary until 1970, when the government required families to have no more than two children. This program was unevenly enforced. The government finally got serious, and instituted the famous One Child Policy at the end of the 1970s. At that time, the government set a population target at 1.2 billion people by 2000. The nationwide census in 2000 returned a figure of

1.3 billion, which was fairly close to the government's target. (Fong, 2002)

Despite its name, the One Child Policy is not really a one-child policy. There are many exceptions granted to Chinese couples possessed with the urge to procreate. For example, the rules are looser for rural couples, which are allowed a second child five years after the first child is born (however, usually this applies only if the first child is a girl). Another big exception is granted to ethnic minorities, who are allowed to have two or three children in cities, and often even three or four. Tibetans are allowed to have an unlimited amount of children in rural areas. (Bulte, et al. 2011) Another well-known exception is that, if both mother and father are only children, they will be allowed a second child. (McLoughlin, 2005)

The government has used a combination of carrot and stick in order to implement the One Child Policy. Bonuses have been paid to those couples that gave birth to only one child, until the child was 14 years old. Those who gave birth to more than one child were subject to stiff fines. In addition, the government would refuse to register later-born children, which made it difficult for them to attend public school, to receive welfare benefits, and to obtain employment with the government. The cost of obstetric care for unapproved births was more than for the first child. First children had priority to attend preferred schools. Preferential access to scarce public housing and health care was given to parents who pledged not to give birth to more than one child. The only child enjoyed free nursery care, free medical care, and free primary school tuition. Maternity leave for the mother of a single child was extended to six months or longer. However, even more powerful than governmental granting or taking away of money and perks was the social pressure in favor of the One Child Policy exerted by families and neighborhoods. (McLoughlin 2005; Rosenberg & Jing 1996)

The goal of the One Child Policy was straightforward – to control China's burgeoning population. But government-contrived social policies are often subject to Milton Friedman's Law of Unintended Consequences. There have been several deleterious effects that have followed upon the adoption of the One Child Policy. The first untoward thing that has happened is that the normal sex ratio has been skewed, so that now there are so many more men than women that it is often difficult for men to find wives. The normal male to female birth ratio across the globe is about 105 male births to 100 female births. In 1964, the ratio in China was 103.5 males to 100 females. In 1992, the rate was 118.5 males to 100 females. (Rosenberg and Jing, 1996) How did this happen? One hypothesis is that there was an unintended reaction of the One Child Policy with the traditional Chinese preference for one son. If parents are restricted in the number of children that they can have, then couples perhaps undertake efforts to ensure that there is a son. They can use sex-selective techniques to kill off their daughters in order to ensure that the only offspring they are allowed is a son. Some techniques employed might be selective abortions using ultrasound technology, even though it is illegal for doctors to reveal the sex of a baby using an ultrasound device. (Laws prohibiting disclosure of ultrasound results can easily be circumvented by means of bribery.) Ultrasound equipment by the 1990s was widely available, even in rural areas. Infanticide or simple neglect might often be employed, even though the government has made those practices illegal, also. This hypothesis, that the One Child Policy, traditional son preference, and ultrasound technology has led to a decrease in the number of women and girls, has been confirmed by research. Bulte, Heerink, and Zhang (2011) claim that the One Child Policy has played an "important role" in distorting recent Chinese sex ratios, and that cultural preference for sons was a "major force."

Another unfortunate byproduct of the One Child Policy is the effect it has had on traditional Chinese family relations. This effect could be one of the most far-reaching of all the effects the One Child Policy has had on Chinese family life. (Rosenberg and Jing, 1996) One does not have to be in China for very long before he is made aware of the importance of family. People are called by family names even when they are not family: Girlfriends call their boyfriends "Brother." I have been called "Grandfather" by dozens of little children I don't even know. Chinese are given generation names so that extended relatives of the same generation can be linked together with a common generation name. An elderly relative will keep track in an ancient book of the names of members of his extended clan who are scattered all over China. I recall a Chinese student staying with us in America who, upon receiving a phone call from a relative in Detroit, exclaimed: "I am so happy! My fifth-cousin is coming to see me!" Fifth cousin! My son, upon hearing the news, expressed skepticism that one could be so thrilled about seeing a fifth cousin. In my personal experience, I never had even heard of a fifth cousin. My student was less than a year old when she had last met this middle-aged fifth cousin at a family reunion. The fifth cousin drove from Detroit, stopped by my home in South Carolina to see his distant relative, gave her a color TV set, and then continued on to Disneyworld. The Chinese language has dozens of different names for family relationships to which English-speaking people only give one word. For example, we say uncle. It's not so simple in China. A father's elder brother is not simply "uncle," but bobo. A father's younger brother is shushu. A mother's brother is jiujiu. Grandchildren and grandparents are given different titles, depending on if they are on the mother's or father's side. In addition, there are regional variations. Many of those rich and varied family relationships depend on brothers and sisters, because without brothers and sisters, nephews and cousins and uncles and aunts can't exist, and the One Child Policy does away with brothers and sisters.

The One Child Policy has not only harmed the family structure, it has also possibly had deleterious effects on the one child, himself. How to educate the only child, and how to care for him psychologically, is one of the most discussed social issues in China. Accounts in the popular press often detail parents' and teachers' perceptions that only children are more willful and spoiled than other children. Much research has agreed with the popular perception, but some has not. For example, only children have been found to be deficient in persistence at a task and behavioral control, and they have been found to be more egocentric than children with siblings. (Jiao, Ji, & Jing (1986), cited in Rosenberg and Jing, 1996) Other negative character traits and behavior problems discovered in the research are short attention span, obstinacy, demand for immediate gratification, disrespect of elders, bossiness, timidity, and lack of initiative (Wan, et al., cited in Rosenberg & Jing, 1996) However, other studies have shown certain advantages for only Chinese children, especially cognitive and intellectual advantages, such as imagination, language, and productive thinking. (Falbo 1982, cited in Rosenberg & Jing, 1996) Other studies have shown no difference between only Chinese children and Chinese children with siblings. (Rosenberg & Jing, 1996)

Finally, the One Child Policy is said to harm Chinese mothers. American opponents of China's One Child Policy have attacked abuses associated with the policy, such as cadres (Communist Party officials) killing babies, or physically forcing women to undergo sterilizations or abortion. (Aird (1990); Mosher (1993), cited in Fong 2002)I know of one incident where a young man in Shanghai, upon deciding that, if his pregnant wife delivered her second baby it would have negative repercussions for his career, insisted (along with several of the mother's relatives) that the wife have an abortion. The woman, a Christian, was absolutely opposed to the abortion on moral grounds, and yet, could not or would not resist her family's pressure. Scholarly studies have chronicled the suffering of women who long for additional children, and the pain of other women who are blamed by husbands and parents-in-law for giving birth to only daughters instead of only sons. Other women have been force to undergo unwanted surveillance, gynecological exams, mandatory contraception, fines, and the loss of benefits or jobs. (Anagnost (1988, 1995;) Greenhalgh and Li (1995), Kaufman (1993); Wolf (1985), cited in Fong, 2002)

I have often asked high school classes what is their opinion of the One Child Policy. Surprisingly, this younger generation of Chinese usually split about 50-50, pro and con. Their knowledge of the effects of the policy is limited; they merely know the purpose of it. The students' arguments about it are either purely instrumental or purely personal - they say it's necessary because of the large population, or they say they are against it, because they want to have more than one child (usually two; I have yet to hear a student say they want three). When I ask them who is going to take care of the older generation because there aren't enough children to do this, they are usually surprised, because they hadn't thought of that before. One thing I have noticed about these discussions, whether with young people or adults, is that the discussion is rarely placed within a moral framework. Nobody asks, is it moral or not for a government to intrude into someone's personal life to tell them how many children they can have? Most Chinese, in my experience, don't think that way. They think about "society," or, "is this policy good for me?" I have been told that there are many discussions on television about the policy, and one can sense uneasiness. But it seems to me that the questions that are being asked are not moral ones, but pragmatic ones – unless one takes "moral" to be a collectivist socialist morality which is offended by any individual choice that trenches upon the rights of "society."

While the sad effects of the One Child Policy have been noted well in the West, there is another unintended effect that has been beneficial for single-child urban girls. These urban girls do not have to compete with brothers for family resources, and are thus better funded for important things, like education. One researcher, having stated this, went on to say that rural women would not benefit from more parental resources being directed towards them, because there were fewer educational opportunities in the countryside. (Fong 2002) I have talked to two young rural women whose brothers were educated before them, leaving no money to educate their sisters. I am not sure whether the first one would have benefited, if she were an only child or not. The first young country girl was our ayi ("Auntie," in our case, our housekeeper) She was the sixth of seventh children, raised in the countryside. Her parents wanted a son, and when they failed six straight times, they tried the seventh time and produced a son. This family was rural and poor. Our ayi never had a toy to play with, and she had no high school education. Public high schools are not free, ironically enough when one considers that China is theoretically a socialist country. Her parents could not send her to school, so they concentrated their limited resources to get their seventh child, the son, through high school. If our ayi had been an only child, would she have been able to go to school? I don't know, but somehow I expect she would actually have been able to. I talked to another young woman who grew up in the countryside, a 26-year old married woman who I met on a tour. We were on a bus in Nanjing, in Zhejian province, touring the famous Kejia (Hakka) people's round houses. Her husband sat behind us, with my wife. This young woman told me she had grown up in the country, with two brothers. Her parents paid for one of her brother's education. The brother took advantage of it and ended up getting a Ph.D. at China's top-ranked university, Beijing University. The sister with whom I was conversing took menial jobs, went to schools, and finally got her high school diploma in her early twenties. She then went to college, and she had just graduated. She contemplated getting her Master's Degree. She was well traveled, and business-savvy. One would never guess she came from the country. I am almost certain that if the One Child Policy had applied to her, and if she were an only child, she would have had her high school and college diploma sooner. However, it should also be pointed out that, although the One Child Policy had not made her to be an only child upon whom all the family resources were focused, not only did this rural girl get her education, but also her brother got a Ph.D. It was sad, however, to hear her tell me she now had absolutely nothing in common with her husband, a simple man from the country who was making pennies in a dead-end government job, while she was making all the money for the family. She was evenly matched when her parents arranged the marriage, but she had outpaced him, and now her marriage was a mere formal shell.

As a side note, when I hear these classic stories of gender discrimination, I am amazed at how calmly and gently the girls describe the situation. There is not a trace of bitterness. I remember, in 1995, a graduate of Shanghai Foreign Languages University, leaving her table in a restaurant in order to come over and help us order. In the course of our conversation, she told me she had applied with another male graduate of the university for a particular job, but had not gotten the job. I asked her why not. She replied sweetly, "Because I am a girl." Then she laughed. Not much feminist rage there.

HOW CHINESE FAMILY VALUES ARE A LOT LIKE DIXIE'S

I had been coming to China for several years, experiencing how strange and exotic everything was, when one day it suddenly occurred to me that there were a lot of things in China that reminded me of my life in the American South. The first was the emphasis on the family. American southerners will talk about their families, kin-relations, and pedigree until the wee hours of the morning, if you let them. I recall a northern professor at the University of South Carolina who came south, got lost, and asked a woman for directions. He later related his amazement to his class. He said the woman, instead of giving him directions to the person's home he was trying to find, began to give him a detailed genealogical record and family tree of the person he was trying to find. The Yankee professor was clearly mystified. I never had noticed that about my own culture. Most things about one's own culture require an outsider to point out, because one is so close to them that he doesn't notice. This attention to genealogical detail is, of course, also present everywhere in China. The ubiquitous family ancestor tablets are a lasting reminder that one's ancestors are always present. Likewise, American southerners worship their ancestors – even if their ancestors were drunkards, thieves, and swindlers.

China is an honor society, where honor is upheld, and shame is to be avoided like death, very much like the American South. Dueling is a relic of times past, in which gentlemen upheld their honor. One of the last duels fought in Western civilization took place in 1880, about fifteen miles from my home in South Carolina. I passed the monument every day for years, while driving to work. The monument is dedicated to Col. Cash and Col. Shannon, the two duelists, the latter of which was dispatched to his eternal reward by Col Cash. Maintaining one's honor is deadly serious business in the South. Closely related to the concept of honor is the importance of maintaining the family name, which American Southerners do with diligence. Growing up, the worst thing a rebellious teenager could do was to sully his family's honor in the community. I recall, as I grew up, references to so-and-so being of "good stock," an old expression that meant "of a good family." If you have read this chapter, you will appreciate somewhat the longing in the Chinese soul to maintain the family name. When children are disciplined, their mother tells them, "you will make your Mama lose face!" Genealogical records are kept tracing family ancestors for generations and generations. Heaven and earth are turned over in order to have a son in order to maintain the family name.

I suspect that the rural foundations of both Chinese and American Southern culture have created a lot of the similarities between the two cultures. I notice that in the rural south where I live, even today people call each other "Miss Jane," and "Mr. Dan," honorific titles of respect, paralleled by similar Chinese titles. The Chinese call each other Teacher John, Policeman Bob, and the like. And just as American Southerners will often call someone who is not a member of the family "Uncle Joe," the Chinese do the same, except even more. Little children repeatedly call me Yeye (Grandfather). Girlfriends call their boyfriends Gege ("Older Brother"). The woman whom one hires to cook and clean is called Ayi ("Auntie"). A foreigner is given the nickname Bobo ("Uncle").

Manners and hospitality are a staple of life in both American Southern culture and Chinese culture. I recall recently an organization created in the memory of Robert E. Lee at a Southern college, perhaps a fraternity, offering public lessons on etiquette. Having become jaded by the crude barbarity of modern American popular culture, this pleasantly jarred me. Southern hospitality is, of course famous, but Chinese hospitality is its equal. I had been coming to China for fifteen years before I managed to pay for my Chinese host's meal. I had to physically hold his hand as he tried to plop the money on the counter, while I fished for my wallet with my other hand. I remember poor students taking me to eat, and me feeling so bad for them when they absolutely refused to let me pay. "You are the guest!" they would protest in indignation as I offered to pay. They even use sneaky verbal techniques to keep you from paying, like saying "Xia yi ci!" (Next time!). Of course, the next time when you offer to pay, they say Xia yi ci! I have said it many times: Chinese treat foreigners like royalty. I recall how, the first time I taught in China in 1995, students rushed to erase the board, and to wipe the chalk dust off my seat. Students insisted that I, the teacher, walk through the door first, even if the student was a woman. This was, and still is, a big problem, because of my Southern training that strikes my conscience every time I walk through a door, ahead of a woman. My Chinese hosts always make me sit in the seat of honor at a dinner table. They drink what I drink, to show respect. I have even been told to sit on the right passenger side of a taxi, because that is the seat of honor. I thought all of this was quaint, at first. I then realized it was endearing me to the Chinese people.

Finally, there is one last parallel between the American South and China that should be told. Our mamas share common values. They unashamedly spank their kids. And they do it without fear of some over-educated social scientist saying they are going to warp the child's personality. And they both know the difference between correction and child abuse. I suspect that if you take the following two values attributed to Chinese mothers, values which were found to exceed "Euro-American" mothers' values (Chao 1994), stack them up against Southern American mamas instead of Euro-American mamas, and there wouldn't be any statistical difference between the Chinese mothers and Southern American mothers at all:

- Mothers must train their child to work very hard and to be disciplined
- When a child continues to disobey you, he/she deserves a spanking.

I suspect that these two simple Chinese beliefs explain quite well the overwhelming courtesy, kindness, and discipline the American professor receives from his students while teaching his classes in China.

CHAPTER REFERENCES

Aird, John S. (1990) Slaughter of the Innocents: Coercive Birth Control in China. Washington, DC: AEI Press.

Anagnost, Ann (1988). Family Violence and Magical Violence: The "Woman-as-Victim" in China's One-Child Family Policy. Women and Language l(2):16-22.

Anagnost, Ann (1995) "A Surfeit of Bodies: Population and the Rationality of the State in Post-Mao China," In Conceiving the New World Order: The Global Politics of Reproduction. F. D. Ginsburg and R. Rapp, eds.. Berkeley: University of California Press. pp. 22-41.

Beijing Review (1981). Changes in the Marriage Conventions," pp. 20-22.

Bian, Y.; Shu, X. and Logan, J.R. (2000). Wage and Job Inequalities in the Working Careers of Men and Women in Tianjin. In Redrawing Boundaries: Gender, Households, and Work in

China, B. Entwisle and G. Henderson (eds.) Berkeley: University of California Press.

Carlson, Darren K. (2005) Americans and Guns: Danger or Defense?, Gallup, http://www.gallup.com/poll/14509/americans-guns-danger-defense.aspx, retrieved February 15, 2012.

Chang, Jung and Halliday, Roy (2005). Mao: The Unknown Story. Jonathan Cape.

Chao, Ruth K. (1994) Beyond Parental Control and Authoritarian Parenting Style: Understanding Chinese Parenting Through the Cultural Notion of Training. Child Development 65(4):1111-1119.

Che, Yan; and Cleland, John (2003). Contraceptive Use Before and After Marriage in Shanghai. Studies in Family Planning 34(1):44-52.

Ching, Man Lam (1997). 'A Cultural Perspective of the Study of Chinese Adolescent Development. Child and Adolescent Social Work Journal 14(2):85–113.

Chua, Amy (2011). Battle Hymn of the Tiger Mother. Penguin Press.

Darwin, Charles (1872) 1872 The Expression of the Emotions in Man and Animals. London: John Murray.

Engel, John W. (1984). Marriage in the People's Republic of China: Analysis of a New Law. Journal of Marriage and Family 46(4):955-961.

Falbo, T. (1982). "Only Children in America." In M.E. Lamb and B. Sutton-Smith (eds.), Sibling Relationships. Hillsdale, N.J.: Erlbaum, pp. 285-304.

Fei, Xiaotong (1982) On Changes in the Chinese Family Structure. Tianjin Social Science 3:2-5.

Feng, L.; Anderson, A.; Wang, S.; Zhang, J. (1995) Research on Marriage, Family and Women's Status in Beijing. Beijing: Beijing Economic Institute.

Fong, Vanessa L. (2002) China's One-Child Policy and the Empowerment of Urban Daughters. American Anthropologist 104(4):1098-1109.

Family Planning Association of Hong Kong (1997). Knowledge, Attitude and Practice Study on Family Planning. Hong Kong: Author.

Family Planning Association of Hong Kong (2000). Report on Youth Sexual Study (Out-of-school Survey), 1996. Hong Kong: Author.

Fox, G.L.; Benson, M.L., DeMaris, A.A. and Van Wyk, J. (2002). Economic Distress and Intimate Violence: Testing Family Stress and Resources Theories. Journal of Marriage and the Family 64:793-807.

Fung, Heidi (1999). Becoming a Moral Child: The Socialization of Shame among Young Chinese Children. Ethos 27(2):180-209.

Gao, L.L.; Chan, Sally Wai-Chi; Mao, Qing (2009). Depression, Perceived Stress, and Social Support Among First-Time Chinese Mothers And Fathers in The Post-Partum Period. Research in Nursing and Health (32): 50–58.

Greenhalgh, Susan and Li, Jiali (1995) Engendering Reproductive Policy and Practice in Peasant China: For a Feminist Demography of Reproduction. Signs 20(3):601-642.

Guo, Baorong and Huang, Jin (2005) Marital and Sexual Satisfaction in Chinese Families: Exploring the Moderating Effects. Journal of Sex & Marital Therapy 31:21-29.

Ho, David Y.F. (1986). "Chinese Patterns of Socialization: A Critical Review." In The Psychology of Chinese People, Michael H. Bond (ed.). Hong Kong: Oxford University Press.

Holroyd, Eleanor; Lopez, Violeta and Chan, Sally Wai-Chi (2011). Negotiating "Doing The Month": An Ethnographic Study Examining the Postnatal Practices of Two Generations of Chinese Women. Nursing & Health Science 13:47-52.

Honig, E., & Hershatter, G. (1988). Personal voices: Chinese women in the 1980's. Stanford, CA: Stanford University Press.

Higgins, Louise T. and Sun, Chunhui (2007). Gender, Social Background and Sexual Attitudes among Chinese Students. Culture, Health & Sexuality 9(1):31-42.

Huang, X.H. (2000) The Present and Future of Caesarean Section. The Journal of the Chinese Applied Obstetrics and Gynecology 16:259-261.

Im-em, W.; Archvanitkul, K. and Kanchanachitra, C. (2004) Sexual Coercion Among Women in Thailand: Results from the WHO Multi-country Study On Women's Health and Life Experiences. Paper presented at the Population of America Association, Boston, MA, August 3-5, 2004.

Jiao, S.; Ji, G. and Jing, Q. (1986). Comparative Study of Behavioral Qualities of Only Children and Sibling Children. Child Development 57:357-361.

Kaufman, Joan (1993). The Cost of IUD Failure in China. Studies in Family Planning 24(3):194-196.

Knodel, J.; Saengtienchai, C.; VanLandingham, M. and Lucas, R. (1999). Sexuality, Sexual Experience, and the Good Spouse: Views of Married Thai Men and Women. In Genders and Sexualities in Modern Thailand, P.A. Jackson and N.M. Cook (eds.), Bangkok: Silkworm Books, pp. 93-113.

Lau, S. and Cheung, P.C. (1987). Relations Between Chinese Adolescents' Perception of Parental Control and Organization and Their Perception of Parental Warmth. Developmental Psychology 23(5):726-729.

Laumann, E.O.; Gagnon, J.H.; Michael, R.T. and Michaels, S. (1994) The Social Organization of Sexuality: Sexual Practices in the United States. Chicago, IL: University of Chicago Press.

Lennon, M.C. and Rosenfield, S. (1994). Relative Fairness and the Division of Housework: The Importance of Options. American Jouranl of Sociology 100:506-531.

Leung, S.S.K.; Martinson, I.M.; Arthur, D. 2005. Postpartum Depression and Related Psychological Variables in Hong Kong Chinese Women: Fndings From a Prospective Study. Research in Nursing and Health 28:27-38.

Levy, Marion (1949). The Family Revolution in Modern China. Cambridge: Harvard University Press.

Li, W. (2007). The Research of the Only Child Parents' Aged Life Question in Urban Area. Journal of Pingyuan University 24(3):32-34.

Liu, D.; Ng, M.L; Zhou, L.P. and Haeberle, E.J. (1997) Sexual Behaviour in Modern China: Report on the Nationwide Survey of 20,000 Men and Women. New York: Continuum.

Logan, J.R.; Bian, F., and Bian, Y. (1998). Tradition and Change in the Urban Chinese Family: The Case of Living Arrangements. Social Forces 76:851-882.

Lu, H.; Geng, X.W. and Liu, Y. (2006) Role Adaptation of Family and Influencing Factors in the Postpartum Period. Chinese General Practice 9:1780-1782 (in Chinese).

Lumbiganon, P.; Laopaiboon, M., Gulmezoglu, A.M.; et al. (2010). Method of Delivery and Pregnancy Outcomes in Asia: the WHO Global Survey on Maternal and Perinatal Health 2007-2008. Lancet 375:490-499.

Ma, Hongnan; and Rosenberg, Ed (1998). Learning Womanhood in China. Anthropology and Humanism 23(1):5-29.

Mao, Q.; Su, S.Y.; Gao, L.L. 2008. Stress and Related Factors in Spouses of Primiparas. Chinese Mental Health Journal 1:37-39 (in Chinese).

Marini, M.M. (1980). Effects of the Number and Spacing of Children on Marital and Parental Satisfaction. Demography 17:225-242.

McLoughlin, Caven S. The Coming-of-Age of China's Single-Child Policy. Psychology in the Schools 42(3):305-313.
Mosher, Steven W. (1993). A Mother's Ordeal: One Woman's Fight against China's One-Child Policy. New York: Harcourt Bracd Jovanovich.

Pan, S. (1993). A Sex Revolution in Current China. Journal of Psychology & Human Sexuality 6:1-14.

Pan, _____. (1989). Quantitative Behavioral Analysis of Public Heterosexual Petting Chinese Public Parks. Sexuality in Asia 173-184.

Parish, William L.; Luo, Ye; Laumann, Edward O.; Kew, Melissa and Yu, Zhiyuan. (2007) Unwanted Sexual Activity among Married Women in Urban China. Journal of Sex Research 44(2):158-171.

Parish, William L.; Luo, Ye; Stolzenberg, Ross; Laumann, Edward O.; Farrer, Gracia and Pan, Suiming. Sexual Practices and Sexual Satisfaction: A Population Based Study of Chinese Urban Adults. Archives of Sexual Behavior 36(1):5-20.

Pimentel, Ellen Efron. Just How Do I Love Thee?: Marital Relations in Urban China. Journal of Marriage and the Family 62:32-47.

Renaud, Cheryl; Byers, Sandra E. and Pan, Suiming. (1997). Sexual and Relationship Satisfaction in Mainland China. The Journal of Sex Research 34(4):399-410.

Riley, Nancy E. (1989) Gender and Generation in Modern Beijing. Unpublished doctoral dissertation. Johns Hopkins University, Baltimore, MD.

Riley, _____. Interwoven Lives: Parents, Marriage, and *Guanxi* in China (1994). Journal of Marriage and Family 56(4):791-803.

Rivers, K.; Aggleton, P.; Elizondo, J.;Hernandez, G.; Herrera, G.; Mane, P.; Niang, C.I.; Scott, S. and Setiadi, B. (1998). Gender Relations, Sexual Communication and the Female Condom. Critical Public Health 8:273-290.

Rosenberg, B.G. and Jing, Qicheng. (1996). A Revolution in Family Life: The Political and Social Structural Impact of China's One Child Policy. Journal of Social Issues 52(3):51-69.

So, Ho-wai and Cheung, Fanny M. Review of Chinese Sex Attitudes & Applicability of Sex Therapy for Chinese Couples with Sexual Dysfunction. The Journal of Sex Research 42(2):93-101.

Tao & Jiang, 1993

Thompson, L. (1991). Family Work: Women's Sense of Fairness. Journal of Family Issues 12:181-195.

Tobin, J. J.; Wu, D.Y.H. and Davidson, D.H. (1989). Preschool in Three Cultures. New Haven, CT: Yale University Press.

Triandis, Harry C. (1989). The Self and Social Behavior in Differing Cultural Contexts. Psychological Review 96(3):506-520.

Triandis, Harry C.; Bontempo, Robert; Villareal, Marcelo J.; Asai, Masaaki and Lucca, Nydia. (1988). Individualism and Collectivism: Cross-Cultural Perspectives on Self-Group Relationships. Journal of Personality and Social Psychology 54(2):323-338.

Triandis, Harry C.; McCusker, Christopher and Hui, Harry C. (1990) Multimethod Probes of Individualism and Collectivism. Journal of Personality and Social Psychology 59(5):1006-20.

Twenge, J.M.; Cambell, W.K. and Foster, C.A. (2003). Parenthood and Marital Satisfaction: A Meta-analytic Review. Journal of Marriage and the Family 65:574-583.

Unger, Jonathan (1993). Urban Families in the Eighties: An Analysis of Chinese Surveys, in Chinese Families in the Post-Mao Era, Deborah Davis and Steven Harrell (eds.) University of California Press.

Waite, L. and Joyner, K. (2001). Emotional and Physical Satisfaction With Sex in Married, Cohabiting, and Dating Sexual Unions: Do Men and Women Differ? In Sex, Love, and Health in America, E.O. Laumann & R.T. Michael (eds.), pp. 239-269.

Wan, C.; Fan, C. and Lin, G (1984). A Comparative Study of Certain Differences in Individuality and Sex-based Differences between 5- and 7-year Old Only Children and Non-only Children. Acta Psycholgica Sinica 16:383-391.

Wang, H.H. and Zhang, C.H. (2008) The Mental Health Status of Primiparas' Spouses During the Pospartum Period in the Rural Area. Maternal and Child Health Care of China 34:4884-4885 (in Chinese).

Whyte, M.K. and Parish, W.L. (1984). Urban Life in Contemporary China. Chicago: University of Chicago Press.

Wolf, Margery (1984). Marriage, Family, and the State in Contemporary China. Pacific Affairs 57:213-236.

Wolf, Margery (1985). Revolution Postponed: Women in Contemporary China. Stanford: Stanford University Press.

Wu, H. and Lu, H. (2009). The Role Adaptiation of New Mothers. Nursing Research 23:596-598.

Wu, D. (1985) Child Training in Chinese Culture. In Chinese Culture and Mental Health, W.S. Tseng and D. Wu (eds.). Orlanda, FL: Academic Press.

Wu, D. and Tseng, W.S. (1985). Introduction: The Characteristics of Chinese Culture. In Chinese Culture and Mental Health, W.S. Tseng and D. Wu (eds.). Orlando, FL: Academic Press.

Xu, A. (1990). Passivity, Decision Power and Low Satisfaction. Xe Hui Xue Yian Jiu 3:105-108.

Xu, Xiaohe and Whyte, Martin King. Love Matches and Arranged Marriages: A Chinese Replication. Journal of Marriage and the Family 52:709-722.

Yang, Kuo-Shu (1986). Chinese Personality and Its Change. In The Psychology of the Chinese People, Michael H. Bond (ed.). New York: Oxford University Press.

Young, N.F. (1972). Independence Training From a Cross-cultural Perspective. American Anthropologist 74(3):629-638.

Zhang, K.; Li, D.; Li, H. and Beck, E.J. (1999). Changing Sexual Attitudes and Behaviour in China: Implications for the Spread of HIV and Other Sexually Transmitted Diseases. AIDS Care 11:581-589.

Zhang, Qian Forrest (2004). Economic Transition and New Patterns of Parent-Adult Child Coresidence in Urban China. Journal of Marriage and Family 66:1231-1245.

Zhang, J. (2009). Analysis on Incidence of Cesarean Section and its Related Influencing Factors for 10 Years In Haidian District of Beijing. Chinese Journal of Family Planning 4:219-222.

Zhang, Zailin (2009). Theories of Family in Ancient Chinese Philosophy. Frontiers of Philosophy in China. 4(3):343-359. FRONTIERS OF PHILOSOPHY IN CHINA

Zheng, X. (1997). On the Phenomenon of Female Retreat to the Home. In Social Transition and Women's Development, Y. Zhao and L. Guo (eds.), pp. 113-120.

Zuo, Jiping and Bian, Yanjie (2001). Gendered Resources, Division of Housework, Perceived Fairness – A Case in Urban China. Journal of Marriage and Family 63:1122-1133.

The Chinese have a well-deserved reputation for respecting the elderly. I recall fondly traveling on a city bus in Yinchuan, standing because there were no seats, when a 35 or 40-year-old woman tried to stand to offer me her seat. I was 59 at the time, and not feeling particularly old. It offended my sensibilities, formed by my raising in the South, to sit while a woman was standing. I had become accustomed to doing this if I was the first to arrive at a seat, and was already seated when a woman arrived. I still feel guilty about doing it, but this is the custom on Chinese buses. But to actually deprive a woman of a seat that she had first, so that I could sit, was going too far. I insisted that she keep her seat. She kept offering. We went back and forth several rounds. I kept telling her, "ladies first." She never told me "old men" first, but I knew that was what was driving her. It was killing her to see me standing there, just like it was killing me to think of sitting down while she stood.

It is interesting to consider the different cultural reactions when one is told that he is old. I suspect I am like most Westerners who don't really like to be reminded of advancing age. But Chinese people love to talk about how old you are – age is good, it isn't bad. A taxi driver in the same city of Yinchuan once asked me how old I was. I told him 59. He said I should not say I was 59, but rather 60. I asked him why. He said that 60 is a very great year for Chinese, because it shows you are getting old. If I say 59, that means I have not reached old age yet, and that is unlucky. This anecdote illustrates several Chinese cultural characteristics: superstition, lying is in many cases OK if higher purposes are served, and how old is good. Everything in China is lao (old). If you want to show respect to an older person whose surname is Wang, you call him Lao Wang. If you want to talk about Santa Claus, you refer to Shengdan Laoren (Christmas Old Man). Colonel Sanders is Kendeji Laoren (Kentucky Old Man). So many Chinese kids whom I don't know have called me Lao Yeye ("Old Grandfather") that it makes me feel old to think about it. The Chinese are so into age that they say you are one year old when you are born. To boot, you get an extra year added to your age on Chinese New Year's Day. So, if someone is born the day before New Year's Day, the next day he is two years old instead of two days old. Only in China could something like this happen. Foreigners quickly learn when asking Chinese their age to qualify their question with "Chinese years" or "real years." I suspect that saying "real years" may be construed as culturally imperialistic, because I suspect the

Chinese considered the two extra-added years to be just as real as the others, but when one is trying to gain his bearings in a sea of confusion, one says what he must.

WANG NIAN JIAO

Literally, *wang nian jiao* means "forget the years friendship." It is a close friendship between Chinese who are about twenty or more years apart in age. It is a friendship just like a friendship between peers, the only difference being the discrepancy in age. I suppose such friendships may exist in the West, but there are more of them in China, and the relationship seems sort of exalted, pure, ethereal, almost literary. The phenomenon usually exists between friends of the same sex, but it can also exist between members of the opposite sex. I first heard about this term while chatting with a coworker, a young single woman about 25 years of age. She routinely kept mentioning a friend she was communicating with on the Internet, and I asked her whether he was her boyfriend. She responded no, he was an "old man" from Australia. If your Western mind is as suspicious and paranoid as mine, you may have immediately jumped to the conclusion that this man was some kind of stalker, or pervert, attempting to prey on a young Chinese girl. Actually, he was a happily married Australian businessman with several children, who met the young Chinese girl on a business trip to China, who maintained Internet contact with her, and who saw her (always in the company of the young girl's other girlfriends) when he came to China on business trips. My young co-worker grew up in the countryside, was laced pretty tight morally as countryfolk tend to be, and she had a boyfriend to boot. There was no sense of hanky-panky at all in the relationship. I was tempted to suggest there might be, thought the better of it, and simply told my coworker that such friendships don't exist in the West. She was shocked, and quizzically asked: why not? My coworker said this was *wang nian jiao*, and Chinese people did this all the time. I still don't have the answer to her question.

Shortly thereafter, I asked another young 25-year-old single girl, a manager of an import food store, whether she knew about *wang nian jiao*. She said, of course, everybody did. I then asked her, did she have *wang nian jiao* friends? She replied that over half her friends were at least fifteen years different from her in age. Several were about ten years old, and several were over 40. Most were the same sex, but some were of the opposite sex, the relationships with the latter not possessing even a hint of impropriety. She was also surprised to hear that such relationships were relatively rare in the West.

There has to be something special about such friendships that distinguish them from such friendships in the West, because the Chinese have put a special universally-recognized name, *wang nian jiao*, on the relationship, and Westerners don't do that. These special relationships are considered to be a very good thing. I suspect that the reason such friendships form is because Chinese really do, down in the core of their beings, respect elderly people in a way that Westerners have trouble conceiving. The 25-year old manager of the import food store told me that the reason the Chinese form such friendships is that young people don't have experience in life, and they like to befriend old people so that old people can share their life experiences with them. I sigh almost tearfully when I hear sentiments like that. When I was young, my hippie peers where screaming to not trust anybody over thirty, giving the finger to anybody old and wise.

In order to get a feel for the concept of *wang nian jiao*, I used the phrase as a search term in a Chinese search engine, and randomly chose two Internet articles which related an opposite sex wang nian jiao experience. The first article was written by a young college girl, who, when visiting her family at home, met a middle-aged businessman who was a friend of the family. The young girl discovered that the businessman had daughters living in the same town as her university, and so their relationship became deeper. I love how Chinese who are strangers to each other seem to light up when they find out the other party has a connection to their city. This is really not such a coincidence, because a small, insignificant city can have over seven million or so people in it. But this girl was happy to hear of the connection, and she was also happy to hear that the businessman had an interest in movie photography, as did she. The young girl went back to her university, and there began to receive telephone calls, and then visits, from the businessman, who was in town to see his daughers. Her suspicions were aroused: was this man a "wolf?" Some time passed, and as they get to know each other more, the girl's suspicions were allayed. She is comfortable in the friendship. But unfortunately, one day the businessman suggests that her figure is somewhat plump. This angers the student, and makes her once again suspicious that the businessman is a wolf. She posts her article on the Internet, and asks for the public to comment and to give her advice: is this man a wolf, or is this an example of *wang nian jiao*? If I had dared to comment, I would have mentioned the umpteen times I have had my girth commented upon by Chinese people, some of them of the inquiring student's age and gender, and none of the comments seemed to be maliciously motivated at all, so why was she so suspicious?

The second *wang nian jiao* article I obtained from the Internet told the story of two well known twentieth-century literary figures, Liu Yazi and Xiao Hong. Liu Yazi (1887- 1958) was a politically active poet who supported Sun Yat-sen, became a left-wing member of the Guomingdang (KMT), was purged from the Guomingdang for his leftist proclivities, and who finally befriended Mao Zedong, exchanging poetry with him, and died a member of the Communist Party and the Communist government. In 1939, on a trip to Hong Kong, he discovered that Xiao Hong (1911-1942) was in a Hong Kong hospital. Xiao Hong, 24 years younger than Liu Yazi, was a leftist poet who idolized Lu Xun, that great socialist Chinese twentieth-century literary figure. Xiao Hong had led a tragic and dissolute life, like country singers and leftwing literary figures love to do. Abandoned in a hotel by a fiancé, she was almost sold to a brothel by the hotel owner in order to pay her bill. She broke up with a newspaper editor she had shacked up with in Harbin, married a husband and had gone to Hong Kong to live. While there, she ended up in the hospital, where she was misdiagnosed and subjected to a useless surgical procedure which left her speechless, and eventually, dead. Before she died, Liu Yazi came to see her in the hospital. Their story is told in the Internet article under the title "Liu Yazi's and Xiao Hong's Wang Nian Jiao" (http://cul.china.com.cn/renwu/201107/08/content_4321851.htm, retrieved January 31, 2012, in Chinese) As soon as Liu Yazi unexpectedly came into the room, Xiao Hong broke into tears. Seeing Xiao Hong on the hospital bed, in an emotionally destroyed state, Liu Yazi encouraged her to become strengthened, to conquer her sickness, to begin to have faith in life. He continued to visit her, untiringly sitting next to her sickbed. One day, he wrote an improvised poem named in her honor, while Xiao Hong's husband looked on. Xiao Hong's husband was merely chatting with Xiao Hong to relieve her boredom, not being capable of soaring poetry. Meanwhile, Xiao Hong was starting to look upon Liu Yazi as the second incarnation of Lu Xun. Liu Yazi was not content with composing poems for his younger friend. He later brought flowers, whose fragrant odors permeated the room. Xiao Hong sniffed deeply the flowers, and immediately felt resuscitated from her illness. She felt a kind of passion bubbling up from within her. Liu Yazi told her to write more books, and that he would wait on her to do so so that he could read them. Xiao Hong nodded her head and asked Liu Yazi to sit next to her on the couch, which he did. They began to talk about life, literature, and other interests they held in common. Liu Yazi suggested that Xiao Hong write a poem, using it to pour out her emotions. She did so, and when Liu Yazi returned later to hear it, Xiao Hong poured out to Liu Yazi, using the vehicle of her poetry, her life's emotions and experiences. Liu Yazi was so touched; he composed a poem for Xiao Hong on the spot, no doubt practicing for the time in the near future when he would pour out his heart in poetry to the great Chairman Mao. I suppose that Xiao Hong's husband had quit talking to her to relieve her boredom, since Xiao Hong was being so lovingly entertained. He probably just kept bringing her tea and medicine. The husband did relate later that Liu Yazi had caused the "master's way" and "friendship" to be gathered together in Liu Yazi's person, and that Liu Yazi always gave other people encouragement and faith.

What may we extrapolate from these two *wang nian jiao* stories? I think it is safe to say that should an older man want a wang nian jiao friendship with a younger girl in China, he better not mention her weight, and he needs to be really good with poetry when presenting her flowers.

STATUS OF THE ELDERLY IN MODERN CHINA

According to the 2000 Census, there were 132 million Chinese who were over the age of 60, who accounted for 10.32 percent of the population. Sixty-five percent of these Chinese who were over 60 lived in rural areas. (Pang et al. 2004) Some demographers project that, by 2020, the number of elderly people over 60 years old is expected to reach 16 percent, a total of 230 million people. By 2050, it is expected that 26 percent of the population, representing 400 million Chinese, will be 60 years old or over, more than doubling the percentage of that age group existing in 1960. (Wong and Tang 2006/2007)

The rising number of elderly in China face problems that are peculiar to that country. The one-child policy has had untoward implications, as has China's forced early retirement policies, as has the relatively large rural population. In addition, the rising number of women in the work force takes potential caregivers for the elderly out of the their children's homes. (Wang and Tang 2007) The one-child policy has given rise to a growing ratio of elderly persons relative to the available number of young people who can care for them. If present trends continue, there will (theoretically) be four old people (both sets of parents) for each married couple to care for. (Olson 1998) A "four-two-one" family generational pattern is becoming the norm across urban China, that is to say, two people in a marriage have four parents and one child to take care of. (Wong and Tang 2007)

China's policy with regard to forced retirement has also impacted the plight of the elderly in China. Men are required to retire by 60, and women by 50, young retirement ages by American standards. This policy, which was implemented in order to open up jobs for younger, better-trained workers, creates a longer period of years during which workers are non-productive and during which they need to be supported. (Olson 1998)

If the problems of the urban elderly are difficult, the troubles of the elderly rural poor are even more severe. Increasing life expectancy has increased the number of years the elderly must be supported. Pensions are rare in the rural areas of China, and children who might stay on the farm and support them are increasingly being lured to urban areas for a better life than one that can be found in the country. As a result, the rural elderly are often required to work until they drop, either from sickness or death. The following anecdote, taken from the field notes of a researcher, highlights the hard, hard life confronting an elderly person in rural China.

Although their son lives in the same courtyard as them, the Yangs cannot expect to rely completely on support from their children and must work as long as physically possible. Yang Guiquan, who is 56, lives with his 53-year-old wife in a poor village, in Liaoning. The couple lives on income from rice cultivation and from raising hogs. Their son, who also farms, built and lives in a separate house and maintains separate accounts. He fully expects to help take care of his parents, in the future. However, despite having a son in the village, the Yangs are planning on working as long as they can. Even though Mrs. Yang had a stroke last year and was unable to go into the fields, she is still doing housework. She is in charge of raising the hogs and taking care of her grandchildren. After telling us that she is in constant pain, we asked why she did not take it easy. She replied, "If you want to eat, you have to work ... it is the key to having enough food in the house". (Pang et al. 2004)

There are fewer government services in the rural areas, and in those areas infrastructure development lags, compared to the urban areas. Affordable health care is not as easy to find as it is in the urban areas. Traditional Confucian values that emphasize the duty of children to parents are eroding. (Xu and Chi 2011). In particular, the traditional extended family is beginning to break down. Traditionally, the great majority of rural Chinese lived in extended families; however, after more than two decades of rapid economic growth, many elderly Chinese live without their children. (Pang et al. 2004) These problems are in addition to the problems mentioned above, the one child policy, the forced early retirement policy, and migration of children to urban areas. Altogether, all of this makes for a hard life for the elderly in rural China.

THE CARE OF THE ELDERLY IN MODERN CHINA

Elderly are taken care of in three ways in modern China. The first is through their own efforts at self-help, the second is through government programs, and the third is through private, non-government organizations. We'll look at all three, in turn.

Self-help undertaken by the elderly, with a view to maintaining themselves in their old age can take several forms. For example, an elderly couple might help their children out by building or renovating a house for a son, thus freeing up the son's capital to invest in a profitable venture. The idea is that, for a given amount of capital, the son will be able to make more with it than can the elderly parents. (Pang et al. 2004) Something else the elderly may do to make it through old age is just to continue working as long as they possibly can. This often means working through pain and sickness. For example, Mr. Liu from Heilongjiang Province was 77 years old, yet was still working every day in the fields. He was suffering from prostate cancer, and was weak, and in pain. When asked why he worked under those conditions, his response was, "If you don't work, you have nothing to eat." (Pang et al. 2004)

The second way an elderly person may find help to deal with his necessary support during his retirement years is through the government. At the same time as the "opening and reform" movement in the early 1980s moved China towards a market economy, the government engaged in a flurry of activity designed to deal with the problem of China's aging population. Publications began to carry lead articles pushing the importance of dealing with the elderly population. In 1981, Longevity, the first periodical devoted entirely to the elderly, began publication. In 1982 the National Committee of China for the World Assembly on Aging was created in order to send a delegation to Vienna for a world conference of the problems of aging in modernizing societies. In 1982, Lu Mouhua presented a very important paper to a gerontological meeting in Beijing. The paper was entitled "'A Very Important Matter For Gerontology to Address--on the Principle of Solving the Social Problem of Childless Elderly in China." This seminal paper advocated several things, including keeping old people active, to utilize the talents and energies of the elderly, to showcase good programs for the elderly in order to show the young that they had nothing to fear from old age, to build on the Chinese traditions which encourages respect and special care for the aged, and to strengthen the role of intellectuals by involving them in the search for solutions to the elder care problem. The next year, 1983, saw the creation of the National Committee on Aging. (Olson 1998)

In addition to committees and publications, actual programs and reforms were established in the 1980s with the purpose of helping the elderly. Pensions were actually established in the early 1950s, reforms of those pension plans were implemented in the 1970s, and pensions were expanded in the 1980s so that by 1982, all elderly, and not just those retired from state-owned enterprises, and including the handicapped, were eligible for pensions. These programs were promulgated not merely as statutes, but as constitutional provisions, such as the ones listed here. (Olson 1998)

Working people have the right to material assistance in old age and in case of illness or disability. To ensure that working people enjoy this right, the state gradually expands social insurance and other services (Article 50, 1978 Constitution).

Citizens of the PRC have the right to material assistance from the state and society when they are old, ill, or disabled. The state develops social insurance and helps make arrangements for the work, livelihood, and education of the blind, deaf-mutes and other handicapped citizens (Article 45, 1982 Constitution).

I think these two constitutional provisions illustrate a basic left-wing ideal, which is not surprising, because China is still nominally a communist state. The first is that government welfare is a right, and not a privilege paid for by other citizens' taxes (see Article 50, above). This contrasts with traditional Western notions that hold that a right is something someone is born with, that costs nothing, and that everyone enjoys, whether he is a pauper or a millionaire (such as the right to life or property). On this view, a state cannot "gradually expand" a right; it exists completely whole at all times – it either exists, or it does not exist.

I talked to a thirty-year old married woman who gave me an interesting insight into the Chinese pension system. She did not object to the government taking out of her paycheck money to fund her pension. But she didn't like the fact that the government didn't tell her how much was being taken out, and that she had to just depend on the government's good graces to accurately and honestly account for the money that was being taken out. If she is typical, it could mean that the Chinese are developing the same angst that Americans are feeling about the solvency of the social security system.

The third way that modern China cares for its elderly is through private, non-governmental agencies. These private care facilities are non-profit in nature. They have arisen because of the state's admitted failure to take care of the needs of China's elderly. The government, in 1998, promulgated the Registration and Management of Civilian-run Non-Enterprise Units, which used tax exemptions and preferential utility rates in order to entice private parties to enter the elder care business. It is somewhat remarkable to see an ostensibly communist government turn to private entities to alleviate social problems, but so they have. During Mao's command economy, the family did the heavy lifting in providing for elder care. The state was a means of last resort, only taking care of the "three-no's," namely, the elderly who had no family, the elderly who had no ability to work, and the elderly who had no other means of livelihood. However, even as a last resort, the state has failed to properly provide for the elderly. China's welfare agency, the Ministry of Civil Affairs, frankly confesses its failures, which to me is a remarkable thing in itself, and I shall comment on this, later. This agency, pointing out that the demands are staggering, states that its resources are too limited, and that many state-run welfare institutions are run-down and ill equipped. In addition, state institutions target healthy older people who are capable of taking care of themselves, rather than frail elders who can't. Also, the management of these government welfare institutions is "rigid, unmotivated, resistant to change, and expensive." Faced with these daunting problems, the Ministry of Civil Affairs has resorted to setting up token model facilities for demonstration and training purposes in each locale, and then pushing the responsibility for elder care onto private entities. (Wong & Tang 2006/2007)

What is required to start a private elder care facility in China? The entity must be not-for-profit, and must not use state resources in starting up. The bureaucratic requirements are heavy, such as registration, license renewal, monitoring, and administrative supervision. A business, social organization, or an individual may start a private care facility, but whoever establishes one must have a professional sponsor who has expertise in management of such facilities, and who can ensure compliance with government regulations. Since the passing of the 1998 Registration and Management of Civilian-run Non-Enterprise Units, which permitted the creation of private care facilities, such enterprises have mushroomed. In 1999, 5,901 units were registered; in 2000, there were 23,000; in 2001, the numbers rose to 82,000; and in 2004, 133,000 units were registered. How well are these institutions faring financially? One study of 130 homes discovered that only 22 (16.9 percent) of them were making a profit (of course, legally, the profits may not be distributed to the owners of the facility), and the profits were small. Sixty-one homes (46.9 percent) reported breaking even, and 41 homes (36.9 percent) reported losses. Remarkably, only 20.2 percent of the homes thought they would recover their investment in the near future, 29.4 percent thought their investment might be recovered, but not anytime soon, and 50.5 percent said they never expected to recover their investment. These numbers cast a pall on the numbers above, which showed a healthy increase in the numbers of private care units. With financial returns as low as this, one may reasonably anticipate that new entrants will be deterred, and that improvements, such as modernization of buildings and professionalization of services will be retarded. (Wang and Tong 2006/2007)

There are other deterrents besides the financial ones, facing would-be social entrepreneurs desiring to establish private elder care facilities. The first stems from the nature of elder care, in itself. Old people are weak, fragile, and prone to accidents, which expose private operators to potentially lengthy and expensive litigation and compensation claims. These claims cannot be insured against, because insurers are not available who will underwrite the risk. In addition to liability claims, private elder care facility operators must deal with a common hostile public perception that these private institutions are exploitative, because the field has traditionally been dominated by the state. I suppose it is not surprising, giving the history of the Chinese Communist Party's decades-long war on non-state private action as evil, that Chinese citizens might hold these attitudes. After all, many American college students subject to the not-so-subtle indoctrinations administered by university social science departments seem to end up with somewhat the same attitudes. Apparently the Chinese public doesn't appreciate the many difficult problems facing the social entrepreneurs who are struggling against many obstacles to fill a huge hole that the state, which is supposed to represent the common good, has failed to fill. Many private care facility operators are explicitly unhappy that the state has not done enough to counter the public's negative perceptions, just as they complain that the state gives no financial aid or other help, nor does it give advice. Some other struggles experienced by these non-profit facilities include the difficulty of finding space. The majority of agencies rent their space, and thus are subject to potential and actual debilitating rent hikes and evictions. In addition, the lower utility rates that the 1998 regulations promised are often refused by the state utilities, which charge the homes commercial rates. The trials of operating a private care facility can be nicely summarized by the words of one facility manager, who stated that "In short, civilian-run care agencies face problem after problem, suffering after suffering, and struggle after struggle…The struggles are really terrible. State homes do not pay rent. They pick the old people they want, often those with better health and self care…Had I known it would be so tough, I wouldn't have started my business"

It appears that, in China especially, getting old ain't for wusses.

CHAPTER REFERENCES

Olson, Philip (1988). Modernization in the People's Republic of China: The Politicization of the Elderly. The Sociological Quarterly 29(2):241-162.

Pang, Lihua; de Brauw, Alan; and Rozelle, Scott (2004). Working until You Drop: The Elderly of Rural China. The China Journal 52:73-94.

Wong, Linda and Tang, Jun (2006/2007). Dilemmas Confronting Social Entrepreneurs: Care Homes for Elderly People in Chinese Cities. Pacific Affairs 79(4):623-640.

Xu, Ling; and Chi, Iris (2011). Life Satisfaction Among Rural Chinese Grandparents: The Roles Of Intergenerational Family Relationship and Support Exchange With Grandchildren. International Journal of Social Welfare 20:148-159.

MANDARIN

The language barrier between Chinese and Westerners is extraordinarily difficult to traverse. I have fantasized about teaching a Chinese language class to English-speaking college students, and using the first day to frighten underachievers to drop the class. My speech would go something like this:

> Class, I admire your courage. However, I do not admire your wisdom in choosing this class. This is not Spanish. If you were learning Spanish, you just add an "o" to each English word, and you've got it. In Chinese, there are no "o's," just thousands of spaghetti-like characters, which will take you years to recognize. And when I say recognize, I don't mean you will be able to write them. That will take years more. Also, don't think you can sound out the characters, because you can't. The characters, unlike alphabetically formed words, do not carry within them the rules for their pronunciation. This means that all Chinese who can read the characters, but who speak different dialects, even though they can understand what they are reading, all pronounce the characters differently. The government has standardized pronunciation for the official language, which is Mandarin. In order for you to speak Mandarin, you first have to master an alphabetically based romanization system, which converts the characters into a sound you can pronounce. This system is called pinyin. Pinyin associates each character with a sound, which sound is represented (usually) by a beginning consonant and an ending vowel.

So let's talk about pinyin. You will undoubtedly try to pronounce the pinyin like English, but pinyin is not English. It has its own rules. For example, "yun" is not pronounced "yoon" like you would think, but it's pronounced "yu-uhn." In addition, there are some pinyin vowel-consonant combinations that no English-speaking person will know how to pronounce; for example, "qiao" and "xu." And to add to your aggravation, there are some sounds that pinyin attempts to reproduce that are never made when English is spoken. But the worst thing about pinyin is this: The consonant-vowel combinations can be pronounced in five different tones, and each different tone carries a different meaning. For example, ma1 (first tone) means "mother." Ma2 (second tone) means "hemp, numb, or pockmarked." Ma3 (third tone) means "horse." Ma4 (fourth tone) means "to scold or curse." Ma5 (fifth tone, or light tone, or neutral tone) is placed at the end of a sentence to indicate the sentence is a question. Therefore, in order to say, "Did Mother curse the pockmarked horse?" one would say, "Ma1ma5 ma4 ma2 ma3 ma5."

But this is not the end of your troubles. I will list briefly some other problems, without going into detail, in order to avoid discouraging you. First, each consonant-vowel-tone combination associated with a character often has multiple definitions. Second, different characters often have the same consonant-vowel-tone sound. Third, many individual characters, even though they have the same consonant-vowel combination, are associated with multiple tones. Fourth, many individual characters are associated with multiple consonant-vowel-tone combinations, each of which has a different meaning. Fifth, some characters have the same meaning, but different tones when used in different words.

Now that you understand characters, lets talk about how characters are formed into words. Most words are a two-character combination. Some are composed of three characters, some of four. The four-character words are usually idioms derived from stories that the Chinese have been telling themselves for millennia, and with which you are totally unfamiliar, and so those words will make no sense at all to you, even if you understand all the characters.

Now that we understand words, let's see how words are strung together in sentences. This will take some knowledge of Chinese grammar. Let me quote you a sentence from a Chinese grammar book, whose back cover says it is an "elementary grammar." Its title is A Practical Chinese Grammar For Foreigners (Dejin and Meizhen 1994). Let's read the English translation of a particular practical grammar rule for students of elementary Chinese: "the adjectival degree complement is descriptive in nature and it tells the degree or extent of the action indicated by the head word (verb), whereas the adjectival adverbial adjunct tells the 'attitude' or manner of an action and it is facttelling." Note the words that I have underlined. Can't you see how practical Chinese is? Is this a great language or what! A word can either be an adjective or an adverb, both at the same time.

I could go on to talk about how difficult it is to listen to the various regional pronunciations, and I could tell you about all of the dozens of dialects that local people speak in different regions, and how the language changes over time, but I don't want to dampen your spirits.

For your first assignment, please be able to write from memory this Chinese character: 龘 This character is da2, pronounced with the rising (second) tone, and means the appearance of a dragon in flight. Once you master it, you can describe any flying dragons you see. And once we teach you how to write this in the cursive style, rather than the print style, you will be able to write it faster. And oh yes, I almost forgot. You absolutely must write the character in the approved stroke order, because if you don't, the character is wrong. This should not be a problem, this character only has 48 strokes. And oh, by the way, sometimes different fonts are used, each of which make the character look different.

See you next class, if there is a next class.

I once asked a forty-something American student of beginning Chinese what motivated her to study the language. She said she had heard it would help her get over a particularly nasty divorce. It makes sense. After she unlooses her wrath on the Chinese language, as all students of Chinese from time-to-time are wont to do, she won't have enough hatred left over to vent on her nasty ex-husband. She probably won't have enough brains left to even remember his name.

One may be tempted to throw his hands up in despair when faced with the obstacles presented by Mandarin Chinese. However, it is necessary to understand the importance of the Chinese language to the Chinese themselves. Mandarin is more than a language. The characters are lovingly painted as artwork using cherished calligraphy techniques. A Chinese person once told me that learning the characters from an early age develops the Chinese mind in a way that Western languages cannot. The condensed nature of Chinese writing is said to stimulate poetic qualities in the Chinese soul. Very few Westerners ever master Chinese, but any foreigner wishing to burrow into Chinese culture needs to learn a little Mandarin.

CHINGLISH

You have just read a short description of the Chinese language. You can imagine that it might be a little difficult also for the Chinese to learn English. That is why I am awed at how China has taught so many Chinese people English. The country is English-crazy. English is everywhere – on signs, on product packages, on TV, on the radio, in the middle of Chinese pop songs. I have listened to a Chinese DJ, a young woman from Yinchuan, Ningxia province, broadcast her show mostly in very good English, interspersed with some Chinese. She played almost all English songs. And this was in China's Northwest, the hinterlands. Almost every Chinese student has started studying English in middle school, and Chinese instruction if fast making its way into the elementary schools, all the way to the first grade.

However, no matter how well the Chinese have learned Chinese, they still have a very, very distinct way of speaking it. I have never heard of a native-speaker having the ability to speak English the way the Chinese do. Even grammatically and syntactically correct Chinese is different – words are used in slightly off-base ways, the phrasing and intonation are different, the words are often poetic. When English with Chinese characteristics is spoken with enough mistakes in it, it is called Chinglish. Now, there are two kinds of Chingish: bad Chinglish and good Chinglish. Bad Chinglish is merely Chinese that is translated into English so poorly that the result is unintelligible. Here is an example of bad Chinglish, found on a store sign: "Smart Noshery makes you Slobber." "Noshery" is unintellible, and so the phrase it's found in is bad Chinglish. Good Chinglish, on the other hand, produces good English words with good grammar, but whose meaning is wacky. Here is an example of good Chinglish which purports to translate "No Trespassing," taken from advertising material for the 2011 Broadway play Chinglish: "Penetration will be dealt with painfully." There are no grammar or vocabulary mistakes, but somehow the idea of no trespassing doesn't exactly come across. I have never met a foreigner who wasn't delighted with Chinglish. I have, however, heard of some rigid stuffshirts who think that when foreigners laugh at Chinglish, we are laughing at Chinese people. Nothing could be farther from the truth. Chinglish is an art form, and should be preserved. Stephen Pucci, a Mandarin-speaking British actor starring in a 2011 Broadway play entitled Chinglish, stated that, in his view "I think it's definitely going to tap into something and encourage mutual awareness and understanding." (Understanding Chinglish, 2011) Oliver Lutz Radtke, a former German radio reporter who is currently working on a Ph.D. dissertation whose subject is Chinglish, and who is considered by some to be the world's foremost authority on the subject, was reported by the New York Times to believe that "China should embrace the fanciful melding of English and Chinese as the hallmark of a dynamic, living language... Chinglish is an endangered species that deserves preservation." "If you standardize all these signs, you not only take away the little giggle you get while strolling in the park, but you lose a window into the Chinese mind," said Mr. Radtke. (Jacobs, 2010) Even someone who was hired to eradicate Chinglish from Shanghai in preparation for World Expo 2010 was guilt-ridden over his deeds. Jeffrey Yao, who teaches at Shanghai International Studies Institute (SISU), my old employer, told the New York Times that some Chinglish phrases tend "to be expressive, even elegant... They provide a window into how we the Chinese think about language." Mr. Yao provides two examples of how Chinese people have translated "Keep off the Grass:" "The Little Grass is Sleeping. Please Don't Disturb It." "Don't Hurt Me. I Am Afraid of Pain." (Jacobs, 2010) Such signs are everywhere in China, but unfortunately, certain killjoys want to deprive the foreigner of the pleasure to be had by reading them. For example, Wang Xiaoming, an English scholar at the English Academy of Social Sciences, felt offended when friends flipped through photographs of Chinglish and laughed. But even she admitted her friends weren't trying to offend her. (Jacobs 2010) Perhaps the thought of the bucketloads of foreign currency brought to China every year by foreigners who are charmed to their core by the exotic and mysterious nature of China, and whom Chinglish delights, should ease Ms. Wang's pain. I know I would be more than glad to have the Chinese come my home state of South Carolina and laugh at redneck stuff.

I am going to give you some examples of Chinglish I have encountered over the years. Treasure them, and pass them down to your children.

A college professor, a Chinese woman, complains in a meeting about a male professor who lives above her, who lifted weights at odd hours of the night: "That man is always banging me every night from 2:00 till 4:00 o'clock every morning!"

A sign is intended to mark an exit through which only cars, and not trucks and buses, can exit: "Private place for getting off."

A huge sign made of red neon letters, hung way up on the upper stories of a very tall Beijing hospital, proudly stated: "BEIJING ANUS AND INTESTINAL HOSPITAL." Alas, the sign has fallen victim to the Chinglish-killers, and now says something like "Beijing Proctology Hospital."

A sign in a restroom: "Look Out For Your Behind."

A small sign in the Hademan Hotel in Beijing tried to warn guests against dying clothes in the tub. It read: "No dying in the tub."

A menu selection offered "Bloody Jew's Nose." I still don't know what food was being represented. Nor do I know what drink was in the cans seen in Shanghai, which were labeled "Jew's Ear Juice."

After showing her class a movie, a foreign teacher's student told her that she had been "infected by the movie."

In a graduate student's journal: "Now I am a girl in the amorous age."

On a sign at Xikou, Chiang Kai-Shek's hometown, a sign helpfully explains the fate of one of the female members of the Generalissimo's family. She had entered a monastery to become a "nun with hair." This was to distinguish her from other monks, who were bald.

Toilet paper at Shanghai's 2010 World Expo was "not made with trees." Judging by the feel of it, I suspect it was made of plastic.

A sign marking the entrance to the Beijing National Ethnic Minorities Park proudly pointed out the entrance to "Beijing Racist Park."

On a menu: "Dumpling stuffed with the ovary and digestive glands of a crab."

In a restroom: "For Keeping the Toilet Clean and Tidy, Please Dump at the Dust Bin"

On a menu: "Fried Crap with Spicy Sauce."

On a sign near a staircase: "Please don't resort and disport at passageway. Don't ambulate in staircase."

On a trashcan: "Poisonous and Evil Rubbish."

CHAPTER REFERENCES

Dejin, L. and Meizhen, C. (1994). A Practical Chinese Grammar for Foreigners.   Beijing: Sinolingua.

Jacobs, Andrew (May 2, 2010). Shanghai Is Trying to Untangle the Mangled English of Chinglish. New York Times, Asia Pacific Edition, http://www.nytimes.com/2010/05/03/world/asia/03chinglish.html.

Understanding Chinglish: A New Play Tries to Bridge the Language Gap. (October 26, 2011). Last updated at 23:16 GMT. http://www.bbc.co.uk/news/magazine-15471753.

www.ingramcontent.com/pod-product-compliance
Lightning Source LLC
Chambersburg PA
CBHW050529190326
41458CB00045B/6770/J